What's the idea?" said the officer. "What d'ye think this is—a dormitory?"
(See page 196)

Copyright 1999 by A.B. Publishing, Inc.
Cover art: James Converse

Republished by:
A.B. Publishing, Inc.
3039 S. Bagley
Ithaca, Mi. 48847

A Child of Divorce

A startling story of an amazing modern evil—its insidious warfare upon all that is high and holy in marriage and its blasting influence upon innocent lives

BY
MARIE LeNART

Author of
"Test and Conquest," "The Phantom Lady," etc.

Copyright, 1922

"And the king said, Bring me a sword. And they brought a sword before the king.

And the king said, Divide the living child in two, and give half to the one, and half to the other."

—*1 Kings 3:24, 25.*

To

"Whiteheart"

*through whose faith in woman-
hood I caught the vision
and beauty of
fidelity*

CONTENTS

	PAGE
CHAPTER I.	
THE UNFATHERED	13
CHAPTER II.	
"WITH BENEFIT OF CLERGY"	16
CHAPTER III.	
DISCRIMINATION	23
CHAPTER IV.	
AN ODD NUMBER	40
CHAPTER V.	
"THREE'S A CROWD"	63
CHAPTER VI.	
APPLYING MATHEMATICS TO BABIES	80
CHAPTER VII.	
THE WORLD, OR HEAVEN, HIGH TRIBUNAL?	102
CHAPTER VIII.	
TO AVOID COMPLICATIONS	131
CHAPTER IX.	
RESPECTABILITY'S FLOTSAM	151

CONTENTS

CHAPTER X.
Fledgling Wings 166

CHAPTER XI.
An Opening Chrysalis 202

CHAPTER XII.
Stripes 223

CHAPTER XIII.
Young Wings Will Strengthen 258

CHAPTER XIV.
A Clear, Imperious Call 271

CHAPTER XV.
"The Chastisement of Our Peace" 295

CHAPTER XVI.
Babbling Tongues 320

CHAPTER XVII.
The Soul of a Woman 341

CHAPTER XVIII.
The Wages of Sin 362

CHAPTER XIX.
What Is Love? 394

CHAPTER XX.
Home 423

LEADING CHARACTERS OF THE STORY

Jean Laval, a child of divorce.

Truman Burnett, a child of shame.

Mr. and Mrs. James Hasbrook, Jean's mother and stepfather.

Mr. and Mrs. Verne Laval, Jean's father and stepmother.

"Mrs." Burnett, Truman's mother.

Jerome Bascomb, a man of the world.

Paul Manson, a man of ideals.

Adele Manson, Manson's niece.

A WORD FROM THE AUTHOR

I have no fear that right-thinking people will accuse me in the following tale of in any way seeking to disparage the sanctity of marriage or the importance of established conventions. It is in defense of a high ideal of the holiest earthly relationship that this story is written, and in paralleling the cases of this child of shame and child of divorced and remarried parents, no attempt has been made to clothe illegitimacy with a cloak of dignity stolen from honorable wedlock, but rather to restore that cloak, spotless, to its rightful owner after stripping it from its usurper, divorce, thereby leaving the latter to stand in its true nakedness.

MARIE LeNART.

NEW YORK, N. Y.,
August, 1922.

CHAPTER I.

THE UNFATHERED

NO moon. Not a star. But out of the airy darkness on either side of Gouvenir Street loomed the still deeper blackness of mass. The damp flags at intervals reflected the flicker of gas-lamps, which seemed to augment, rather than relieve, the pervading dismalness by their further revelation of the sultry August night and the gloomy contrast in which they threw everything beyond the limit of their feeble rays. The buildings faced each other (two large institutions), separated visibly by the pavement, but, in reality, by a span immeasurable, because unseen. In the still obscurity, you were almost conscious of a hanging, ethereal bridge between them, a bridge as long as is the way from birth to death, for one was a gateway of this transitory life, the other its final port. One was the Florence Crittenden Home, where penniless women who have loved indiscreetly bring forth their children of shame; the other was the Refuge for the Aged Poor.

A CHILD OF DIVORCE

In a wing room of the latter a shaded lamp burned near an unpretentious bed. Old Dr. Bayliss, long an inmate of the Refuge, having spent all his substance in succoring others, was about to yield up the spirit that for eighty-seven years had animated his frame. Over him leaned the house physician, and close behind crowded the matron, chaplain and nurse, while a few sad-hearted, silver-haired contemporaries anxiously watched for the visitant whose next summons might come any hour to one of themselves. But the old man was beyond the aid of them all, or the need of their aid. While thus they stood tense, he was relaxing into rest; while thus they gazed through tears, he alone smiled. Mayhap those two ends of life draw nearer together again than we think, for surely his old eyes, when they opened once more, reflected the glow of a long-left youth. Yet they seemed not to behold his surroundings, but, rather, some vision which no earthly eyes until this hour may see. He began to mumble words. Perhaps he had sung them years before in some little chapel at eventide by the side of his dear mate Martha:

"How should we reach God's upper light—
If earth's long day—had—no—good night!"

THE UNFATHERED

And then the Reaper came for him and gathered his soul and bore it away, and, because life must be balanced on the earth, he called to a fellow-messenger in the far firmament, and, through the raised windows of a room in the building opposite, the plaintive cry of a new-born babe pierced the night.

Not with the peaceful anticipation, the reassuring song, which had ushered out the son of godliness, came this new spirit into the world; or groped his young mother back through the valley of the shadow with her hand in her mate's. She was alone. From the "upper light" he had descended to where the dreary fog without seemed now symbolic of the cloud under which he was born.

CHAPTER II.

"WITH BENEFIT OF CLERGY"

"HELLO!"
"H'lo!"
"Where you goin'?"
"To the store."
"Decker's?"
"Uh-huh."
"So'm I."
"What's your name?"
"Truman; what's yours?"
"Jean Frances Laval. Aren't you got any other?"
"Yep—Burnett."

By mutual consent the two children fell into pace along the semi-rural road. For some distance no other person was visible, and in juvenile frankness they welcomed each other's company. The girl looked about nine. Her bobbed chestnut hair partly framed a round face, healthily tanned and set with clear, level hazel eyes. She was straight-backed, of sturdy build, walking with a firm, yet graceful, swing. The boy must have been eleven, inclined to rapid growth, and, as a result, too thin. Indeed, his bones were quite apparent even under his striped percale blouse and corduroy bloomers. He was visited by the usual sprinkling of freckles, nor had he yet achieved all his second molars, but, looking up into his blue, long-lashed eyes, imaginative Jean, who loved the open, was reminded of the way the sun sparkles through the dark fringes of forest-trees. She liked him, and further queried: "Whose class 're you in?"

"Miss Sibley's."

"Oh, *that* ol' crank?"

"Is she? I on'y been here 'bout three days now. She wasn't mean to me—yet."

"That's cause you're new, then. *You'll* see." Her tone waxed ominous, calling a slight shadow to his sensitive face, whereat her quick feminine sympathy made her supplement: "Well, maybe she won't be to you —if you do ever'thin' she says. Maybe I oughtn't to 've said that, but let you find out for yourself. *Some* of the kids think she's all right, and, if I was her, I wouldn't want to put the sun out—the sun in your eyes." Instantly the sun rebroke as Truman laughed: "That's right, 'cause then Hurray-shus couldn't find his way."

"Hurray-shus?"

"Uh-huh; see that one there?" He paused in the middle of the dusty road and quite soberly drew her attention to an extra capacious freckle which might well have captained the small host. "That's Hurray-shus on the bridge—of my nose. When I was a little kid, mom uster say if I cried the bridge 'ud overflow, so he couldn't get across, but if I kep' the sun shinin', why, bime-by he'd march away with the whole army."

Jean giggled with delight. There was something so pleasantly naive about this thin little boy. He lacked the precocity so evident in most twentieth-century youngsters, and, although he referred to his mother by that familiar appellation—"mom"—it was in a tone which at once conveyed the impression that "mom" loomed a predominant factor in his life and affections. Jean felt, rather than observed, this, and it prompted her next interrogation: "Aren't you got any father?"

He shook his head, his warm smile once again fading. "Mom says I have, but I never seen him. Mom says I will some day, though, 'cause she's prayin' for it. But seems like it takes 'n awful long time to get answers to prayers, an' I sure do wish he'd come!" he finished, with a little choky sigh.

"That's funny!" Jean exclaimed. "My father went away, too, and I *know* he ain't

"WITH BENEFIT OF CLERGY"

dead, like Margie Reynolds' father is, 'cause ever' time I asked mother if he'd a-went to heaven, she'd jest kind of laugh 's if it was funny. Now, Margie's mother *cried* when *her* father died, so I know mine ain't dead, but I aren't never seen him since that day, and after awhile I got tired askin'—"

"What day?" Truman grew tense with interest.

"The day they took me—there."

"Who took you where?"

"Well," her voice lowered suddenly, and then went on in a key of mysterious confidence: "Mamma told me not to tell this, but if you'll promise—cross your heart—you'll never say I did, I'll tell you, 'cause you told me 'bout *your* father, 'n it'll be our secret. First, mamma took me to a big house where there was lots of other kids, 'n' left me there for weeks 'n' weeks. I didn't like it, an' I wanted to go home. I kep' cryin' for mamma, but I guess they never told her, 'cause she didn't come for ever so long, till that day, an' then—I was so glad, 'cause I seen her an' papa again, but it wasn't home. It was 'n awful big room, an' there was policemen in it, an' lots of people. I was jest little—teeny-weeny—but I can remember all right. There was a man with the crossest face you ever saw. I was scared of him, an' he sat behind a 'normous desk up high—you had to go up steps to get there. He had a long black thing on like a wrapper, and he hit the desk with a thing like a croquet-mallet with the handle broke off it, and made the people keep quiet when they started to talk. An' there was two men down in front o' him that he lissened at, only they both tried to talk together, an' once I thought they was goin' to fight, but they didn't. Then, at last, he made my mother come up the steps an' sit by him. I cried—I was so scared. I thought he was going to hit mamma with that hammer, but he didn't. The other two men talked awful loud at her, and onct in awhile *he* talked. Papa came over, then, an' took me on his lap; so I wasn't so scared after that. But bime-by mamma came down an' took me, an' papa went up the steps, an' they talked at him, an' then he came down again, an' the man in the black thing said sumpthin,' an' papa came over an' hugged an' kissed me, an' he said, 'Good-by, Jeanie; be a good little girl an' mind your mother,' an' I cried again, 'cause I didn't want him to go 'way, an' I didn't know why he was goin' or why he said that, an' I—I—don't yet!'' The child's voice faltered with the graphic recollection of that courtroom scene, but she quickly recovered enough of her normal curiosity to put another question to her wondering confidant: "Have you got any brothers an' sisters?"

"Nope. Have you?"

"Well, I got a baby brother by my second father."

"Your second one?"

"Yes, mamma went an' got another one, but I'd lots ruther of kep' my own first one—on'y they never asked me. He was awful good to me. Ever' time he come from town he brung me presents."

"Gee! It must be great to have one like that!" husked Truman, wistfully. "If he didn't die, whatever d' you s'pose happened to him—an' mine too—I wonder?"

"You know, Truman, there's a-lots o' things in this world us kids can't un'erstand," Jean observed profoundly, "an' nobody wants to bother to tell us. I don't see why, though; I don't see why we haven't got any rights at all!" Sudden tears rushed to her eyes as her staunch little breast began to heave with a passion of rebellion which one would scarcely have suspected could smolder in a heart so young. And the boy was in accord. Just what impulse moved them then they never knew, for children do not analyze their feelings, but they reached out there on the lonely road and clasped each other's hands, and, by and by, awkward as it was, each realized an odd new sense of comfort from this common sympathy.

" 'Tis queer," Truman marveled at length, "the way you've got two fathers, an' I ain't got any; an' you don't want two, an' *I'd* be glad if I jest had one!"

"Well, if they'd on'y let me have my first one back, I—I'd give you my second one!" Jean broke out generously. "On'y," hesitating, "I guess you wouldn't like him so much neither. He's cranky 'most all the time, 'cept to Junior. An' that's 'nother funny thing—havin' a brother which has a different father from you, and the same mother—aw-w-w!"

Truman squeezed her fingers. "I've got the goodest mom all to myself," he smiled once more. "You come to *my* house some time an' see!"

CHAPTER III.

DISCRIMINATION

"LISTEN, Truman," stage-whispered Jean between the tall pickets dividing the boy's and girl's playgrounds during one recess when the two children had been friends for over a month, "come up to my back yard after school. Our tree has got loads of apples, an' I'll give you some so's your mother can make some more of those pies. Then I'll come down—maybe to-morrow. I'll wait for you on the rock underneath. Papa an' mamma an' Junior are goin' to Oxford till suppertime, so I have to mind the house" (this by way of reassurance).

"All right," Truman accepted immediately. "I'll bring a bastick."

"All right; bring a big one."

Women are noted for being late to appointments, so perhaps it was because Jean was only the beginnings of one, and not yet versed in all their ways, that she scuffed her swinging heels against her rocky perch for half an hour, incidently consuming three

A CHILD OF DIVORCE

generous samples of overhanging fruit, before Truman arrived at the trysting-place. She slid down, gulping the last half-masticated mouthful, and wiping juicy hands on her gingham frock.

"Ain't there packs?" she glowed. "We've got a ladder. It's down cellar, if you'll help me bring it out."

"We don't need any ladder," scorned Truman, lifting anticipatory eyes to the boughs of flushed pippins. "I'll shin up." And very soon his presence was manifested only by a violent disturbance of the thick foliage and a resultant downpour of apples from which Jean scurried, laughing, to safety.

"Pick 'em up!" presently directed the voice from the leaves. "I'll shake the other side now."

"Say, sissie, give us some, will yer?" Jean was stooping when this other voice startled her, and she looked up to find two large and rather dirty boys lolling over the fence. Her response encouraged them only in departure.

"You get out o' here, Kenneth Sykes! An' you, too, Milton Steiner. That's our fence and this 's our yard, an' nobody asked you!"

"Aw-w-w-w, go on, ye little pig! Are yuh gonna eat 'em all yerself?" challenged Kenneth, who was spokesman. "Let's wait

DISCRIMINATION

an' see 'er get drunk, like Eli Stanton's pig,'' he added in an audible aside to his comrade, whereat Milton grinned appreciatively.

"Get out! D'you hear?" Jean rasped, clutching a rotten pippin, which she poised threateningly.

"Oh, gee! Here go!" Kenneth clapped his hands and spread them out as if to play ball.

"Pooh! Whoever seen a girl as could pitch straight?" Milton scoffed. "Betcha she couldn't hit a—" *Thump!* For sometimes the unexpected happens, and, by a vagary, the missile squashed between his chest and chin, spreading like a dumdum, so that he could taste its fermenting spray, while a goodly portion of brown mush slid the other way down his unbuttoned shirt.

"There's your apple!" sang out Jean.

"Confound you!" hissed the boys simultaneously. "You just wait," Milton boiled, vaulting the fence. "I'll wash 'er face with it, I will!"

"Say! What's up?" Truman's agile descent from the tree abruptly curbed the hostile advance. Milton backed a step, while Kenneth paused half over the pickets, but Truman was quickly recognized.

"Ho-ho!" Kenneth jeered. "Look who's here! Is *that* yer beau, Jean?"

A CHILD OF DIVORCE

"So he's yer feller, huh?" Milton spat out. He was learning that there are two ways in which apples may tickle the stomach, and that, while both may be exhilarating, one is less desirable, wherefore he finished with impressive malice: "That *bastard!*"

"*What!* What did you call me?" Truman approached him, two sudden flames aleap in his cheeks. Milton, a bit shorter and much more stocky, ran a sneering look of appraisal over the other's form, quite evidently mistaking its wiry slimness for frailty. "I said you was a bastard," he repeated, "and that's what you are, 'cause I heard my father say so! What 're you gonna do about it?"

Now, Truman had never heard that word, and he had no full idea of its meaning, but his instinct told him it must be something bad because of this application, so he answered grimly: "I'm gonna make you take it back!"

"Oh, y' are, huh? Wanna fight?" Milton began to push up his sleeves.

"I can fight you all right. I can fight you both, but one at a time. That's fair," as Kenneth belligerently sauntered up to his ally. "Ever'body knows his mother wasn't never married," the latter supplemented spitefully. Without a breath of warning, Truman struck his mouth. They clinched, and the fray was

DISCRIMINATION

vigorous. When, however, it became apparent that Kenneth was getting the worst of it, he yelled to Milton for support, and these primitive rowdies, quite oblivious to the etiquette of the manly art, both pitched their strength against the single boy's.

However, Truman was not minus a second, either, though he raised no cry. Stirred from pertrifaction by this unfair attack, Jean sprang to his aid like a young jackal, applying so many decomposed apples at short range that they were finally forced to desist from obstructed vision. Milton slipped on some of the fruit, knocking Kenneth's feet from under him. "Down?" he sputtered. "It's no use tryin' to fight a girl—they don't fight fair!"

"You're a great one to talk about *fair!*" shrilled Jean.

Kenneth muttered an oath worthy of any pirate as he scooped the refuse out of his eyes, spat, and wiped his face with the remnants of his shirt. Just to what extent they were injured, only a bath would reveal, but from all three noses and from all three sets of knuckles oozed blood, and Milton dragged himself up, whimpering: "Y—ye've busted my rib—I know ye have!"

"If you don't take back what you said, I'll bust *all* your ribs!" flashed Truman. "D'you hear that, Kenneth Sykes?" He emphasized it with a sharp kick. "Get up an' apolergize, or you won't get away yet!"

The prostrate one groaned, but managed to comply. "All right," he mumbled, doggedly. "We'll—apolergize."

"F'rever?" Truman panted, quivering with temper and weakness.

"Ye-ah!"

"Well, if you don't, I'll—I'll fix you so you'll keep your dirty mouth shut all right! Go on now—get out o' here!"

They went with all the alacrity possible under the circumstances, Milton openly blubbering, and his pard limping exaggeratedly. At the road, however, they turned to look back, with knotted fists. "Aw-w-w!" Milton bellowed, his face contorted by dirt, rage and pain. "We *don't* 'polergize an' you jest wait'll my big brother gets you!"

Truman started after him again, but Jean snatched his torn sleeve, imploring: "Please, Truman, don't mind the old things any more. Ugh! you're all bleedin', an there's a cut on your cheek an' a bump on your head, an' goo'ness knows what you've got un'erneath! Please come in the kitchen, an' wash it off." And her pleading prevailed, for the high-strung boy was trembling in reaction, and his breath seemed to draw with difficulty. He followed her docilely. She put an agate

DISCRIMINATION

basin into the sink and seized a dish-towel, while he dropped on a chair, trying hard to conceal his real faintness. With only a little girl's tender heart to prompt her, she drew him a clear, cold drink, which somewhat revived him, to the gratification of her anxious gaze. "Does it hurt awful?" she queried.

He made a rather sickly effort at a smile, his upper lip being split. "Naw! I jest feel kind o' funny. I mustn't mind little things like this; 'cause, you know, when I grow up, I'm gonna be a doctor."

"You are?" her eyes widened in admiring wonder. "You never told me that."

"Well, I'm tellin' you now. I jest didn't think to tell you before."

"Then I know what!—" Jean clapped her hands, which was an impulsive habit of hers whenever an especially bright thought struck her. "*I'm* gonna be a nurse!"

"All right; then I'll have you come an' work for me when I'm head of a big hospital, I will."

"Oh, let's make b'lieve now! You play you're sick, an' I'll be your nurse, on'y you have to be the doctor, too, 'cause there's no one else to play."

"All right," in a tone of assumed gruffness. "Wash all the blood an' dirt off my face an' hands."

A CHILD OF DIVORCE

Jean wrung out the dishcloth, and, though her feelings recoiled from the open cuts and scratches, went bravely about the task.

Truman threw back his head, relaxing in the chair as she bathed his forehead with the cool water, and closed his black-fringed eyes. He was growing drowsy.

"Gee! that feels good," he murmured. "Jean, I won't let you go 'way with the other nurses, 'cause then—when I'm a man an' a doctor—I'm going to marry you."

She laughed.

"You'll let me, won't you?" he pleaded dreamily.

"Course," she frankly assented. "An' I'm awful glad you want to, 'cause I know I'll never want to marry anybody else."

"Hello! What's this?" A shadow darkened the kitchen door, and metaphorically fell across Jean's heart. Was it supper-time already—and the table not set? Her "second father" entered, and after him her mother, with the baby.

"Well, for pity's sake!" chimed in Mrs. Fannie Madden Laval Hasbrook. And they both stood surveying the medical scene. They were, however, no more astonished than Jean and Truman.

"What's all this mess, anyway?" James Hasbrook demanded.

DISCRIMINATION

"This is Truman, papa, an' he got hurted in a fight," Jean explained.

"Truman—who?"

"Burnett, sir," the boy spoke up.

Hasbrook tossed a significant look at his wife. "Burnett, eh? What 're you doing here?"

"I asked him, papa. The fight was in our yard. It was about the apples. Kenneth Sykes an' Milton Steiner tried to steal some, an' Truman chased them away," Jean eagerly championed her chum.

"He did, eh? And what was *he* doing in the yard?"

"Why, we was playin'—"

"I saw a basket out there."

"That's mine, sir," Truman confessed. "I—I—was goin' to take some home. I didn't know you'd mind. I'm sorry, sir."

"I *offered* 'em," Jean interposed. "I *asked* him to take 'em!"

"You did, eh? And who said you could give my apples to everybody? And why did you wait till I was out, huh?"

Jean hung a guilty head, her cheeks flaming, but managed to assert: " 'Twasn't *ever'-body.*"

"No; one robber routing the others, so's he could get more himself, and then posin' for a hero, while you swallow it—hook, line

A CHILD OF DIVORCE

an' sinker. That's a smart one!" Hasbrook laughed unpleasantly.

Truman sprang up, his pale face flushed again, his voice shaking. "I ain't a robber, sir, an' don't you dare to call me one! I'm not tryin' to be no hero neither. I said I was sorry, an'—I'll go, sir."

Calmly Hasbrook reached out, and, nipping the boy's ear, twisted it till the smart brought mist to his eyes. He was not generally known as a cruel man, yet deep in the strata of his nature ran a malicious vein which tempted him to play upon the feelings of weaker brothers.

"I never let a kid sass me," he told the lad.

But here his wife intervened. "Let him go, Jim," she advised, in a tone which, for some reason, sent chills, instead of gratitude, to Truman's heart. "You could hardly expect him to have much principle. Consider the source, Jim—and we mustn't keep him near our children."

Reluctantly Hasbrook loosed his fingers, and the boy, too full of emotion for another word or look, strode out the back way. Swift as a bird from its cage, Jean flew after him. Her stepfather caught her, but she tore away and raced across the lawn, sobbing: "Truman, Truman!" He made no sign of hear-

DISCRIMINATION

ing, but at last she gained him. "Oh, Truman—dear Truman! It's all my fault; I'm so sorry!"

For an instant then the boy turned back, but in his beautiful gray-blue eyes was an accusing defiance which shocked her like a lance-thrust. "Your second father is sure a peach!" he said stridently. "Why did you ask me if you knew what I'd get?"

Too deeply chagrined and hurt to answer, Jean could only stand and watch through brimming eyes as he stalked proudly on down the road. Proud, was he? She could not see the stinging teardrops that presently broke forth from beneath his eyelids and slid down in the October gloaming, tears that bodily pain had been unable to draw from him. Under the shredded front of his blouse, his bruised chest began to heave with the pain of a heart still more bruised.

"Consider the source!" "His mother was never married!" What did they mean, anyway? There grew upon him the sense that some hitherto unsuspected, intangible monster was threatening him and his mother. It made him feel that hereafter they must be closer than ever; but he wondered, with the first shade of resentment, about his tardy father. Not for an instant did he doubt his mother's faith, but now there arose within him vague questionings as to his father's worthiness of it. If he loved them as fathers ought to, why did he not come and defend them against these insults? Oh, how he yearned to be grown that he might search him out and bring this suspense to an end! But to-night there was no one to answer his queries, for he somehow felt that he must not tell his mother what had happened. Out of all this travail was being born into his boyish soul the chivalry that marks the dawning man, and it told him that knowledge of the incident would hurt her. Yes, he must keep it secret. Could he, though? Her love-clear eyes were so keen, and there were his betraying wounds. He wished that the bordering woods might yield, where he could find it, some herb of instantaneous healing, such as one reads of in fairy tales. But he could explain about the apples. He needn't fib. He simply would not tell it all.

Firm in his resolve, he approached the shabby little bungalow. The lamp was lighted in the front room and the shade was up for him. He could see his mother still sewing, and the two uncanny, headless "Judies" standing ever at attention, and the billows and billows of frock stuffs spread over the table and chairs, for she had turned to that trade which has proved a raft to so many

DISCRIMINATION

shipwrecked women. She was a dressmaker. Something made him pause out there to watch her for a moment, and the same something tugged at his feelings with a strange new pathos. He had never exactly thought before how tired she must get. He wasn't a baby any more. Why should he play while she worked so hard? To-morrow he would hunt a job to fill after school!

He entered very softly, but she heard him.

"Is that you, sonny?"

"Yes, mom."

"Supper's ready, dear. I'm just waitin' for you."

"All right, mom; soon as I wash." And he went on out to the pump, trying hard to whistle through his swollen lips.

. . . .

After many hesitant minutes Jean turned back home, passionately wishing she could die there on the path. Whippings, in lieu of supper, had been borne ere this, but, combined with the loss of her playmate, her prospects left little indeed worth living for. She was almost overwhelmed by the impulse to run away, but it was getting dark. She stole around to the rear yard and lingered once more, coaxing courage to go in. She could feel her stepfather, through the very clapboards, waiting, like a lion in his lair, to pounce upon her, and she shrank and shuddered. Her little heart was so sore to-night, it seemed as if blows would kill her. But, then, she wanted to die. She wanted to, and yet, when she raised her eyes, they welcomed, with bounding relief, a suggestion of escape. Her own small room completed an extension over the woodshed. This woodshed was enclosed by a wide lattice that climbed to within three feet of the second-story back windows. Her window was open! In another moment she was creeping cautiously upward. The lattice, being old and rather flimsy, shook some, but Jean was light. Just as she gripped the sill, however, a sinewy arm shot from the interior. In her panic she let go, and would have fallen had it not caught her.

"Come on," James Hasbrook urged grimly; "I'll help you."

"Don't! Don't touch me!" she shrilled.

"What're you squalling about before you're hurt? You'll get what's coming to you pretty quick, though—you little smart aleck!" He deposited her on the matting with a shake. But Jean was keyed to the limit of endurance. She struggled frantically against his grasp, kicking, scratching, biting. Never had she been so unmanageable, and, as she was a strong, nervous, agile child, Hasbrook had a mighty handful.

DISCRIMINATION

"You let me go!" she shrieked. "You're not my father, an' I hate you—I *hate* you! I HATE you!" This challenged all the man's innate brutality. His teeth clenched, as with one big hand he squeezed her wrists together and beat the other upon her twitching body. Finally, he flung her upon the bed, muttering: "There, I guess that'll do you for awhile!" strode out and banged the door, to leave her retching hysterically. Had she been of more delicate physique, she might have succumbed to merciful unconsciousness. However, her fibers were finely strung, and the effect of that night's agony was something she never quite outgrew. Thoroughly exhausted at last, she dozed, only to start, a little later, from a nightmare, crying: "Mamma—mam-ma!"

Her mother came in. "Hush, Jean, you're waking the baby!"

"Mamma—I saw papa—my own papa—I saw him! He was comin' to me—but that man—in the black thing pulled him away!"

The woman flushed. "Nonsense, child," she exclaimed; "that was a silly dream. And I've told you before to forget him, Jean. He wouldn't have been as good to you as the father you have—"

"He *would!*" sobbed the child; "I *know* he would! Mr. Hasbrook ain't good to me!

A CHILD OF DIVORCE

He don't love me, an' I hate him—an' I'll—I'll never call him 'papa' again!''

"Jean," her mother said sadly, "you make me feel very bad. I've tried to do the best for you, and what your father has done is for your own good too. You'll understand it some day. You were a naughty, naughty girl this afternoon. You don't seem to care how these things hurt mother. I'm sorry papa had to spank you, but naughty girls must be punished, Jean. Get undressed now and go to bed and keep quiet. Junior's asleep.'' She moved to go out, and Jean implored pitifully:

"Please, mamma—kiss me—good night!"

Mrs. Hasbrook hesitated; then, with a little regretful sigh, shook her head. "I can't, Jean, till you've told papa you're sorry for naughty things you said. You must do that, and then mother will kiss you again,'' with which she softly departed. This was her idea of enforcing discipline, and it is the mistaken one of many parents. Perhaps there are few forms of punishment we can afford to spare in dealing with the willful child, but to deny its cry for affection is a useless, if not dangerous, course. Love is not plentiful enough in this old world to be frost-bitten to death in its tender stage, even for the sake of "discipline." Jean turned over and stifled long, moaning sobs in the pillow. Her temper had subsided. She was sick and utterly desolate. All the grievances of her short life welled over her in a passion of self-pity, beginning with those long weeks in the "protectory" while the divorce proceedings were in progress, where a certain hawk-eyed matron, who possessed as much knowledge of child nature as a grim-visaged Buddha, had terrified her into silence with a bookstrap when she cried for her parents. In her juvenile imagination this individual glowered, beside her "second father," like the ogre of some fable, leaving its indelible portrait upon her memory.

During a lull in her spasm she heard Hasbrook mumbling in the hallway outside her door, and her mother answer fretfully: "I'm sure I don't know how to manage her, Jim. She's getting more like *him* every day." They seldom referred to her own father, and never in ways complimentary, so that through the medium of their occasional remarks he had become to her a synonym of something evil. Yet, strangely conflicting with this was the memory of that one who had kissed her last in the voluminous courtroom. Could there have been, somewhere, still another? How many fathers did a child have?

CHAPTER IV.

AN ODD NUMBER

THERE were migratory germs in the Hasbrook blood which could have explained the family's several changes of residence during the next nine years, and Jean at eighteen had fading reminiscences of a stock farm "up State," of a coal-mining region in Pennsylvania where her stepfather "owned shares," and of a furniture-shop in lower Brooklyn, over which they existed in a cave-like apartment, till it burned out mysteriously one midnight. Hasbrook then confessed that he had always wanted to go into the hotel business, for, if he could not travel himself, this would at least bring him into contact with people who could; and so we find them again, backed by the insurance money, at their latest venture —"The Two-ways Inn"—an establishment for public convenience on a lonely stretch of the famous Merrick Road, some eight miles out of Jamaica, Long Island.

This morning ushered in Jean's birthday. She slid out of bed, and, after regarding the date on her calendar for several serious minutes, turned and surveyed herself still more earnestly in the mirror. She was a woman! But she did not feel like it—that is, she did not feel grown up—and certainly there was no one else who seemed aware of the transition. At her heart, however, a gnawing unrest had been at times quite alarming, and now, in the dawnlight, she saw her own large eyes peering back at her with a questioning hunger in the hazel depths of them; she saw, too, through the sheer muslin of her nightgown, her rounding breast and shoulders, and did not know how much—except that her skin was too tinted for marble and too white for bronze—she resembled a statue, for Jean had very little acquaintance as yet with statues or art of any kind, and there were few girls in the neighborhood by whose figures she might gauge her own. But beneath that young bosom were ripening two all-absorbing, if still unexpressed, desires. She yearned to love some one unreservedly, to serve for the sake of that devotion, and to be loved in return—for her soul and mind, as well as her flesh. And she craved beauty, harmony. For some reason, to this fanciful girl, her life often seemed like a song which had been started on the wrong key and played out of tune ever since. Corresponding notes in the proper chords might have rendered

A CHILD OF DIVORCE

melody instead of discord. She was growing flinchingly sensitive to her present atmosphere, though it was the only one she had ever known. She felt intuitively now that "duty" alone, albeit of a lower conception, moved the Hasbrooks to share with her the house they were still essaying to build on split foundations, for as she waxed in the likeness of Verne Laval, she became—even to her mother—the constant reminder of an early *misalliance*.

The decoration of this narrow retreat up under the eaves, limited as were her materials, had afforded something of an outlet to the girl's æstheticism and reflected the inborn delicacy of her taste. She had wanted one of the larger, lighter rooms, of which the house held several, but these were reserved for patrons. However, her fourth-story refuge afforded her one consolation: she was on a level with the birds. An old maple, reaching to caress her window, held in the crook of its fingers a big robins' nest, just near and low enough for her to see all that transpired therein, and throughout the spring the sweet little drama of family life had proved to her more fascinating than any stage production. She had watched the nest grow from nothing, woven of the twigs and grasses the tireless mates carried in. How they did work together! And once she had seen the tiny mother pluck

AN ODD NUMBER

feathers from her own breast to line it softly. Then, one morning, with a thrill of awe, she beheld five azure eggs, and, a little later, cried all alone, in tender delight, at the emergence of the funny, speckled babies. The young parents had become quite tame, and, when she hid behind the curtain, would steal to the sill for crumbs. Out of her affection she even dug revolting worms for them, and it was wonderful to witness how they tore and nipped these creatures into morsels that the greedy birdlings might not choke on their repast. With a reversal of feeling, Jean would pity the worms, and hope they were really as senseless as the naturalists claimed; and then, while the babies slept, she would gaze off into the rich green folds of the leaves, shut her eyes and open them suddenly, trying to imagine how it must feel to be a bird and wake up to find one's self enveloped by such exquisite tapestry.

She began to dress slowly, listening the while for the clear call of her little friends. This had become a habit. Many other birds sought transient lodgings in the maple, even as did people at the Two-ways Inn, but she knew the voices of Bob and Betty Redbreast, and would have missed them.

"There!" Her heart gave a bounding response to the trill of a joyous treble. "They

A CHILD OF DIVORCE

are saying 'Happy birthday!'" But as she glided to the window for a sly peek, a summons of rasping contrast reached her through the keyhole:

"Jean, are you up? That new waitress ain't showed up yet, and there's some men downstairs, and pa wants you to take 'em their breakfast. You better hurry."

The girl's spirits dropped as they had mounted, but she answered tolerantly: "All right, Junior."

This waiting on strange men in the intimate capacities that belonged to home was a thing she instinctively loathed. Servants in that vicinity were susceptible to epidemics of "spree-itis," due to which Jean was frequently expected to substitute. She had done about everything in the scullery line except tend the bar, and only her mother's intervention spared her that. Mrs. Hasbrook was prompted here, not so much by tender consideration for the girl's feelings, as by a certain vanity of blood, the "rights" of which she still made forlorn efforts to assert. "Mercy!" she had exclaimed upon the first provocation, "*my* child a barmaid? Why, General Beaugarth would turn over in his grave!"

"Well, let him turn," her husband rebutted, sullenly, "or else turn *out* somethin'! We can't live on ancestors' reputations!" On that extreme occasion, however, the woman had her way, but Jean's springing gratitude was chilled by the shade of her defense. Quarrels between her parents, over more or less trivial questions, not only relating to herself, had become more and more frequent, and in the silence of her heart Jean somehow felt that the Hasbrook walls were trembling, even as the house of Laval had trembled prior to its collapse. How, indeed, could it be otherwise? No one can build firmly over broken basebeams. Even the laws of physics disprove such a thing. Her mother had sipped of the wine of extravagance until she had become its slave. She was a gentle, cultured, shallow woman, whose weapons were the more dangerous because so unapparent. They usually procured her eventually whatever she wanted, if need be, at the expense of others, but always in a manner visibly correct. Indeed, she had no direct intention of cheating any one. She was simply one of those creatures dominated by desires without the moral backbone to work for their fulfillment, though possessing enough sense of proportion to guard appearances. She was, in short, a parasite, with whom no mate could have prospered, because, as fast as he gathered substance, she sucked it from him, ever demanding more. James Hasbrook, in his rovings, had acquired a certain sophistication, which only the close relationship of matrimony betrayed as a very thin shellac over a "coarse origin." He had hailed into her life like a stimulating wind just as she was growing bored with her refined, but unaggressive, husband, and he, not being an heir to the delicate gift of analysis, had no comprehension of the reason for their increasing discontent. He could not understand his wife's moods. True, all his beguiling word-pictures had not materialized, any more than had the business prospects of Verne Laval, but, then, every man was not "lucky," and she had taken him "for better, for worse." It did not occur to him forcibly that she had taken a former mate with the *same* promise. He only felt dully that he had been good enough for her once; then, what did she mean by "acting so snobby"? And so the trying years wore away the poor shellac, leaving the real man bare, and exposing, too, that vicious vein in him before referred to. He grew taciturn and irritable, and Jean lived under the impression of some vague, submental foreboding.

As she slipped downstairs and passed the door of their bedroom, she heard them arguing again: "But I *want* it, James!" her mother's voice rose petulantly. "You've dragged me out here to the end of the world, and now you don't even want to let me have

AN ODD NUMBER

that little pleasure! But I tell you, I can't stand it. A woman has got to have something to love!"

"You've got the kids, haven't you?"

"But they're big now. Even Junior's running wild; he won't let me even kiss him any more."

"D'you want a cat to kiss?"

"You needn't be so sarcastic. I never said such a thing!"

"Well, that's what it sounds like. If you've got to have something to maul, then, why don't you have another kid!" (the girl in the passageway winced); "that would give you something to do."

"Yes, and cost you a lot more than $50."

"And wouldn't be worth it, either, if you bring it up as good-for-nothin' as the others. Well, I'm not shellin' out $50 for any old cat to mess around the house!"

"But it's *Angora*," desperately; "it would catch the mice!"

"Catch mice, your eye! Those stuck-up breeds of cats have about as much idea of catchin' mice as you have of workin'. Any old tom could beat 'em at that, and there's a whole litter at Pearsall's. You can have one for nothin'."

"One of those common things full of fleas! I'll go without first!"

A CHILD OF DIVORCE

"Well, then, I guess you'll go without all right." The gruff voice approached the door, and Jean hastened on to the dining-room with a mind unhappily disturbed.

Lolling over one table waited two loud young fellows, typical "representatives," and in the farthest, darkest corner, as if he desired seclusion, sat another man.

"Here she is!" greeted one of the drummers, thrumming the board with his fingers.

"Ah there, bright eyes!" chorused his mate. "How's chances for a little feed?"

"What would you like?" Forcing down her repulsion, Jean approached in her fresh gingham dress, looking suggestively at the fly-specked menu-card.

"Ah, let's see. Adam an' Eve on a raft, I guess. What's yours, Jack?"

"Ditto—and wreck 'em!"

Jean hesitated, whereupon "Jack" grinningly modified: "Over, and don't be stingy with the bacon."

"Fried murphies, if you've got 'em."

"Same here, and double on the Java."

Jean was glad to escape to the kitchen, though she knew that would not be the end. The third man appeared a gentleman, yet his one swift glance had caused her to recoil as keenly as the others' raillery, and for some more sinister reason. She returned with her loaded

AN ODD NUMBER

tray, mentally striving to forget that she was a woman, or anything else just then but a waitress, upon whom rested the obligation to be courteous; but her smile was poor camouflage.

"What's the funeral, sister?"

"Feelin' sore this mornin'?" Over their steaming breakfast the drummers waxed cheerful. "Maybe her sweetie didn't come last night," "Jack" offered by way of solution.

"She should worry. Say, cutie," the other leaned forward and lowered his voice, "we're hangin' out around this burg for awhile. Come and take you for a spin to-night. Are you on?"

"Do you wish anything else?" Jean asked coldly.

"Huh? Oh, you ain't? Well, if that's the way you feel about it"—the two exchanged significant looks, shrugged and laughed—"nothin' doin'," she heard one add as she turned to the man in the shadow. She had felt the latter's searching eyes before she met them. Those eyes drew her, even while the rest of the man's personality repelled. They were splendid eyes of dark gray-blue, and Jean had the aggravating consciousness that she had looked into them before—but where? Not here, or she would have remembered. It seemed to be long ago. He was tall, slim,

49

clean-shaven, just beginning to be bald, one of those men upon whom time registered his passage so slightly that he might have been anywhere from thirty-five to fifty.

"My wife is in the car," he explained softly. "Will you please *take her a tray*—the best you have?"

"Certainly, sir."

When the chauffeur saw her coming, he slid down to open the door of the limousine, and a young woman peered out. Satin, jewelry, "summer furs," combined to render her a living fashion-plate, and over Jean flashed an impression of how beautiful she would have been had she not looked so worried—nay, more than worried—desperate! She drank the coffee eagerly, but pushed the food away, fretting. "I told—my husband I didn't wish anything; I'm not hungry. Shut the door, Charles!" The servant obeyed. Incidentally he caught Jean's eye and deliberately winked.

"Your wife wouldn't eat, sir," she reported to the gentleman; "she cared only for the coffee."

"Oh, very well." A small, queer smile drew his mouth—cruel, it seemed to Jean. "She isn't used to such early rising. Do you work here, child?"

"When we are short of help. My father is the proprietor."

AN ODD NUMBER

"Oh, I see." His eyebrows lifted slightly; then once more he looked directly at her. "I hope you won't misunderstand me, Miss, if I take the liberty of saying that it seems to me you are wasting your time."

"Why—how?" stammered Jean.

"I have a friend who would pay you a good salary to pose for him."

"*Pose?*"

"Yes; he's a sculptor. Now, don't mistake me," as Jean shrank back. "It's nothing. Simply the arms and shoulders. I'm no dime-novel or movie seducer, telling you you're beautiful when you're not. Your face is all right, but nothing extra—good and honest—but your neck and arms are fine!"

"How do you know that?" Instinctively the girl caught together the rolling collar of her blouse, flushing deeply, her voice a little sharp.

"Don't think me bold," he said; "I'm only frank. I'm old enough to be your dad—an old married man." He arose, now openly, though quietly, laughing, and, reaching for his panama, continued: "I don't wish to urge you at all, though I'm sure you could better yourself; but if you should take a notion to seek your fortune soon, and want to try it, come and see me. I have offices both in New York and in New Jersey. This is nearest."

A CHILD OF DIVORCE

He drew a card from his case and slipped it into Jean's surprised fingers. The next minute he was gone. In vain did the drummers clap their spoons against their glasses. Jean hastened from the dining-room. But just outside stood Hasbrook, appraising her grimly. He tried to block the passage.

"What's the matter with you?" he growled; "what d'you mean by treating customers like this? Go back there and see what those men want!"

"I won't—*I can't!*" Jean gasped, and, tear-blinded, rushed to her room. Her nervous hand still crushed the card. She glanced at it curiously and read through the blur: "Jerome Bascomb, Attorney at Law, 809 Fladison Bldg., New York City."

"No wonder," came the passionate thought; "he's a *lawyer!* Lawyers stole my father—my father! Oh, father—if you knew this—wouldn't you care?" She tore the card into bits, and, sinking beside the bed, her face in her arms, cried recklessly.

How dared any man insult her with such intimate remarks? Was she entitled to no respect—just because she must work?

So began her nineteenth year, and each ensuing day stretched nearer to the breaking-point the strained relations at the Two Ways Inn. Following that episode, her step-

AN ODD NUMBER

father seldom addressed her, except to give some terse command.

One afternoon, several days later, when he was in town on business, her mother returned from a drive and smuggled a covered basket into the house.

"What's that, mother?" Jean queried.

"Something I want," Mrs. Hasbrook answered, through lips stiff in defiance. "You needn't say anything, Jean. Let him find it out if he wants to. I don't care, though—I've got it now!"

There came a scratching sound from the basket. "Is it a cat, mother?"

"Yes, it is; how did you know?"

"I heard you ask for it."

"Well, I'm getting less and less what I ask for, Jean, but I don't intend to be denied *everything*—as if I were an irresponsible child. The Lord helps those that help themselves. It's a beauty, Jean. Look!" She lifted the lid, and out bounded a yellow, shock-headed Angora feline, appearing larger than it really was because of its bushy fur, its neck adorned by a huge baby-blue bow. It began at once a sniffing investigation of the strange quarters.

"Isn't it pretty?" enthused Mrs. Hasbrook.

"I should say!" Highly pleased, Jean stooped to pet it; but the golden bundle evaded her hand.

A CHILD OF DIVORCE

"Get her some milk," Mrs. Hasbrook suggested. "She'll feel at home then."

The girl hurried to comply, bringing, too, a plate of scrap-meat, all of which the stranger relished without, however, manifesting any signs of gratitude. It is well known that this breed of cat possesses a fierce nature, and is seldom as affectionate as the ordinary tabby; but to Mrs. Hasbrook her relative value was determined by what she had cost, and the resultant fact that she was not "so common."

"She'll soon feel at home now," she reassured herself and Jean, which proved true, for in a few hours "Trixie" had the run of the inn, coming and going upstairs and down, quite independent of them all, and at last submitting ungraciously to being locked up in the cellar for her first night. Next morning, Junior released her before his mother knew it, and she strolled with aristocratic leisure to the edge of the barroom to introduce herself to the liege. Hasbrook, having imbibed rather generously after another domestic tiff, looked up and blinked at the yellow splotch on the threshold, "What the devil!" he grumbled. 'Where'd *you* come from?"

"Me-ow!" saluted his caller; then, as he stared, her golden presence illumined his mind. "It's that cat—that $50 cat; she's gone and got it, after all! I'll be—" He started so

AN ODD NUMBER

suddenly for the door that the cat retracted and bolted up the stairway, flying past Jean on her way down, and, directly, the girl was arrested by angry voices.

"So long as it wasn't *your* money," her mother was defying stridently when she reached the room, "what need you care? I hope I have some rights left, James Hasbrook."

"Not my money, huh? Where'd you get it, then? And who d' you think's goin to pay for the food? I tell you, *one* ornamental brat of yours is enough to feed? And, by the way, it's time that girl was shiftin' for herself. She's more than of age now, and if she won't work, she can get out, that's all! I've done *my* share—and more!"

Jean shut her eyes as she braced herself against the pang of those words. She stole in and stood regarding, in agonized silence, the quarreling pair.

"Yes; did you hear that?" Hasbrook demanded, spying her. "I've done my share—all I'm going to—you lazy young snob! Just like your mother; but I'm not married to you, and you can get out now, and see how the world will stand for you!"

Jean bowed her head before his coarse wrath. "All right." Her voice was low and strangely hollow. "I'll go—I'll go—to my father, if you'll give me his address."

A CHILD OF DIVORCE

"Your father? Ho, ho! Much *he'll* do for you! He was through with you before I was."

Jean looked up, then, crimsoning. "I don't believe it! He never said so! He didn't know!"

"You don't, eh? He didn't, huh? You just wait—wait'll I show you. I guess *this'll* prove who's taken the most from you!" He strode to a dresser, jerked out a drawer, and, after rummaging for awhile, withdrew an open letter to her mother, which he flung at her.

Wonderingly, Jean's eyes traced the lines, beginning with the letter-head: "Mackenzie, Reed & Mackenzie, Counselors at Law, East Elair, N. J." It was dated two years before.

"DEAR MADAM:—On behalf of our client, Verne Laval, from whom you were awarded a decree of divorce in 1903, we wish to advise you that, whereas the child, Jean Laval, who was the issue of that union, and whom the courts gave into your custody, has now attained the age of sixteen (which, by this State, is set as the age of maturity), it is no longer incumbent upon our client to be responsible for the child's maintenance, and, therefore, the sum of $30 per month which the courts allowed from our client for this purpose during the minor years of the child is being discontinued as of the present date. We enclose herewith the final payment.

"We assume, of course, that, according to the agreement, this money has been used toward the support and education of the said child with such discretion as will have by this time thoroughly equipped her for self-support.   Yours very truly."

AN ODD NUMBER

Jean looked up, stunned, to face Hasbrook's leer. Her mother had turned away, whimpering.

"But I haven't been 'equipped for self-support.'" She grappled at last, numbly, for some defense. "I've never even finished school!"

"You didn't want to go, Jean," sobbed her mother. "You know what a time we had to make you!" This was true. Something in the girl's nature had rebelled at mental molding and physical confinement, and the Hasbrooks, having more immediate interests than her future welfare, and also finding her useful at home, had simply followed the line of least resistance, making no special effort to train the child's whims. In this respect, their migratory habits had afforded them many excuses for evading the law of compulsory education. Jean's "discipline" had been wholly contingent upon whether or not her conduct interfered with the pleasures of her parents.

"Is this where my father lives—East Elair?" she asked mechanically.

"Yes," her mother replied. "That's where he was two years ago, and I s'pose he's still there. He owned the house. He got married again, you know."

That was an added shock. Jean had never known. For a few minutes she stood, dazed;

A CHILD OF DIVORCE

then, turning, she dragged herself heavily back to the only refuge the world afforded her—the little room. But, in its doorway, a sharp cry tore from her lips. While her heart was being virtually severed below, another tragedy had transpired above, another home had been wrecked! Under the open window crouched the yellow cat, growling and chewing, her eyes like cinders, her long claws impaling the remains of Bobby Redbreast, about her the trophies of her conquest—feathers. Then, before Jean's eyes a black veil seemed to fall. She groped for support, reached the bed and fell across it. When the curtain lifted, her mother was beside her with smelling-salts.

"Oh, dear me, Jean! How you scared me!" she complained. "What made you faint? Are you all right now?"

"I think so, mother." Jean turned her face to the wall. "Don't worry about me," she added listlessly.

"Jean, I came up to tell you—I'm awfully sorry." Her mother's tone was nervous. "I'm sorry you didn't get more schooling. But you didn't want to go. You remember that, don't you? And, perhaps," brightening, "you won't find it so hard, after all. Why, I've seen some college graduates that didn't know very much, and, with all the girls there are working nowadays—they can't *all* have had more schooling

AN ODD NUMBER

than you, but they get positions. No, you'll get something, something genteel, too—of course you will. Where are you going, Jean?"

"Please, mother, let me think a little. I just can't decide yet. But by to-night—"

"All right, dearie, but don't you worry. Your mother was wiser than you think. I saved some of that money from your father, Jean. I've got fifteen dollars left, and you can have it all to start out with. It'll pay your board till you get a position, and you're smart, Jean—you'll get along all right. It's not as if you were a poor, helpless, dumb animal—like Trixie." She patted the girl's shoulder and went softly out. Jean stared up at the ceiling. Her eyes were vacant. Her lips twitched into a little cold, hard smile. She would rather have gone out penniless, with a real mother's deep faith and yearning affection, than with fifteen *hundred* dollars, under such circumstances. But what was the use of repining? No one understood. The hope of ever being loved and loving was nothing but a silly dream. She ought to have known that by this time! There was only one way to live in this world— that was to give blow for blow. Well, she would do it, and let those who tried to cross her look out for themselves. Why should she waste her time and feelings on any one else's troubles? Yet, under all this bitterness gnawed the persis-

A CHILD OF DIVORCE

tent longing to see her father—her own father —who had kissed her good-by twelve years ago before the Vice-Chancellor. Was he really as indifferent to her as they said? She fell to speculating. Even if he were married again, it could not alter the fact that he was her father— the man who had given her life. Surely he could not forget that! She resolved presently to go first to East Elair and hunt for him, trusting fate for what might follow. She still had the lawyers' letter, and they would know his address, if she could not find it in the directory. At length she arose. Trixie had followed her mother out, leaving the scattered feathers and some blood-stains on the floor, and the sight shot pain through her breast. She crept to the window and gazed out pitifully. Only a few shreds of that toil-gathered, love-built nest swung in the breeze from the fingers of the maple. Gone—her cheerful little serenaders— all gone! She leaned against the sash, while slowly once more the smarting tears slid down. By and by she gathered the feathers with tender hands, and washed the stains from the matting. "But you loved each other," came the thought, "and you went together. Oh, little friends, it's better to die like that than to live with your heart torn in half!"

That night she packed her possessions, her mother and Junior helping. She would leave

AN ODD NUMBER

them so till she got settled somewhere, then send for them, taking only a suitcase. The process was not as sorrowful as it might have been, because of that secret star of hope, that vague faith in her father. Not that she wanted his material support. She could work. But perhaps he would *care!* She had made many overtures to her little half-brother. Junior, however, was too much like James Hasbrook for her to gain much headway there. We dislike to think of a child as calculating, yet certainly they are quick to seize a point of vantage. Junior had seized his in babyhood and held it ever since. His father's patronizing tolerance toward her had been, perhaps, only naturally absorbed by and reflected in the boy. He was excited to-night over the novelty of her departure, and, besides, she was bequeathing him some of her old playthings, long stored away.

"Gee!" he broke out suddenly, when their mother had gone out for some cord, "if I can have them roller-skates, I'm glad you're goin', Jean."

The girl flinched. "I thought you'd miss me," she answered wistfully.

"Oh, sure we will, at first, but we'll get used to it. Oh! can I have that pencil-box too?"

"Yes, Junior," she choked. Nothing could have hurt much more than this, because we know that children are candid. And still she could not resist the temptation to probe him for one appreciative word. "Who'll sweep and wait on the tables when Stella don't come back?" she queried.

"Oh," he answered easily, "papa'll buy a woman."

CHAPTER V.
"THREE'S A CROWD"

"THE next stop is East Elair!" suddenly sang out the train conductor, and Jean started, though she knew from the time-table they were due there. Her heart thumped. She straightened her hat, plucked her rumpled dress into order and fumbled once more through her handbag to be sure she had lost nothing. She had sifted somehow through the bustling maze of the Long Island Terminal in New York, found the ferry to Hoboken, and was being whirled at last toward her destiny. She felt rather dizzy and her head ached. She had never traveled so far alone. After they had drawn clear of the railroad yards, emerged from a long, smoky tunnel and skimmed the Meadows, the landscape unrolled somewhat monotonously, and, sprinkled here and there, appeared groups of small, frame houses, not artistically dispersed over the wide green acres, or even individually planned, except for alternating coats of paint, but clustered together like unexpected litters of cubs—all the same but for their markings, and not much variety

A CHILD OF DIVORCE

even in those. Yet it might have been interesting had she been less anxious. Each revolution of the wheels was cutting off the distance between her and her father! What was he like? How would he receive her? Her imagination conjured up various situations, and she counted the stations, as one might tell the minutes to some crisis, growing tense and tenser. She clutched the grip handle for long minutes ere the train ground into the depot. Then she alighted mechanically. The locomotive regathered its forces and chugged on; the few other passengers discharged started off as those who are certain of their destination. Only Jean remained, bewildered, on the asphalt platform. Presently she stole into the waiting-room and inquired a bit timidly of the ticket agent: "Have—have you a directory?"

He jerked his thumb toward the telephone sign.

"There's one in the phone booth."

"Thank you!" She found it, set her burden on the floor and opened to the "L's."

"Laval, Laval"—her finger traced the column—"*Verne*—37 Vernon Place!"

Can you tell me how to get to Vernon Place?" Once more she appealed to the railway oracle. He complied with terse directions, which only augmented her mystification. However, she was launching courageously out when

"THREE'S A CROWD"

her glance was caught by the black type of a placard on the wall.

"Is divorce Christian? Come and hear the answer of Holy Scripture. Sunday, June 17, 11 A. M., First Union Church, Paul Manson, Pastor."

"Today's Saturday—it's to-morrow," Jean recalled her thoughts long enough to observe, then off they flew again to her father, and thereafter afforded room to no other subject.

East Elair had really begun as a suburb of the city of Newark. It had reared quite a business district of its own, but, to a great degree, retained its suburban characteristics, and was extensively residential. Jean, passing a small lunchroom near the depot, remembered that, though one o'clock had struck, she had eaten nothing since her early breakfast. She was too excited to be hungry, but the hope asserted itself that perhaps a bite would steady her nerves and fit her better for whatever awaited; so she entered, climbed a tall stool before the counter, and ordered some milk, with a corned-beef sandwich. It being late, there were no other customers, and, as she swallowed hurriedly, she became subconscious of the same placard she had seen in the station propped up against a cheese globe. The stout, blond proprietor, apparently having not much else to do, threw her curious glances, inclined

A CHILD OF DIVORCE

toward conversation. Upon finishing she felt encouraged to ask him about Vernon Place.

"Oh, ja," he responded, "but dot vrom here iss a long valk, unt dere iss no gross-town trolley. You got mit a pig pag, no? Mine poy, he drive der taxi. You vant I should call you vun?"

"No, I want to walk. I've been sitting in the train—*hours!*"

"Phew! Mit dot so heavy pag in der hot zun! Vell, den, dis vere you iss now iss Fourd Avenue. You should go on till id iss"—he scratched his head and counted—"nine—ja, nine plocks, den to der right you should valk fife plocks, den you should turn vunce again yet to der right, unt it iss apout two plocks. You vill see on der gorner vun pig red brick houze, unt dot is Vernon Place."

"Thank you!" acknowledged Jean, slipping off the stool. She did feel stronger. The cool milk had refreshed her. But the crosstown blocks proved long and the sun burned indeed. Soon she was shifting the valise very often from one hand to the other, and a few times she set it down to pause for breath. At last, by dint of pains and persistence in following directions, she came in sight of the big red brick house, and then a sign on the lamppost reading "Vernon Place." The red brick house was No. 508! Tears of fatigue and chagrin rushed to Jean's eyes. She wanted to drop down on the curb and sob, but, instead, she blinked resolutely and braced herself to trudge on to "37," though the pavement scorched through her soles, her palms began to blister and her heart beat far too rapidly.

Verne Laval belonged in that sad category of twentieth-century Americans who, to please themselves or their families, will have a pretentious dwelling, though they eat canned beans in the kitchen behind it—when there is no company; who will have a car, though it means a second mortgage on the home, and a liveried chauffeur, periodically at least, though that may mean a mortgage on the car. Nor is this observed in hasty condemnation of that very prevalent weakness which often springs from something deeper than mere love of show, or even an ambition to keep up with the neighbors, beginning in a true appreciation of beauty and a really commendable desire for the niceties of life. The curse of these people, however, lies in the fact that their enjoyment of the things acquired is naturally spoiled by worry as to how they are going to pay for them, so that what might have made for happiness becomes a cause of friction, and often despair.

Laval had not progressed in business. His was too sensitive a nature to push toward prospects which might have been realized for the effort. As a young teller in a large bank in New York, he had married Jean's mother. Then, when his vision was clearer, he had attempted a feeble remonstrance against the folly of extravagance, but this was the seed of the trouble which reached its fruition in the advent of James Hasbrook. His second matrimonial venture involved a poor stenographer, who, he thought, would appreciate the need of economy. But she was sick of poverty, and lo! with another to meet her bills, she spent as much as her predecessor. Laval's position had not advanced beyond an occasional raise in salary, but, judging from the home which Jean now approached, he had ceased in his middle age to struggle for a principle, and was letting himself drift with that swift throng which lives but in the present.

It was a fine stucco house, with a deep veranda, set in a wide, velvety yard, over which a revolving hose fixture swept a crystal spray. On either side of the walk unfolded well-planned flower-beds, and the porch base was bordered with several varieties of dwarf evergreens in blending shades and graduated sizes. Two children sprawled on the grass, taking liberties with the hose. A boy of about eight would squeeze it, shrieking with delight at the resultant fluctuation of the water, while his little sister gleefully followed his every move.

"THREE'S A CROWD"

Jean stopped to regard them, the strangest emotion suddenly surging within her. Prominent on the screen door shone the number "37." Wearily, half fearfully, Jean advanced. The boy dropped the hose, and sprang up, calling: "What d'you want?"

"What's your name?" Jean asked, but she knew already, because, peering speculatively at her from around the boy's elbow, shone a pair of hazel eyes strikingly like some she had seen in the mirror. Yet her breath caught at the crystallization of that fear in words.

"Berty Laval. Why?"

"And yours?" to the tiny girl.

"Luthie L—Laval."

"What d'you want to know for? D'you wanta see my dad?" persisted Berty.

"Yes—is he home?"

"He always is Saterd'y af'ernoon."

"But muvver not—she gone out," piped up Lucy. Jean felt a quick mingling of relief and increased agitation. Her hungry gaze sought Lucy, nor could it have beheld a sweeter bud of femininity. Suddenly she knelt on the grass and flung her arms around the plump little body, sobbing: "Lucy!—kiss me—love me—I'm your sister!"

"Go on," interrupted the suspicious voice of Berty; "you're kiddin'. We haven't any big sister like you!"

Jean stared at him, the shadow of pain darkening her wet eyes. "Then, your father never told you—about me?" she choked.

"Nope," decisively. "I dunno who you are, but you're not our sister—'cause we haven't any!" Lucy, however, as if drawn by some mutual sympathy, was squeezing her neck, her round cheek pressed against the hot, moist one, and lisping, "No cwy—poor, bid dirl— Luthie 'ove oo!" Lucy loved every one who her unfailing juvenile instinct told her needed it.

"But I *am* your sister," Jean asserted, still looking anxiously at the boy, as though upon his response depended in a large measure her fate.

"Then, why don't you live with us?"

"I—I—went away before you were born— when I was only as big as Lucy."

"Aw, shucks! Girls on'y as big as Lucy can't go 'way."

"But some one took me."

"D'you mean they stoled you?"

"No—not exactly. Oh, I can't tell you it all now, but perhaps some day you'll know, and first I want to see papa."

"Are you goin' to live with us now?"

"I don't know—perhaps—if papa don't think I'm too big."

"Well, c'mon, I'll show you where he is." Jean arose and limped after him, half dragging her luggage, Lucy's affectionate fingers clasping the other hand. He burst through the screen door, boylike letting it bang, and she could hear his shill "Oh, daddy, daddy! Here's a big girl wants to see you!" Then quickly he reappeared, announcing: "He says for you to come in—he's in the lib'ry."

"Thank you, Berty, and now will you wait outside and play?" They seemed disappointed, but obeyed, staring in wonder after her as she relinquished her burden and stole into the hall. The library was just beyond the parlor, and between the Japanese portieres Jean could see a man sitting there, a handsome man still, after the slender, nervous type, though many gray strands emphasized the chestnut of his hair, and worry lines seared his face. He had laid aside a newspaper, and was looking expectantly toward her with large, almost feminine, dark hazel eyes, and he filled not only her vision, but her total consciousness. Yet on the threshold she halted, transfixed.

"Well, Miss?" his voice broke the spell— that voice of long ago! In one vivid flash Jean was back in the courtroom feeling his last embrace and hearing "Good-by, Jeanie, be a good little girl and mind your mother."

"What is it?" he pressed, frowning slightly as she stood there speechless. Then her tongue loosened, *"Papa—Papa!"*

"What?—Why—" He arose and came toward her, tense, yet incredulous.

"Who are you, child?" and now his voice sounded thick.

"Papa! Don't you know me? I'm Jean."

"Jean!"

She flew to his breast and there cried out her misery. And Verne Laval wept a little too—at first. Then dawned upon him the complications of this situation. He led her to the divan, keeping his arms around her, till she calmed, when he brought her a cool drink.

"Lie down here," he invited, piling the pillows for her; "you must be very tired, dear." She was glad enough to do so, and then, for a long interval, he sat opposite and studied her thoughtfully.

"So this is Jean," he observed finally; "my little Jean—come back to me a woman! To think I have a grown-up daughter—it doesn't seem possible. I've thought of you so often through all these years, Jean. More than once I've been on the point of going to see you, and only one thing kept me back. I thought it would only aggravate things and make you unhappy. I thought it was better to leave things as they were; then, perhaps, you might forget me."

"Oh, papa! I could *never* forget you!" cried the girl, with a fresh break of tears.

"THREE'S A CROWD"

"Yet, Jean, I almost wish you had tried to—for your own happiness—and—"

"And what, papa?"

"Jean, you are a woman now, dear; and I feel that I can talk to you as one; one who will understand, for your own sake first, and then—your mother's—and mine. You love—both of us, don't you? So you will understand. If I had come, it would not only have made you unhappy because I couldn't stay, but I would have had to see—your mother—and *him*. And now I have a family and—for you to be here—you know I love you, Jean, and I'm *very* glad to see you; yet, dear, I wish you had written me first, so I could have been prepared. My wife—"

Under Jean's heart crept a dull, chill pain—a sickening pain—and she hid her face in the pillow. Understand? Only one agonizing realization overwhelmed her—that, after all, he did not want her! He was sorry, of course. He would do what he could, out of a sense of "duty," even as the Hasbrooks had—but he did not *care!*

Seeing her gestures, he continued, plainly distressed: "My dear child, don't misunderstand me—don't think me harsh. Only sometimes we must be reasonable for the good of all concerned. I'm sorry you've been so unhappy, Jean, even indignant at what you have told me. Your mother chose—*him*—and I hoped he would make you a better father—even than I—"

"Oh!" the girl broke in. "How could anybody else take the place of my own father that God gave me? If *He* had meant me to have another—wouldn't He have given me that one at first? Don't God know His business? I tell you I *don't* understand anything —*anything*—except that you're my father and she's my mother—and all I want is you both and a home—like other girls! Oh! I don't see why we should be divided like this!" She was close now to hysterics.

A strained expression shaded Laval's face, and it cost him an evident effort to be patient, as he argued: "That is impossible, my child. You are tired and nervous. When you have rested, you will see things in a saner light. Lie there now; don't cry any more, and try to take a nap. I'm going to find you a place to stay." He arose once more and left her for the telephone. She heard the conversation as a submental mumble. She was not enough interested to listen. Her star of hope was snuffed out, the light that she had dimly seen was gone. Nothing in all the dark earth mattered now.

Having made arrangements with the party on the other end of the wire, Laval could ill disguise his haste to get her away before the return of his wife. "Come, dear," he bade her gently, donning his hat and lifting the suitcase; "we'll go to a place where it's much quieter, and you can have a good, long rest." Jean acquiesced absently. Just as they descended the front steps, a long, dark-red car swerved in at the driveway, controlled by a richly dressed lady. Catching sight of them, she threw on the brakes, and called, "Where are you going, Verne?" but her eyes lingered on Jean. The man laughed a little nervously, as he walked toward her, explaining: "I'm taking this young lady to Harland's—she's strange here."

"Since when were you appointed housemaid's guide?" Mrs. Laval asked, with poorly concealed suspicion. Here Berty inserted, "She ain't a maid, Muth; she says she's our sister."

"What!"

Laval swallowed, then confessed. "Yes, Alice; this is Jean. You remember my speaking of her?"

"Oh! How do you do, Jean?" Coldly gracious, she reached down a hand—a stiff, formal ring-rack. But Jean shrank back, her taut sensibilities recoiling from such insincerity. It takes a big-souled woman to be cordial to the child of her marital predecessor. Alice

Laval was not a big-souled woman, and this move of Jean's piqued her. However, she feigned to overlook it. "I hadn't heard much of you lately. Where've you been keeping yourself?"

"On Long Island," Jean murmured, though she wanted to scream, "What do you care?"

"Well, I hope you've enjoyed your visit. Here, Verne, I'm through with the car. Don't walk along the street with that clumsy satchel —and every one doesn't know who she is"— her tone implied "thank goodness!"—"get up in the back seat, Jean, while Mr. Laval drives."

When they had cleared the neighborhood, Laval slowed down, flung open the door, and invited Jean to come into the front seat beside him.

"Did your really tell Berty that?" he queried anxiously.

"What?"

"That you were his sister?"

"Yes—why?"

His answer was a look of annoyance, and Jean could say no more. He took her for quite a spin before winding up at Mrs. Harland's, out to the foot of the Orange Mountains and back over the white roads of a rolling, lake-gemmed park; but it held no enjoyment for her. She was in a mental stupor, and the

"THREE'S A CROWD"

only thing real was the pressure of the long, empty future.

Mrs. Harland proved to be the very fat custodian of a boarding-house in a section near Newark, which had developed several manufactories and a subsequent need of such human hostelries. She was known as a good-humored lady, though, as she suffered from high blood pressure, one could never tell just when she might "go off," a condition which the boarders soon found it the better part of three square meals a day to accept with respect. However, whether from altruism or an eye to business, she kept an effulgent manner for strangers, and welcomed Jean profusely upon her father's introduction. "This is the daughter of a distant relative, from Long Island," Laval explained; "she wants to go to business as soon as we can land her a suitable position, but first I want to see her fixed in comfortable living-quarters."

"Yes, sir, yes. She'll sure be comfortable here, sir. Won't you come up and see the room? Lucky! I just happened to have it—gentleman moved out yesterday, and soon as you 'phoned, I tidied it up. Best one in the house, sir. I advertised to-day, and it would soon've been took. Lucky!"

"I'll take your word for it," Laval smiled; "and if Jean don't like it she must tell me.

A CHILD OF DIVORCE

You run along up, Jean. I'll wait for you here."

Mrs. Harland wheezed up two flights of stairs like a small trench tank, followed by the still dazed girl. The room was of average size with south and west windows, stocked with the usual odds and ends of furniture least desirable for the family's own use. Even the patched matting displayed a variety of patterns wherever they were not too faded to be recognized. The south window gave over a garage, but from the west one caught the perspective of a board, maple-bordered avenue which Jean later learned was Park Road, corresponding in New Jersey to the Merrick Road of Long Island. Although the late sun rays betrayed the furniture's dinginess, they lent the room a generally cheerful aspect.

"Clean beds," boasted Mrs. Harland, turning back an inch or two of the sheet; "no bugs *here!* You'll sleep fine, Miss. Tired? You look so. Come a long piece, didn't you?"

"Yes," Jean answered wearily; "I'd like to lie down soon as I've said good-by to—Mr. Laval."

There was little more to be said. Jean told her father quietly that she liked the room, and after Mrs. Harland had waddled back to the kitchen to oversee the dinner, an awkward interval elapsed. Then Laval drew a twenty-

"THREE'S A CROWD"

dollar bill from his wallet, offering: "Here, Jean, make it last as long as you can, for I don't know when I can give you another. It's not as if I didn't want to, Jean, but a family these days—don't be too hard on me, child. I thought you'd understand better, and I believe you will when you're rested—" But Jean had drawn back with her head high, a strange, cold light glinting in her eyes.

"No, thank you, papa," she refused, her voice hard with repressed feeling. 'I'll stay here till Monday, because you've treated me like a kind stranger, and like a stranger I accept your courtesy—and thank you. But don't think money—even more than this—could pay me for your love. If you won't acknowledge me as your daughter, then I can't take your money. Oh, yes, I know"—as his lips parted to remonstrate—"but don't worry, papa. I won't disgrace you. I'm going away just as soon as I can to take care of myself."

Other boarders began to come in, and he did not kiss her farewell for fear of being seen, but went out at last, obviously dejected.

Hungry as she was, Jean could eat very little that night. Food not only choked her, but the loud company of strangers was unbearable, and hours later, depleted of bodily and nervous strength, she sank into a trouble-haunted sleep on a damp pillow.

CHAPTER VI.

APPLYING MATHEMATICS TO BABIES

JEAN was awakened by sunrise cathedral bells, still under a heavy sense of depression. She lay for a long time trying to concentrate her thoughts on the problem before her and adjust herself in some measure to her impending life, though as yet it was too early in the stage for her to fully comprehend all that being a young woman, homeless, penniless, virtually friendless, would involve. This was a merciful circumstance. Presently, more from restlessness and habit than interest in living, she arose and dressed. No one else in the house seemed to be astir, for most of the boarders were of that variety which takes the "day of rest" literally, and as Jean crept downstairs for a breath of summer morning air, she was greeted only by many-toned snores sifting through crevices and keyholes. Even the kitchen was silent.

Park Road to the west offered an inviting walk. From its long canopy of trees bird notes responded to the distant echoes of early service

APPLYING MATHEMATICS

chimes, enhancing that caressing charm which belongs alone to a June Sunday. Over Jean's heart poured an unaccountable balm. It seemed as though any one who could sleep through such a morning must be hopelessly sunk in the carnal. Trouble belonged with the lovers of darkness and no more than midnight's gloom could his ugly specter survive this cleansing flood of newborn sunshine, or his lamentations the blended harmony of bells and birds. Youth, too, contributed, and the dash of buoyant French blood fused in her veins with the hardy Norse of her grandfather; for the germ of persistence which in her mother had developed only to serve selfish ends, would rise, intensified, in Jean to nobler purposes. Spontaneously her steps quickened.

Several blocks covered brought her to a large, gray-stone church, gracing a corner at both angles. To Jean, churches stood for boredom. Out of deference to good form (this was the only apparent reason) her mother had attended one of high ritualistic persuasion whenever "possible," the girl reluctantly accompanying; for somehow the program of religion always seemed nebulous to Jean. She was passing on when a casual glance at the bulletin-board sent her thoughts back to the placards in the depot and lunchroom. This was the First Church of East Elair, pastored

A CHILD OF DIVORCE

by Paul Manson. All its doors stood open to the morning zephyrs, and, while she lingered to read the sermon titles, the sound of a song stole upon her consciousness; not the finished melody of a soloist, but the untrained lilt of a man, halting a bit, sometimes a little off key, as if he were moving about, but withal so sincere that it quickened her pulses.

A sudden desire possessed Jean to enter those open portals. Somewhat timidly, she stole up the side steps and found herself in a vestibule, with a closed door on the right lettered "Study," and to the left double swinging doors into the auditorium. These she pushed open a crack and peeped in. For many rods the floor inclined gently to where some steps ascended to the distant pulpit, which she could see across an amphitheater of mission pews. All the woodwork was finished in the same subdued mission, now christened by the warming sunlight, as it filtered through the beautiful windows in streams of crimson, emerald, purple and amber. A healing peace pervaded the place, potential strength seemed hovering beneath the lofty dome, and it wooed her to penetrate farther. Then she could see the Roman gold pipes of the organ, and the raised choirloft with its brass railing and curtains of dark red plush matching the carpet. Drawn on, she was tiptoeing toward the pulpit when the singing rose again—

> "Lord, for to-morrow and its needs
>   I do not pray;
> Give me a thankful, faithful heart
>   Just for to-day;
> Help me in season to be grave,
>   In season gay—
> Still keep me, guide me, love me, Lord—
>   Just for to-day."

The last line broke out clearly with the sliding back of a partition to the annex which revealed the aging sexton.

"Mornin', Miss," he hailed cheerily; "pretty day, eh?"

"Lovely!" Jean responded.

"You're an early bird," he observed; "never would o' thot o' havin' an aujience this time o' day!"

"I like your song—and I wanted to see the church inside."

"Wasn't you never here before, then?"

"No. Aren't you open early?"

"Well, no. I always get here ahead, so's to have the Lord's house all fresh and sweet and fittin' for worship. You want to come to mornin' service, Miss. Come early, though, so's you'll get a seat."

"Is it so crowded?"

A CHILD OF DIVORCE

"Crowded? See this here annex? It'll be jammed, and all them pews and the balcony, and then there won't be room for 'em all. He's preachin' to-day about divorce. I don't s'pose you're divorced"—he stepped nearer and his blue eyes twinkled—"but it'll be good for every one—'specially young folks, for it's young folks have got mighty loose notions these days 'bout divorce. Think they can pick up a husband or wife and drop 'em when they're a mind to, like an old shoe! Didn't you see in last night's papers where he give out a special invitation to folks who was divorced, or thinkin' 'bout bein'? He's had crowds for the whole series, and this'll be the biggest drawin' yet."

"No, I didn't. I hope it'll do some good!" More emphasis than she realized rang in her voice. Of course the old man could not know how the subject stirred her or why she so abruptly changed it. "I hadn't thought of coming, but maybe I will. That was a nice song you were singing. Is it a hymn?"

"Why, yes," in visible surprise; "ain't you never been to church, Miss?"

Jean flushed slightly, yet the question was too kindly put to offend her. "Not like this one," she confessed. "I know some hymns, but I never heard that one. It's so simple somehow—it helps you. The ones I had to

APPLYING MATHEMATICS

learn are hard and grand. Do you have canticles and creeds and catechisms and things?"

"Whew! what's all them?" Jean could not help smiling at his expression.

"Why," she explained, "they're what you have to learn to get confirmed, so you can join the church."

"Oh! Are you a Cath'lic?"

"Not Roman. They call it 'high church'—it's a lot the same, though. All *I* can see different is the name."

"Humph, I never heard tell o' more'n one kind o' Cath'lic. Do they let folks get divorced in that one?"

"I guess they do. I—I—know some that are."

"What d'you have to do to get confirmed?"

"Why, after you've learned all those things I told you, and all the places in the prayer book, and the church seasons—like Trinity and Epiphany and Advent—and then the Holy Days, you have to kneel down and let the bishop lay his hand on your head, and say a prayer."

"Why can't you say your own prayer?"

"I don't know. They make you do that. You can say your own prayers too, and the ones in the book, only the bishop has to say his so you can go to communion."

"And do they think that's goin' to save folks?"

"Yes, I guess they do."

"Jiminy! Then there's a mighty sight o' folks won't get saved, 'cause all of us ain't got enough brains to remember all that. But it don't seem's if the Lord would send us to Hades for not havin' what He didn't give us, does it? Take me f'rinstance. I never could learn all them things—not now, nohow —and if I could I don't see as it 'ud bring me a mite nearer the dear Lord. I think I'd feel farther away."

"Yes, I guess you would. Can anybody join this church, then?"

"Anybody that believes *He's* the Son of God. That's all the confession we have."

Jean looked down thoughtfully, and a deep silence ensued. At last she raised a puzzled face back to the old man's, for his homely earnestness drew out her confidence. "But I don't see how you can tell. How do you *know*—He is the Son of God—and that He cares about you?"

"You know in *here*," the sexton pressed a work-calloused hand against his breast; "somethin' tells you. You can't hear it, but you can feel it. Not all of a sudden, though. With most folks it has to grow. You jest go to Him first, like you was His little girl, and tell Him, simple, you want it, and keep doin' that till bime-by you feel it."

APPLYING MATHEMATICS

"Like I was His little girl—" Jean echoed, quick tears nearing her eyes.

"Yes, Miss, and don't worry nor fret about nothin'. 'Fore I come here I kep' a farm near Boonton. One day Tess, our dog, was a-chasin' the chickens, and a hen flew up to the fence and didn't know how to get off again, though she wanted to mighty bad, for it come feedin'-time. I went to lift 'er down, but she kep' a-cluckin' and squawkin' and a-flappin' her wings so, I couldn't noways git a grip on 'er—when if she'd only kep' still I could've lifted 'er down gentle where the corn was. That's the way the Lord is, Miss. He's lovin' and powerful, but even He can't help 'less you *believe* He can, and then keep a-prayin' without fussin'—jest doin' right what your hand finds to do and waitin' for His will."

Jean felt a swelling in her palate. She rose from the arm of the pew where she had been half perched, husking: "Thank you. That's helped me already—as much as a sermon. I think—I will come back. I wish I knew your name."

"My name? Borland, Jim Borland. And yours, Miss?"

"Jean Frances—" She stopped, for Borland might know of her father.

"Well, Miss Frances, I'm awful glad you came by this way and I sure hope you'll come again, but wherever ye go, try—what I told you, won't ye?"

"Y-yes."

The sun now shone brilliantly, and though something on her lashes broke its rays into a thousand kaleidoscopic rainbows, Jean's hopeful mood had been augmented. Perhaps her dread of the world's unkindness was largely imaginary.

Upon re-entering the house, she was almost choked by the smell of coffee and the smoke of pancakes. However, this appeared not to trouble the boarders now chatting in the dining-room, they doubtless being accustomed to it. The brisk walk and mental stimulus had sharpened her own appetite, so she sat down with the rest and ate a good breakfast while listening eagerly to several comments on Paul Manson and his "moral crusade." Diversified opinions combated each other across the table, but, from whatever angle, he had certainly compelled attention.

Following the sexton's advice, she returned to the church in generous time, and was then a little chagrined at being ushered to a seat very near the front, for fear she might not act correctly in this strange congregation. But as the human streams poured in, she soon forgot herself and even shrank with a feeling of insignificance, for Borland had not exag-

APPLYING MATHEMATICS

gerated. Hunger for truth, mere curiosity, or just the church-going habit, were probably all factors in bringing them; however that might have been, the crowds came.

As the organ's voice soared into the prelude, a door beyond the platform opened to admit a man of striking physique, a man in splendid prime, probably above six feet, broad and deep-chested, with a fine, yet essentially masculine, face, its strong lines softened by the touches of silver to his black hair over the temples. Jean watched him in a sort of fascination. The prayer, the hymns, all that ensued, but led up to the moment when these two thousand and more souls would stir in response to this magnetic person's words. It fell with a pause of still expectancy. Then he stepped slowly forward, easily erect, independent of notes, combing the packed congregation with his keen, expressive eyes.

"And the king said, 'Bring me a sword.' And they brought a sword before the king. And the king said, 'Divide the living child in two, and give half to the one and half to the other!' "—his voice, deeply mellow, hinted of volumes in reserve—"never mind the context of that bit of Scripture. I am to call you to a modern scene analogous with it—to a later 'court of Solomon'—the law court of the present day. Let Solomon represent the judge;

his attendants, the counselors; and there is the sword—*divorce!*"

The tensity could be felt.

"Friends, in approaching this subject, let us deal with it on the only fair ground for dealing with any question, the basis of *motives*. He whom every professing Christian must acknowledge, at least outwardly, as the mouthpiece of God the Creator, said, 'Whosoever shall put away his wife, *and shall marry another,* committeth adultery; and whoso marrieth her which is put away doth commit adultery.' I had almost chosen those words for my text, and it is not because I feel them in any way inadequate that I have reached still farther back for one which leaps correspondingly as far ahead in its appeal, but because I believe their underlying motive to be protection against the very thing now expressible through the one I have given you—the ruined lives of children. Moreover, even these words do not seem strong enough for some people to-day—yes, people who go to church—perhaps because, by constant repetition, they have become trite; perhaps because, in spite of the prevalence of Christian theories, Jesus is not yet conceded by every one to be infallible authority. But, whatever your personal views on that point, He is the *highest* authority the world has ever known, and the

APPLYING MATHEMATICS

absolute worth of His ideals regarding the sacredness of marriage—even as weakly lived up to as they have been—has been proven through twenty centuries! Loyalty in marriage means *homes*. Homes are the cornerstones of society. Where they have been preserved, nations have risen mightily; where they have been made secondary to passion and greed, kingdoms have crumbled! . . .

"Research shows that the Aramaic language, in which the New Testament was first written, was largely devoid of connective particles, which means that the conjunction *'and'* was often used where a modern writer would use the connective *'in order that'*; therefore, we of to-day can get the best sense of those words of Jesus by translating them thus, 'Whosoever shall divorce his wife *in order to marry* another, commits adultery. And if she divorces her husband in order to marry another, she commits adultery.' So, you see, our Lord, too, had in mind motives. Yet He leaves no easy loop-holes, for it is not at all probable that He meant it only necessary that the heart be free from a design to remarry *at the time the divorce was sought*. Remarriage was not to be permitted at once, or later, under any conditions during the lifetime of the first partner, save one—infidelity, which left the guilty one as dead, the other free. For marriage was not an invention of man for his own economic convenience, but a divine ordinance, a holy sacrament. It was part of God's original plan when He made the world! Incidentally, if we counted only those who seek divorces for other reasons than the hope of marrying again, and never do marry again, our cause for alarm would be greatly reduced. Though separations may sometimes be justified and even, in rare cases, beneficial, they are beset with unexpected temptations, and bad enough in their effect on the home. Still, there is always a chance that through the influence of their children, or the softening of the years, such persons may become reconciled. Where remarriage occurs, this is impossible. There is *no* hope of reunion! And whereas the unnatural influence of merely separated couples usually ends with their unhappy lives, that of the remarried divorced person lives on in the horrible mixup of his families, each generation tending to a looser conception of its 'privileges'—a downright social menace! . . .

"Brethren, we pride ourselves on our civilization. Do we mean to use its prerogatives to choose our way back to the herd? Socialism—anarchism—you shrink from them! How are they worse than divorce? They strike at the home. Divorce does the same! You

APPLYING MATHEMATICS

women, who have the future in your keeping, you throw up your hands at the idea of the harem in Turkey—at the nationalization of your sex in Russia! You're fighting for your 'rights' in America. You're going to get them. Then, will you dare to sanction glib laws, which permit men and women to break pledges made on the altar of the most high God, and go forth under the illusion that they are as free from responsibility as they were before they took them? *I dare to stand here and tell you there is no human law under heaven which can controvert the laws of God—any more than there is one that can turn back the universe!* . . . In our country to-day, there are discontented aliens spreading seeds of unrest and jealousy, but it is only a nation vitiated by its own follies which need fear outside opposition! I'm an American. And I'm with America for stamping out the bacteria of all such disorders, but as a loyal citizen, too, I say let America first cure her own cancers, that she may be in a better condition to resist foreign contagion! . . .

"Where is it leading? What will be the end? Have you considered it *seriously?* Every decent person shrinks from the thought of immorality—even 'legalized immorality.' Yet here, threatening the fabric of our homes right under our eyes, is something *worse!*

A CHILD OF DIVORCE

License we know for what it is, but this thing is stealing upon us beneath the sinister mask of respectability! . . .

"And if, in the sight of God, the union of a divorcee with another is no purer than adultery, how are their children better than the children of shame? Indeed, the children themselves are quite as miserable. Surely friction comes soon enough when they must begin their own battle for bread. As we grow older, much of the pleasure in life is in reminiscence, and there is nothing quite so sweet or strengthening as the memory of the affection between our parents who were lovers to the last—the last we saw of them, whether that may have been back in the old home on earth or on the threshold of the home beyond. We think of them waiting for us—believing in us, their mutual, all-absorbing interest—and it lends us fresh stimulus to resist that which would otherwise overwhelm us. But the child of divorced parents has no such saving memories. 'A young man or woman facing life, and entering the world without the faith and love of a home in the background, is destitute of one of the most valuable assets!' Statistics show that the largest percentage of all the criminals in the jails are those who have no recollection of good homes in childhood. They take refuge in the pleasure of

APPLYING MATHEMATICS

yielding to the lower appetites which there is no incentive to conquer since, one way or the other, no one *cares!* And nearly all who become converted prove to be influenced by some memory of a Christian home from which they have strayed. Outgrow the impressions of childhood? We never do! They haunt us all our lives, looming only clearer again as we near the end. . . .

"Fathers and mothers of to-day, and days to come, do you realize that to create a human life is as serious a matter as to take one? That you will be held as accountable for the soul you inflict, unprepared, on the world through birth as if you had consigned it to the unknown by murder? And yet many 'cultured' parents of to-day care less for their child's happiness and success than did the poor, branded harlot who came before King Solomon, pleading the birthright of motherhood, in what they please to look back upon as that 'heathen age'! What did *she* do when the king ordered her baby cut in half? We are shown how much she wanted that baby, but, in order to save its life, she sprang to the only alternative of an absolute personal sacrifice. What do *they* do when the court says, 'Six months to the father and six months to the mother'? Sit quietly by, and, without a breath of protest, watch the descent of the sword! . . .

A CHILD OF DIVORCE

"You think this analogy far-fetched? I tell you it isn't strong enough—for the child cut bodily in half would be out of its misery; but a child of divorced parents must live on physically, paying the price of their disloyalty. Only his heart is torn in two, so he must carry that bleeding wound around with him for years ere the sensibilities are numbed at last in death! . . ."

As he stepped down from the pulpit to greet the many people who surged forward to shake his hand, Jean remained wedged in the pew, her eyes still riveted upon him, wide and strained, her face colorless. Yet with that instinct for detail which we often have in the tensest moments, she noticed a tall, modish man among the others, whose back was vaguely familiar, lean close to the pastor and murmur something which instantly changed his expression. His smile fled, his eyes struck fire. However, he retorted only with a curt nod and turned to his friends. The other pushed up the aisle, the twist of a sneer still on his lips, and Jean's startled mind made lightning connections. Jerome Bascomb! He had repelled her that first time at her stepfather's inn; now for some psychic reason she at once detested him. She lowered her face lest he should recognize it, and caught the back of the next pew, for everything seemed to sway. The hot,

APPLYING MATHEMATICS

breath-laden air, and her emotional reaction to the sermon, combined with this shock, nearly overpowered her. Trembling, half supported by those around her, she wormed towards the doors, but there a stream of people from the balcony inflated the throng. She was pushed far aside, and found herself clutching the footpost of the stairway, which was now comparatively clear. With no design save the urge toward a refuge from public gaze where she might recover her strength, her feet took her up the stairs. Open windows permitted a circulation of air through the deserted balcony, and, still dizzy, she crouched down on one of the tiers between two pews, leaning against the seat. She hoped no one would see. It was not likely. Soon she would feel stronger and could get out. But, as she huddled there, over and through her with a terrific force flooded the truth of Manson's words. She saw all the naked horror and hopelessness of her position; lived again through the strife-wrought past, and tried to face the arid future; and every shadow across the floor took on the shape of a sword. The wounds of her mother's indifference seemed to gape anew beside the fresher ones of her father's shame, and all the blows from Hasbrook's hand to wake and smart once more, for he had practiced "physical suasion" not infrequently up to her eighteenth year, the last time being when he had thrown her down and lashed her with the clothesline, as an emphasis to a lesson in "gratitude."

The rumble of voices below diminished and finally died, but she had ceased to listen, nor did she hear the sexton lock up, latching the annex door behind him as he departed for dinner. She was unconsciously gnawing her lips to get control of her nerves. Yet she could not hold out long. Like a broken dam her resistance gave way, and her anguish burst forth in smothered, quivering moans. But presently she felt the vibrations of soft approaching footsteps and then a hand, gentle as an autumn leaf, fell upon her shoulder.

"Why, child, what is it?" Her sobs increased while the strong presence tarried, seeming to understand. When the worst was over she glanced up shyly. He who had come was Paul Manson, but he whom Jean beheld in the amber light, of which her tears made a halo, was the Good Shepherd. The warmth of his hand radiated through her, so near her own that she wanted to grasp and cling to it for the help it offered.

A little later, under the urge of Manson's sympathy, she had somehow unburdened everything, concluding brokenly: "Oh, I just can't tell you how queer I felt when I saw *her*—

APPLYING MATHEMATICS

my father's wife—and thought of my own mother still alive! I—I—guess I must have felt like—the Sultan's children—!" He smiled a little, then his grave look returned. "So you must fly with your own wings," he reflected gently; "that's a serious business. I don't suppose you have had any sort of training."

"But it's not that I'm afraid of, sir," she responded with the assurance of ignorance; "what worries me is the feeling that's growing in my heart—about—my mother."

"I wish, my child, that you could go back to your mother. I feel that is the right place for every young girl who has one."

"But, Dr. Manson," her voice shook, "my mother isn't—*true!* She broke her promise—the one she made to God. That isn't right. Didn't you say so?"

"Yes," he admitted, "I said so, I said so."

"Then, don't tell me to go back to her. Oh! I couldn't live with her now—since I've seen what it all really means! If I ever love any one, I want to be true—whatever comes—I want to be a *woman!* Oh, Dr. Manson, I'm afraid—I don't know what it is—but something—inside me is beginning to—hate her."

"Hush! she is your mother."

"My mother—yes, I know. But an animal can be a mother, can't it—as much as that?

I didn't ask for her. No! and I tell you, if I'd only had the right to, I never would have chosen a woman like that—a woman who could lie to God—and pass from one man to another like—'

"Hush, Jean! You don't know what you're saying. You are all unstrung. My poor girl, you have suffered too deeply. You were not in a fit condition to hear that sermon to-day, and I'm sorry you did. None of us choose our mothers, Jean, and you are here as the result of natural law and God's will. God has a plan for your life. Now I'll tell you what I want you to do. I want you to go home and rest all afternoon, and try to forget this subject for to-day, and then come back to my study to-morrow at twelve o'clock, and we'll see about some work. Other things later. I'll find you a place, so don't worry about that. This is the Lord's Day, Jean. I want you to respond to the spirit of it, and trust in Him. We need only solve our problems as they come to us. Just let yourself live in the spirit of to-day. Will you do that—for me?" She could only nod now as, half hysterical, she dashed away the fast-coursing tears. He waited for her to gather some poise, which she finally did by a brave endeavor, then led the way downstairs. A merry voice broke upon them.

APPLYING MATHEMATICS

"Uncle Paul, Uncle Paul! Are you here yet?" The doors sprung apart, and into the vestibule rustled a pretty girl of seventeen. "Oh, here you are? Had you forgotten that we're invited to Pearsons' for dinner? Come, unky, we'll be late—oh, excuse me! I didn't know you had an appointment." She flashed Jean a bright, apologetic smile, the smile of a free-hearted, kindly girl.

"Adele, this is Miss Jean Laval. She's been visiting us, and if she stays here I want you to be friends. Jean, my niece." Adele proffered her hand, and Jean tried to respond in kindred mood, but that was hard just then.

"Remember, to-morrow at twelve," Manson's voice followed her as she went down the steps. By and by the couple overtook and passed her on the other side of the street, walking briskly, happily, Adele's plump arm linked through her big uncle's. She gazed after them wistfully. Of course she could not hear their conversation.

"Unky, dear, what was she crying about?"

"Musn't ask me, pet."

"Oh, 'scuse me again. I just felt sorry."

Manson smiled down at her, looked away once more and sighed. "I fear, Adele, that—as usual—my sermon probably went through the heads of those who needed it, and only disturbed the ones who didn't."

CHAPTER VII.

THE WORLD, OR HEAVEN, HIGH TRIBUNAL?

"For God looketh not upon the outward form of man, but upon the heart."

PAUL MANSON took his holiday in the middle of the week—when he took one—and usually managed to keep his regular hours of interview in the church study on Mondays, for a psychological reason. He preached to rouse consciences. He desired to give those who were honestly stirred, but unsatisfied, by his messages, an opportunity for questions as soon after delivery as possible, and before secular demands should crowd out their interest. By this personal touch he had not only convinced many a wavering soul of truth, but it enabled him to gauge the influence of his preaching, sound the depths of human need, plan his program accordingly. Years of contact with people had rendered him keen to sense in those who came any object of mere curiosity or exploitation, and such were quickly, though politely, requested to excuse him.

THE WORLD, OR HEAVEN?

This morning several individuals had preceded him to the study, and were waiting in the outer hall where Borland had placed chairs for them. The first comer was a short, debonair man of perhaps thirty-eight, whose muscles were in constant activity. He popped up the instant Manson entered, and followed him to the inner sanctum without waiting to be invited, beginning his story before the pastor had hung up his hat. "Say, Doctor, you've got me worried."

"How?" Manson motioned him to a chair, and dropped into the one opposite. The man sat down, but was not still.

"I'm leading a damnable life," he confessed nervously, "and I want to know if I understood you right yesterday. Do you mean to say that in order to get back his freedom a man has got to—er—be immoral first?" A dull flush stained his cheeks.

Manson looked his astonishment. "That's an odd interpretation of my message," he exclaimed, "I hadn't thought of it being taken that way, and certainly meant to give no such impression."

"But that's about the only way out I could see it left a chap," fidgeted the other. His fingers began to pluck imaginary specks from his clothes.

"Out of what?"

A CHILD OF DIVORCE

"Out of the mess I'm living in. I've been married eleven years, and—you mightn't believe it, Doctor—but I've been straight with her. I've always been a decent chap, and that's what's got me worried. I don't want to do anything but what's decent—but it gets worse every year, and I've decided I can't stand it much longer. I want my freedom back."

"What do you mean by your freedom?"

"Why—my freedom, Doctor. I want to get away from her everlastin' naggin' and complainin'. I like pleasant things around. And she's always got some kick comin'."

"In other words, it's turned out for 'worse' instead of 'better,' so you want to recall the bargain—after eleven years."

"Well, if you like to put it that way."

"There's no other way to put it. How does your wife feel about this?"

"Why, she don't know," sheepishly; "I hadn't got that far yet, but it's been worryin' me a long time, and after I heard you preach yesterday I thought I'd come an' see you first."

"I see. What business are you in?"

"Insurance."

"Then, I suppose you're away a good deal."

"No, I'm not on the road."

"Then, you're home evenings?"

THE WORLD, OR HEAVEN?

"Well—sometimes. Half the time—I do stay out—to get away from her naggin'."

"What does she nag about?"

"Everything! She's always wanting something. A man is dunned enough outside without getting it in his own home."

"But it costs you something to spend the evenings out, doesn't it?"

"Well, that's different. A man has got to be a sport."

"Yes," echoed Manson, "a man has got to be a sport. But why limit it to the poolroom? Why not be one all the way through—sport enough to make the best of a bad bargain—if it *was* a bad bargain?"

"Well, now, I—"

"I don't know your wife," here the preacher twinkled, "maybe she's all you say, but let me ask you one question. Do you treat her like a partner—share things with her? How long since you've made love to her, played with her, showed appreciation of little things she does—like perhaps you did before you married her?"

"W-why, I don't know. Our courtin'-days are over—we aren't kids no more—and she never seems to want—"

"Do you wait for her to ask?"

"Well, but she knows I've cared about her. I'm not rich, but I've earned a pretty good livin', and we got as good a place as most people."

"Listen here, my man, there may be some women who only want *things*. But I think they're exceptions. If flowers could think with logical brains, they would know that the clouds held rain, yet, if the rain never fell, the flowers would die in spite of knowing it. Eleven years of marriage takes a lot out of a woman's life—her youth, her fresh beauty—yet most of them give freely without regret if they're only sure of being loved in return. They like to keep the courting-days fresh, at least the spirit of them. My advice to you, sir, since you ask for it, is to make friends again with your wife—send her flowers, or take her something if you will—something intimate and not too prosaic, maybe something foolish, but let it be a symbol of affection, and confide in her so she'll understand the transformation. If she survives the shock, go on with it—spend some evenings with her, or take her to a good show now and then, or to anything you can share together. I believe you'll find it worth all it costs. Anyway, try it for a month and then come back and tell me if you still want a divorce."

The man's eyes were blinking. "Well, I —I'll say," he stammered, "that's the queerest advice I ever thought of gettin' from a

THE WORLD, OR HEAVEN?

preacher." Manson laughed as they rose, and thrust out a cordial hand. "Perhaps, but give it a chance, won't you? And the next time you come to church, sir, bring your wife along."

Into the vacated chair swept a corpulent matron in plum-colored satin, modeled to fit like the skin of that fruit. Numerous beads and bracelets dangled and clinked from her person, which immediately filled the study with the scent of heavy perfume. She appeared annoyed at having been obliged to wait, and regally presented a card whereon could be deciphered amid chirographic flourishes: "Mrs. W. Chesterton Jones."

"I'm glad to see you, Mrs. Jones, and what can I do for you?"

"Nothing," stiffly; "my caw is waiting, and I have an impawtent engagement, but I felt I must run in and express myself regawding your sermon yesterday. I must say, Dr. Manson, that I had no idea such antiquated notions still prevailed anywhere, and it is surprising, to say the least, to observe a man of your influence and intellect advocating them."

"Oh, indeed! To just what 'notions' do you refer?"

"To that absurd comparison between remarriage of divawced people and adultery. I think it is vewy fah-fetched, not to say insulting. They are as different as black and white. Immorality is illegal, divawce is sanctioned by law."

"Whose law?"

"The laws of our great commonwealth, which should be sufficient for any one."

"But there is a higher law, Mrs. Jones. I was preaching that."

"Yes, on what authority, pray? All our laws are derived from the 'higher law,' but we were given common sense with regawd to their application. *Perhaps* the interpretation of one fanatical dreamaw is more credible these days than that of the great, sane body of our legislatuh. If so, though, then in one point I agree with you—we *are* revuhting to the primitive when supuhstition and belief in witches and prophets was rife!" It needed no connoisseur in human nature to see that the shoe which Manson had flung out yesterday not only fit Mrs. W. Chesterton Jones, but pinched; and like most spiteful females, in retaliation, she resorted to personalities. Goaded by his calm tolerance, her resentment finally bested her dignity. "What do you know about it anyway?" she demanded. "Perhaps if you were married, you'd have your eyes open. But I've always noticed," with irony meant to be sizzling, "that it's spinsters

THE WORLD, OR HEAVEN?

and bachelors who know the most about how married people ought to live."

Manson glanced at his watch, stood up and bowed courteously. Again there shone just a glint of humor in his dark eyes. "I am aware, my dear madam, that I have missed a great deal, and even that misfortune has been made the basis for criticism of my 'theories' before. But, you see, if I were married it would probably only take another shade. It would be said that I was so lucky in having an angel for a wife that I couldn't appreciate other men's troubles. If that is all, will you pardon me now? Some one is waiting." She took the hint reluctantly, passing out like a ruffled pullet.

Next came a woman in real distress, whose husband was unquestionably moral, but cruel and profane. The mother of three impressionable children, she had been driven to the edge of seeking a divorce with alimony.

"Your sermon seemed to sear my heart," she told Manson; "but, Doctor, there are things that make marriage quite as unbearable as infidelity—coldness, selfishness, constant neglect. Sometimes, it seems to me, I'd rather have my husband do one big, terrible thing than be the way he is all the time. I could forgive that—but he—he's just gradually *killing* my love. He seems all right to people outside, but they don't see him when he's home. If it was only myself, I might go on bearing it; but he has a bad influence on the children. He's always picking quarrels about something, no matter how I try to please him, and they can't help hearing. That isn't good for them. Then, he often uses bad language, and, one day when he was angry, he struck me before my oldest boy. Yet, they need a father too. Oh, Doctor, I wish you—or some one—could tell me what to do! It seems as if I must choose between loyalty to my ideal and my children, or to my husband—and is *he* worth such a sacrifice?" Her voice quivered, tears began to trickle down her cheeks, and she pushed them away with a labor-roughened hand. She was rather small and bent.

Manson never felt more sympathy for any one, and he told her so most earnestly. "Yet," he added, "the problems of a man and wife can rarely be solved by a third party. Wise counsel may help, but in the main it is a matter between themselves and their Creator who joined them in one. I fear, my friend, I can give you no more to-day than I did yesterday—the word of Scripture. As the great apostle says, we can not always tell when faith and patience may convert a wayward mate. Sometimes the results appear suddenly after long, loyal years. Every holy

THE WORLD, OR HEAVEN?

injunction is against the separation of husband and wife, and on this you must base your actions as a Christian. It might be temporarily beneficial to the children to take them away from him, yet there is another question. In the after years, when these children are mature, and their own true natures have triumphed over the rough externals, which memory will inspire them most? Of mother clinging like a little soldier to her marriage vow and father, through her patience, perhaps softened and saved at last—or mother leaving father to go on alone down his way of darkness, while she looks to their safety and her own? They are his as much as yours, little woman, though I know they seem nearer to you; but, somehow, I feel that if you do your part as a wife, God is going to look after those children's characters. The question is not so much one of their immediate as of their future good. They'll grow up soon; they'll realize all the experiences of fellow-humans, and then they'll single the wheat from the chaff with capable, grown-up eyes. Will you kneel with me now while we lay this matter before the Father? For He is the only One who can really guide you."

When he escorted her out a youth had risen and was leaning against the door-jamb anticipating his turn. But just as the pastor greeted him, a look of chagrin broke over his face, and, following his gaze, Manson saw a girl enter the vestibule. In another minute, their confusion was mutual; then they both glanced at him shamefacedly. He, however, quickly gauged the situation, and, the ice rather melted by his hospitality, they followed him. In the study, he asked to be excused for a moment and disappeared through a far door. This was really to give them time to recover, for the place was nothing but a store-closet. Guarded though their words were, he could not avoid overhearing:

"What are *you* doin' here, Mary?"

"Maybe that's what I'd like to know about you."

"Did you hear that speech yesterday?"

"Yes—did you?"

"Yes."

Manson emerged, beaming. "Your name, my fine young man?"

"Frank Grimm, sir."

"Ah, a good name; means you'll always stick to the ship. They say 'What's in a name?' But I think they are great incentives. And this young lady, fresh as a rose? Now, what can I do for you?"

"My wife," informed the youth, diffidently; "I—I think maybe we'd better see you apart, sir."

THE WORLD, OR HEAVEN?

Manson's warm eyes searched their faces. "Why, certainly, if you wish."

Between them the story unfolded. He was a telephone lineman, she was an ex-office clerk. Barely a year previous, they had met at a dance and proved to be perfectly matched for the turkey-trot and the one-step. Speedily it developed that they had other common interests, such as a kindred taste for pineapple sundaes and melodrama at the moving pictures. Three months of this thrilling fellowship had convinced them that they were created for each other, so they went before a justice of the peace to acknowledge their bonds and be sealed in matrimony. Then, the sad tale of disillusionment. Frank had seen Mary take part of her hair off; she was pale in the mornings, and he presently dogged her complexion to a little box in the bureau drawer. This was by no means the only respect in which she had grossly deceived him. Shortly after their introduction, she had treated him to some fudge of her own making. It was delicious, from which he innocently concluded that she could cook. Why, she couldn't at all! Even the eggs were either hard or raw, and *everything* was burnt! She sulked when he would not take her out as often as formerly, never stopping to think that he had to pay rent now and a million other bills. And she spent the afternoons and the house money at matinees, or gadding around the shops with other young matrons just like her. When he came home from work, the flat was either dark, or she had arrived on a breathless margin of five minutes with some cold ham and stale salad from the delicatessen and a thin, watery old pie! He thought every man needed a wife, but felt that he had been badly "stung."

As for Mary's side, she had never imagined such a long, ugly neck as Frank had without his collar on, or that any human being could snore so. He kept her awake nearly all night and also, being stronger, wound himself up in all the covers, never caring any more whether she was cold. And she had blistered her fingers and scalded her face trying to please him, and all he did was make fun of her meals; and he was a regular grouch about every little pleasure she took. All this she imparted to the pettiest detail like a child. They had wanted her at the office enough to pay her; *he* expected her to be his slave—for nothing! She wished she was back with the other girls.

Gently, appealingly, Manson endeavored to rouse these young souls to the deeper meanings of life and the grave dignity of their partnership; to show them how the state

THE WORLD, OR HEAVEN?

depended upon them as the founders of a home. They were not a boy and girl engaged in a game which either might terminate by a whimsical "I won't play!" They had assumed responsibilities—the soberest in the world—to which they *must* do justice, or join the contemptible rank of slackers. These petty grievances must be absorbed by tolerance, even according to their marital oath. Had they not realized that such a union meant utter self-abnegation for both, first in the service of one another, then of the generations in which they had become a link?

No, they had not thought of these things. They had just wanted to be together, so they had gone through the contract because that was necessary. In fact, they had not even heard all the words. They were too much excited. It had been about as spontaneous as the mating of sparrows. But before they left the study, their countenances began to brighten with the new revelation, for, underneath the glaze of an artificial and pleasure-drunk environment, they were tractable young humans. They departed reconciled, promising each other and Manson to "begin again" in the light of this broader outlook, their impulsive thanks echoing back to him. Alone once more, he breathed a silent prayer that it would endure. He felt glad and yet he sighed,

A CHILD OF DIVORCE

for they were one couple in similar thousands, not all of whom would hear sane counsel or heed it if they did. Blind infants trespassing on the ground where surer feet might fear to tread, tampering with the things God meant for mature men and women. He thought of the child which might come to them; he thought of all the untimely children of all such half-developed parents—poor first babies, born without the advantage of full physical organisms, then to be the brunts of maternal experimentation.

Succeeding the Grimms appeared another anxious parent. Indeed, she was quite distraught. Her girl of sixteen had eloped with a "fascinating" widower of forty. The man was eligible, but the family felt disgraced, for the daughter had come repentantly home with sorry tales of incompatibility. So they wanted to have the union annulled.

"Surely, Doctor," she pleaded, "you can't believe *all* marriages are made in heaven."

"Too many of them are not; but then, from a Christian standpoint, madam, I can see only one truth to face. Your daughter has simply been ruined."

"Oh, no!" she cried sharply in visible pain; "they were married!"

"But you don't wish to acknowledge that bond. It is possible to eradicate the vows, but not the fact that they lived together. Don't you see where that leaves her?"

"Yes; I see what you mean. But it isn't as if my child had meant to be immoral. She was his wife—at the time."

"I would venture to say, madam, that very, very few girls fall through a deliberate intention of sinning. They are seduced by affection, whether they have gone through a ceremony or not. If the fact that your daughter went through the form of becoming a wife, though she now wishes to revoke it, seems to you to modify her case—as it may seem to many others from a worldly standpoint—surely you are welcome to all the comfort you can get from it. You came, I believe, for my opinion as to the Christian viewpoint; so, as much as I would like to help you, I can only tell you the truth, that I am positive that in God's sight, if she was his wife at that time, then she is still; if she is not his wife now, then she never was."

"You are unmerciful!" She pressed a rumpled handkerchief to her shaking lips, the hand that held it none too steady.

"Indeed I am not, my friend," gently; "merely to call a situation by its right name is not always to condemn. Judgment rests with God alone. He looks beneath the surface to our motives. He will freely forgive your child and start her on the road to a better life—but just as He forgave the Magdalene—for what will weigh with Him is not the formality she may or may not have respected, but whether she seeks His pardon now in the proper spirit of meekness and contrition."

"But I—I—don't like to think of Dorothy classed with Magdalenes."

"Then it would seem to me that her only course is to remain true to her husband."

"But, Doctor, he's old enough to be her father! She didn't know her own mind. They are utterly unsuitable, and she would be very unhappy. Must the child's whole life be wrecked because of one ignorant mistake?"

"Not at all. That would not be Christian. Still, like all of us, she must learn the law of sowing and reaping. Whichever course you decide upon now, you must face the fact that her life can never be just as it was. She must pay in some measure, for that law is inexorable. God can temper it with mercy, but He Himself can not dissolve it, or at least He does not will to. You seem, madam, like one who cares for your child's welfare. How came she to do such a thing?"

"Oh, I don't know, Doctor. We never even knew about the man till we got their telegram."

THE WORLD, OR HEAVEN?

"Then, you hadn't trained Dorothy to confide in you?"

"Well—I hadn't *trained* her to—but I just thought she would if anything extra happened. She grew up so fast and was a good girl—but I thought of her as a child. I never thought about her wanting to get married—that is, for years yet—and I was so busy. We have a big house and two other children—" Once more Manson sighed. Always, it seemed, must material claims crowd out spiritual kinship. Three meals a day, a bath and music lessons was the average parental conception of rearing offspring "well."

"I fear," he said at last, "that I have not helped you much, and I am sorry that I can not say all that you would like me to. Two courses lie open to your daughter. Whichever way she turns, she must expect, and you with her, to meet trying circumstances. She appears to stand between lifelong discontentment and present shame. You must choose the road that seems to your consciences to afford the wider scope for spiritual improvement, whether that shall mean the sacrifice of her future to a promise, or sin acknowledged and forgiven and a new start made. I can only hope you will meet it like Christian women and not try to hide anything from Him who knows every secret."

A CHILD OF DIVORCE

"Well—th-ank you." She departed still downcast, and he knew that she was not satisfied.

"Good morning!" snapped out rather as a demand upon his notice than a salutation, and Manson had to step backward to discern the gender of the personage on the threshold. She was one of those modern productions who nurse a constant (though secret) grudge against nature for having turned them out of the female mold, and so retaliate by confiscating all accessible masculine attributes, barring actual trousers—and result in making themselves poor nonentities. Her skirt approached as nearly as possible, in semblance, the coveted pants, being very short and narrow above heavy, low-heeled boots. Her jacket, setting off with tailored precision a stock collar and four-in-hand, might have been the bequest of a graduated brother. A severe little sailor hat topped all this, nor was any softening wave of her hair permitted to escape from under it.

"My name is Hefferndyke—Clotilda Hefferndyke—and I represent the New Jersey chapter of the Women's League for Political and Civic Uplift. I've come to talk to you about your sermon yesterday."

"Yes? Sit down, won't you, Miss Hefferndyke?" Something had always made

THE WORLD, OR HEAVEN?

Manson shrink from women of this particular type.

"I was here in person," she began brusquely, "and I hope you will pardon me for saying that your ideas struck me as rather radical, and somewhat unreasonable. In fact, they are at variance with the ideals of sex equality and economic independence we are endeavoring to inculcate in the women of this State, and I want to say, straight from the shoulder, as man to man, and as a representative of our League, that we object to the advocacy of any program which argues for the repression of woman within the old-fashioned bonds of domestic slavery from which she is at last on the verge of emancipation."

This delivery may not have had anything to do with Manson's wiping his forehead, for it was a hot June day.

"Indeed, you surprise me," he answered; "my whole object in speaking as I did was to emphasize the dignity of family life, and in that way protect both womanhood and childhood."

"But you preach against divorce. We believe in the availability of divorce, especially for women, as a mark of advancement. A new day has dawned for woman. We stand your equals, if not your superiors. Many doors are open to us, and one of these privileges is

A CHILD OF DIVORCE

divorce. No woman need any longer prostrate her body and degrade her soul to a man whose conceit and brutality have killed her love. There is a way back to freedom and self-respect." Suddenly Manson's dark eyes flashed, and he leaned forward, tense, his big fist clenched on the desk.

"You mean to say," he demanded, "that you, a woman and a delegate for a woman's league, are teaching such insidious rot to the young mothers of our State?"

"Rot!"

"Yes, rot! Look here, Miss Hefferndyke, you've come to my study to talk 'man to man.' You've disrespected me already, but we'll let that pass. From all your words and actions I gather that you wish me to treat you like a man. Very well, I will; I'll be courteous enough to your womanhood to comply with your wish. You talk about freedom and self-respect. The kind of freedom you refer to knows no true self-respect. It is only a freedom of the lower nature, a rein given to self-seeking. There is a higher freedom than that, a spiritual freedom of choice of sacrifice and womanly duty—as God ordained it, *not* as man imposed it. I mean the freedom of Christ who chose the cross. You are no more our peers to-day than you ever were, and sometimes I fear less. God knows we men have

THE WORLD, OR HEAVEN?

fallen far short of appreciation in many ways. But why do you want to come down to our level, you to whom we have always looked up? Oh, I know just what's in your mind, and perhaps it isn't fair to expect so much of you, and grant ourselves so many prerogatives as we have done, seeing, too, that we have stronger bodies. But that is the only way in which our strength is superior to yours, and poor it is compared with strength of soul. Every one of you who isn't stone blind ought to rejoice in her womanhood, for it pleased God to bring you, somehow, nearer to Himself. You are His instruments of life. Woman, think of it! Within a few short months, by your very thoughts, you can so mold the minds of men as to determine the destinies of years. Is it possible that your sex can be so shortsighted as to wish to throw such a privilege back into the Creator's face for the one of grasping the lesser and more perishable right of material supremacy? You seem to have a very distorted sense of values, and, believe me, if you and those with you teach such philosophy to our women, you will have yourselves to blame for the day when the safe walls of home crash down entirely, and you find yourselves ravished by those in whom the spirit of chivalry has died because you no longer inspired it to live.''

A CHILD OF DIVORCE

Miss Hefferndyke was biting her lips. "Oh, indeed!" she retorted, "that's all very high sounding, and just what I might have expected from you—after yesterday. But it happens we're living in a very practical world, Dr. Manson, one where every woman isn't blessed by the 'safe walls of home,' and where, unfortunately, a lot of men, though the prerogative and advantage are theirs, *don't seem keen about their duty of offering them to her!* Your viewpoint is visionary and typically masculine. You want to put us on pedestals without the bother of maintaining us there, and then go your own sweet way, come back and find us where you left us."

"Pardon me, but the man who has such a shrine in his life is not likely to go any way but toward that of achievement, and when he comes back it will be to share it with her."

Miss Hefferndyke squirmed with impatience. She laughed harshly. "Really, Dr. Manson, you don't seem to belong to the twentieth century. You may be behind our time, or far ahead of it, but in either case such ideals don't fit the present, and therefore it is hardly fair to make them the basis of a standard. We're facing practical issues, and if you can't help us there, we would only ask that you will not impede us by advancing impossible theories."

THE WORLD, OR HEAVEN?

"My ideals, madam, were conceived by a higher mind. Had they been 'impossible,' God would not have given them life. I fear that your outlook has been limited to material satisfaction, and I tell you once again, so long as woman keeps her place in that spiritual realm which is peculiarly her own, no matter what her *hands* may have to do, she will draw men up to her; but when she deserts that to throw her energies into mere physical combat, she will find she can not compete with him, for there he is the stronger. For my part, I can not understand why she should want to do this, for the office God has already appointed her is so much finer than she can ever win for herself."

"Finer? Finer for you, oh, yes! It worries you, doesn't it, to think of us threatening your sovereignty?"

Manson relaxed with a slightly impatient gesture. "If the voice of your own womanhood can not convince you, nothing I can say will," he concluded. "We do not seem to be gaining much by this discussion, Miss Hefferndyke. Perhaps we had best both save our time and breath."

But for her pride she would have harangued him further. However, she sneered, backing toward the door: "*You* are the very type of man who hinders progress. You have no wife,

A CHILD OF DIVORCE

and know nothing of our feelings, and yet you presume to set a criterion for us"—they were now in the hall—"but you won't always succeed. Our eyes are open at last. We've made good headway, and we'll maintain our rights in spite of you."

Manson silently bowed and watched her strut down the steps. She was the last caller, and the sexton, sweeping out the vestibule, too obviously pretended not to have heard. Manson turned to him smiling, a little wearily, "That, my good man, is a lady politician." Borland looked undecided as to whether this might be meant for an apology or simply a statement. A stubborn expression darkened his face. "Humph," he grumbled, "mebbe she's a politician, sir, but she ain't no lady."

The pastor returned, dropped down again by the desk and leaned his face in his hands a moment. He felt tired and, perhaps because of that, a little discouraged. There never existed a great soul which opened to pour out its riches, no matter how freely, for its fellows, that was not sometimes tempted by the human query, "What good does it all do?" In review there floated before his mind these questioning faces of the morning, and many, many others. Their owners came seeking for truth, yet so often when he gave them what he believed with all the strength of his nature to

THE WORLD, OR HEAVEN?

be truth, they seemed disappointed. What numbers of them really wanted, whether they knew it or not, was salvation, not by truth, but by salve. Manson had grasped for the text of his life that assertion of the brave apostle for whom he was named, "I determined to know nothing among you save Jesus Christ and him crucified." He would not swerve from this to compromise with other religions, or vagaries of his own religion, though sometimes it all rushed over him like a tremendous burst of idealism. Those words had rung down nearly two thousand years, yet in their actual application they proved almost as much "foolishness" to modern Americans as they had to ancient Greeks. "I am convinced," he told a colleague once, "that if the whole New Testament church would maintain her authority to preach strongly against definite intimate evils, instead of slurring over them with 'nice' generalities and platitudes, we would in a short time witness a social revolution." Alas! such a realization, too, was scarcely more tangible than a dream. Still he kept a grip on himself, knowing all the while that his Redeemer lived.

Much earlier his unfolding devotional power had been laid at the feet of an unattainable woman, for she favored his elder brother. Not long after the wedding that brother drowned in Culver's Lake, and such was the shock that the bereft bride did not survive the birth of Adele. Eagerly Paul adopted the baby to fill his gaping heart. Through care for her his paternal instinct found expression, while the deeper love, time-mellowed, flowed out into a broader channel, and his work became to him as his wife.

Now, in his reflection, one face stood out from the others, the young, wistful face of Jean Laval, and suddenly his heart warmed in renewed defense of every high contention. The girl was like an embodied argument for the verity of them—one which could not be refuted. And then, feeling another presence, he turned and saw her in the doorway, as if she had stepped from his thoughts, and heard the noon whistle blowing.

"I've made up my mind, Dr. Manson," she told him after his cordial greeting, "to go back to New York and work. I've heard there's more chance there, and I—I'd rather not stay here where—my father is."

"Do you know any one in New York, Jean?"

"No."

Manson shook his head slightly. "I can't say I like the idea, Jean. New York has always seemed to me too big for a little girl alone. No doubt it offers many oppor-

THE WORLD, OR HEAVEN?

tunities, but mostly to skilled help. For the kind of work you can do there'll probably be a hundred applicants at each place. I don't want to discourage you, but I was rather hoping you'd stay near here where we could sort of look out for you. I think I could get you some clerical work at the Magneto Company. They employ a great many girls, and have never turned me down yet, though these are the slack months, I know."

"That's kind of you, Dr. Manson, but, really, I'd rather not stay. I think I can get a place through the 'Y. W.,' and a room too."

"Well, Jean, I won't urge you—under the circumstances. I'm slightly acquainted with the 'Y. W.' secretary, and I'll give you a letter to her." He reached for paper, took out his fountain pen, thought a few seconds, and began to write. Jean waited quietly till he folded the sheet and addressed the envelope.

"There," he said, handing it to her, "many good wishes, Jean, and I want you to promise me that you'll keep in touch with me; will you?"

"Yes."

"If you get in any bad hole, you must come to see me—don't forget. And whatever happens, my child, keep up your ideals of truth and loyalty. Remember, you have a Father in heaven anyway. Keep near to Him, and remember, too, Jean, that a girl may not always go where a boy can go. Be very careful, my child, of your precious heritage. I look to see you, in spite of all handicaps, grow into a real and noble woman.''

Jean was too deeply touched to say much more, but the warmth of his handclasp charged her with fresh courage, and, as she hurried back to Harland's to get some lunch and collect her things, those stimulating words kept ringing in her mind.

She was stepping off the curb to cross the street, when the shriek of a claxon drew her eyes up just in time to catch a bright smile and wave of the hand from a girl beside the driver. Quickly though it passed, she recognized them both, and gazed after the limousine in astonished wonder. Where could Adele Manson be going with Jerome Bascomb?

CHAPTER VIII.

TO AVOID COMPLICATIONS

INSTEAD of rooms at the Young Woman's Christian Association on Fifteenth Street, Jean found herself preceded by a very long list of applicants. There was not even half a room, or a lesser fraction of one, in the dormitory.

"But what shall I do?" she implored of the secretary; "I haven't any place to go." Her limbs trembled with the fatigue of her search for the place through the unaccustomed city commotion.

The secretary scrutinized her with that experienced glance which people of her calling acquire.

"I suppose you want work too?"

"Yes, I do."

"Any experience?"

"No, I haven't."

"Business school?"

"No."

"What do you think you could do?"

"Why, I thought office work—"

A CHILD OF DIVORCE

"Everybody wants office work. You might get some substituting for a week or two. Go in and see the employment secretary, and then come back. I'll see what I can do about a room for you."

On the threshold of the employment office Jean's heart dropped still lower. Flanks of girls filled the long benches awaiting their respective turns to be interviewed. She approached the nearest desk.

"Have you filed your application, Miss?" asked the young woman behind it.

"No."

"Well, you'll find some on that table. It'll be necessary for you to do that first."

Jean went over to where some other girls were writing on blue cards, or making studious efforts to, between intervals of vacant staring. She sat down, drew one of the blanks toward her, and became enmeshed in a maze of printed questions. All the cardinal points of her history, plus a few other things, this card wanted to know. When and where was she born? Who were her parents? Did she live with them? If not, why not? Was she single? What could she do? What schooling had she, not in general, but by given years? What preparation for the desired place? Who were her last three employers? What other references, etc., etc.?

TO AVOID COMPLICATIONS

After an agonizing half-hour, the card still presented gaping lines, but she could satisfy it no further, so she returned to the desk, as she saw others do, confiding, "I filled it out the best I could."

"All right. Here, take a seat till your number is called," with which the clerk proffered a little check bearing the numeral 79, and Jean found space on one of the rear benches.

"Aw, heck," yawned a girl in front of her, "what was that, Molly? Forty-three?"

"Yeah."

"Swell chance for us. It'll be one before they ever get to us. Some speed to this joint."

The tension a little relaxed, Jean surveyed her contemporaries, a representative gathering of working-girls, a few of them obviously timid and shrinking, yet pushed by the cold hand of necessity over the threshold of home into this world of commerce; others led to it by the lure of adventure, and the enticing prospect of making their "own money," quite self-confident till they reached the door; still more of them comprising a portion of the city's constant turnover, girls who worked from place to place, and glibly discussed their various bosses. There are thousands of these latter to whom each successive "job" serves

A CHILD OF DIVORCE

only as a plank in the bridge to matrimony. Perhaps the prevalence of this drifting type is one of the strongest factors contributing to the low wages of young workingwomen. Yet were it not so, the future of American home life might be even more dubious than it is at present, and it is perhaps pleasantest to think of these girls as the instruments through which wary old nature is still maintaining her own.

Jean witnessed interview after interview, and thought how the secretary must grow very weary. She had for each a smile, but Jean imagined it was not the same one she would have used on really smiling occasions. It was too stereotyped. It belonged with the equipment, like her desk and the blue cards. Forty-three was approached, called and passed, and in the course of hours, it seemed, her straining ears caught "Seventy-nine." She responded, almost choked by the high beating of her heart, and received her allotted smile. Then the secretary scanned her card with pursed lips and a flickering frown.

"This doesn't tell anything very definite," she complained; "is it your first?"

"Yes."

The secretary fingered through a card index. "Can you sew?" she asked presently.

"Yes—a little."

TO AVOID COMPLICATIONS

"The Blumenstein Company on Fourteenth Street, lace importers, want a girl to help mend curtains and wind lace. It doesn't call for any experience. This seems to be all I have just now. You might take it till we have some office calls. Shall I give you a card?"

"Well, if that's all," Jean assented, oppressed by the weight both of disappointment and necessity. The secretary filled out and handed her a card of introduction, advising, "You had better go right away, and let me know if you get it."

Blumenstein's occupied the third floor of a senile building on Fourteenth Street, near Broadway, one of those which the growing city was gradually squeezing to death, having already choked off its influx of light and air. A wobbly elevator, that shared passenger space with freight, lifted Jean to her destination.

"You got it eggsperience?" asked the Russian Jewess in charge of the "reception-room."

Jean shook her head. "They said I wouldn't need any."

The daughter of Abraham reflected, fumbling with the card. "Vell, ve couldn't pay you so much den. Ve giff you fife dollars a veek. You should be glad for dot midoud no eggsperience."

A CHILD OF DIVORCE

"Well," Jean hesitated, "I don't know what my board will cost yet."

The other shrugged. "You should get board if you ain'd too fussy. You vant to come?"

"Yes," decided Jean, "I'll come."

"Awride, in the mornin'. Ve stard by sefen and vorg till fife, mit a half-hour for lunch."

Jean went back to report her success, and was found a berth that night in an East Side transient house, a parochial institution provided for just such strange and unescorted girls.

June mornings break early, even in the city, and at seven o'clock next day, though rather sleepy, she reported bravely for work. But Blumenstein's obviously had not much use for the sun. Miss Silverberg convoyed Jean through several gloomy, linty-aired compartments stocked with bolts and cases of all descriptions of lace, to the workroom in the rear. This was large, but so dirty were the windows that even the light from the court had much ado to penetrate, and the girls were sitting in circles under shadeless electric bulbs. It was somewhat surprising that the mercenary mind of Blumenstein's had not perceived the economy of making an effort to utilize the daylight, but then old Sol is often uncertain, especially when hampered in his

TO AVOID COMPLICATIONS

good intentions by skyscrapers. The whistles having just blown, the girls were already at their sewing, and Miss Silverberg did not bother with the formality of an introduction. She gave Jean a chair, scissors, needle and thread, and a snagged lace curtain, with instructions to "sew it up so good no one should know the difference." The others stitched on industriously until her temporary departure, when they leveled curious eyes on the new arrival. With the exception of two Irish girls, they proved to be all Italians, chiefly emigrants, and many of them, it later developed, could speak very little English. But an observation of their prowess with the needle soon put Jean in despair. The keenest eye could scarcely have detected their delicate joinings of the damaged lace, while Jean's own efforts—her fingers seemed to have swollen. They felt clumsy, numb, and, try as she would, her stitches were awkward.

"Gevalt!" cried Miss Silverberg, upon returning for inspection, "is dot vot you call sewing? You should vorg mit circus tents, not lace."

"I'm sorry," Jean murmured, "I—I never did it before."

"You got no need to tell me. Here, Rosa, take this, und you come over here und vind till you get it some decent fingers for lace."

A CHILD OF DIVORCE

Hot and close to tears, Jean followed her to the winding-tables in the next room, where the light was dimmer still. In front of these stood huge boxes of loose laces, beadings, insertions and edgings, and clamped by a thumbscrew to the edge of each table was a winding device, near piled-up oblongs of beaver-board finished off with glaced blue paper. Miss Silverberg grasped one of the boards, snapped it into a holder, pinned to it the tag end of a strip of lace and turned the crank. The board revolved, wrapping the strip about it. "Dot's all you got to do," she informed. "It's all cut out—ten yards each piece—but loog oud you should get it on even, but don'd pull so hard as to stretch it from shape."

It appeared simple enough, but swiftly proved exasperating work. One hand must turn the crank, leaving only one to guide the lace in symmetrical layers, and these strips, being narrow, persistently twisted and tangled. Moreover, it required constant standing. Before long Jean's limbs and shoulders ached, her nerves tingled and her eyes smarted from straining in the dismal light; and yet the rows did not look very even. Miss Silverberg's next examination elicited no enthusiasm, but she let it pass. "Only," she stipulated, "you got to get it some speed if you vant to vorg here."

TO AVOID COMPLICATIONS

The transient house limited the stay of its guests to a fortnight. By the end of that time they must have found residence elsewhere. Working from seven to five did not leave Jean much energy for room hunting in the evenings, but her visit to St. Barnabas' lasted as long as her "job." The change from her fairly open-air life to one of such constant confinement was acute. The second day she suffered tortures from neuralgia. Night brought no relief, and the third morning saw her late. Naturally, her productive capacity was also affected, not for the better, and the Blumenstein combine held no compunctions about showing its impatience. The short lunch period afforded meager opportunity for recreation, even had it been possible to find such in running a gauntlet of bold stares from loafers in Union Square Park. Despite its incessant industry, New York seems always to have enough men to fill its park benches at any hour of the day, and, of course, noontide finds the ranks much inflated. Sometimes between the shoulders of them one's eye may catch on the back of a bench a few half-obliterated letters of the satire "Reserved for women and children." Women do not avail themselves extensively of the invitation, either because they do not get a chance, or they do not dare. The law

A CHILD OF DIVORCE

can protect them from open insult, but no law under the flag can prevent the surreptitious solicitation which is conveyed through stare and gesture. Also, with nearly all New York dining in the restaurants at the same hour, more time is consumed in waiting for an order than it takes to eat one. So Jean soon noticed that her associates usually brought packed lunches, often not moving to eat them from the chair in which they had sewed all morning, and would sew all afternoon. During the summer months Blumenstein's granted them the convenience of a small refrigerator in which to keep these viands, and daily Sidney Greenbaum, the "generally useful," brought up the ice.

Friday morning witnessed no variation from this routine, except that while the senior partner happened to be present, the cube of ice slipped from Sidney's numb fingers into its zinc casing with an unwonted bang, causing Saul Blumenstein to jump.

"Hey there, you Sidney," he demanded, "vot you doin' to dot ize-bogs?"

Chafing his fingers, Sidney whimpered: "The chunk was too wide, I couldn't get it in 'thout smashin' my hands."

He turned on the boy wrathfully. "Your hands, huh? D—— your hands! Do I pay for your hands or my ize-bogs?"

TO AVOID COMPLICATIONS

"Oh," broke out Jean, "that's cruel!" Instantly, but too late, she knew her mistake. Saul glared at her. "Huh? Cruel? You talk up to me, do you? Vell, ve got no room for such lazy people like you anyhow. This place is to vorg, not preach. You're fired."

Jean stared incredulously. "Go on!" he prodded, "get oud. You ain't vorth keepin' another day." Dazedly she took off the apron, picked up her hat and bag and went to the office for her wages, which came to $2.97, minus a "dock" for the morning she had been late.

Not knowing where else to go, Jean drifted back toward St. Barnabas'. In her heart was the panic of one who, alone in a little bark at sea, has lost the oars, and glimpses no sign of land or ship. Not much over $3 remained of her original capital, and Jean had no idea which way to turn. St. Barnabas' being downtown, her instinctive route led past an immense department store near Astor Place. It was an emporium of the most exclusive type, its wide plate-glass windows offering displays luxurious, but of exquisite taste. One filled with pictures arrested Jean's already lagging steps. Then the clang and roar of traffic, pierced by the shrieks of police whistles, claxons and bells, the ceaseless clatter and thunder of feet and voices, died for a time to her

A CHILD OF DIVORCE

consciousness. She was one with the beauty she surveyed, borne far away on the wings of imagination to sweet streams and pastures, firesides—and love. Soon enough, however, a rude jostle broke the spell, for she was near the big, main revolving door, which kept up a constant operation of at once disgorging and devouring people. All sorts of individuals were flowing in and out, along the pavement, or to and from their sleek, monogrammed motor-cars, where chauffeurs waited, with impassive faces—society leaders; business men; ladies' maids; priests; nurses; newsboys; venders; long-haired, Windsor-tied, soft-collared geniuses, with brief-cases and pinched faces; courtesans; staring sight-seers, and, occasionally, a pair of nuns. Three clerks emerged from the store bearing several bolts of glistening satin for the approval of one madam in a limousine, who looked at each piece through her lorgnette, and turned away in plain disgust, which she confided to a fluffy chow-chow.

So many people! How much help it must take to serve them all! An idea struck **Jean.** Perhaps they needed some one in the picture department. If they would just let her dust— or do anything! Some instinct told her that not much would be gained by another trip to the Employment Office, and she decided **to inquire** for herself, though not without several

TO AVOID COMPLICATIONS

futile efforts to clutch her courage by the forelock.

But no. When her turn of many came, she was curtly informed that there were no openings in any of the art departments. Still, having summoned so much initiative, Jean lingered, hoping against circumstances.

"Isn't there anything—*anything*—I could do?" she implored finally, reapproaching Mr. Smith, the employment manager. He frowned, but deigned her a look. "Not unless you want to wipe glasses. They need some one in the restaurant—fifth floor. I suppose you wouldn't care for that, though."

"How much is it?"

"Five dollars a week and lunches."

"And what hours?"

"Eight to six."

"I—I'll take it."

Mr. Smith looked a bit surprised, but made no comment, simply referring her to a clerk who engineered the hiring process. After the usual inquiries she was given a card and assigned to a small group of girls who had preceded her to different vacancies. Something over an hour had passed when a matron, wearing a red ribbon diagonally across her breast, showing the name of the firm in gilt letters, appeared to guide them to their respective places. She glanced at each card,

A CHILD OF DIVORCE

Jean's last, with its printed "Employed as . . ." completed in the scribbled words "glass polisher," and led them all out, dropping them, one by one, where they belonged.

It was then about eleven o'clock, an hour which found the restaurant kitchen in a rush of preparation for lunchtime. The guide turned Jean over to the department head, who allotted her a part of a locker, and at once set her to drying and polishing freshly washed tumblers and goblets. This was no slipshod process, as occurs in most restaurants. The firm prided itself on appearances, and, after each usage, the glassware must be cleansed and rubbed till it shone with the transparency of a diamond, nor dared she leave a mite of lint on any shining surface. Once the department head—a thin, weasel-faced woman whose eyes escaped nothing but virtues— "called her down" for this. To perform the task at once thoroughly and swiftly was Jean's new problem, shared with several fellow-workers. The glasses were then slid along a broad shelf to be partially filled with cracked ice by another kitchen hand. The place was a bedlam of clattering dishes, rolling carriers, shouted orders, etc., and, of course, insufferably hot. Jean soon oozed with perspiration, but there was no sitting down— that would have impeded speed.

TO AVOID COMPLICATIONS

"Hisht, Molly? Yez know whir Aggie landed fer thot!" cried the washer warningly to the "icer," who, steadily disdaining the ladle, was dishing up the ice with her hands.

"Aw, shut up, Maggie Ryan," good-naturedly, "what the ould woman don't know won't hurt 'er." The others giggled. They seemed very much disposed toward cordiality, notwithstanding that conversation during work-hours was taboo. They threw Jean sidelong glances to see how the "new one" took their overtures; but Maggie Ryan let no reticence interfere with her friendliness. Her superior age (forty-seven) and her long standing with the firm—at that particular sink for thirteen years—gave her the responsible feeling of a hostess toward "new ones," and she immediately manifested her interest by a series of personal interrogations, in exchange for the gratification of which she quite readily regaled you with her own confidences.

"Shure, now, yez ain't married, Jean?" she asked, when about every other thinkable question as to name, age, residence and relations had been applied.

Jean smiled. "No."

"Good, 'n' I thought ye was too sinsible fer the loik o' thot. Yer young yit, an' it's plinty o' time yez hev. Shure, now, 'n' ye want to be careful, dearie, about the men.

A CHILD OF DIVORCE

They're mostly a bahd lot, an' it's me that's tellin' ye. Two 'usbands I've 'ad, an' it's standin' by the sink I am day afther day—an' not me own nather. There's thim that's fair, but more o' thim that ain't, an' the most o' 'em's on'y good about a month, Jean."

"Shure 'n' it always takes the married wimmin to give advice about not marryin'," thrust in Molly. In addition to being naturally homely, she was squint-eyed. It was plain that she would have been willing to take a chance, and equally plain that she had never had one.

"Well," Maggie parried, "I'm thinkin' it's us as shud know. There's thim, Jean, as don't know whin they're well off."

As time wore on thus, Jean, growing conscious of an emptiness within, wondered when they would have the promised lunch. She had supposed she would eat with the waitresses after the rush hour, but she presently discovered that there existed a very marked social distinction between them and her own toiling mates. Her place was with the dish-washers or "pearl-divers," and the charwomen, to whom those professional ladies in white would scarcely condescend to speak. The latter had their own lunchroom, and about one o'clock the first shift of them chose what they liked and betook themselves thither for the business

TO AVOID COMPLICATIONS

of self-nourishment. At two they returned to release the second shift, but the Ryan detachment went on working. Jean grew faint and almost wavered, which did not escape Maggie. "Shure, don't yez feel good, Jean?" she queried.

"Not very. I feel sort of faint."

"Mebbe it's hungry yez are. We eat at three, an' it's most thot now. Mebbe ye nivver et so late before; but yez'll git used to it. Hisht! Mary be praised! Eat it b'fore Mis' Quackenbush gits 'er eye on yez!" From a newly deposited tray of soiled dishes Maggie rescued a plate containing one fat, partially nibbled chocolate *eclair*, passing it to Jean in a glow of generous triumph.

But Jean shrank back with a wave of nausea. "I don't want it—thank you. It's —too sweet."

"Shure, now, is that it? Yez don't mind the little bite out of it? Bether eat it, darlin'."

Jean shook her head. "You eat it if you want to, Maggie," she murmured.

Maggie surveyed her anxiously, but complied in two gulps with evident relish.

"Ye big fat pig!" Molly protested. "Yez mighta divvied it thin!"

"Go chase yourse'f, Molly. Findin's keepin's, sez I. Mary be praised, there goes the

A CHILD OF DIVORCE

bell! Come along, Jean; I'll show yez the way.''

Though Jean had heard no bell through the numerous other noises, she was glad to follow docilely. Her environment was beginning to swim. The scullery workers formed a long line, Maggie keeping just in front of her and handing back a large, thick plate from a stack on the counter. Thus they filed by a long table of food, which the male cooks behind it dished out, all on the same proffered plate, as they voiced their limited preferences.

"Pork or mutton?" scowled the meat-cook to Jean, for he was uncomfortably hot. Though bare of hairy chest and arms, he perspired profusely, and some of it dripped into the skillet where the chops were frying. Jean hesitated. She had been hungry, but by now her appetite seemed to have fled, and with it her power of expression. Impatiently the cook jabbed his fork into the nearest chop and flung it across the counter. It landed on the plate, splashing hot gravy over her dress and hands. That was too much. Right there she broke into uncontrollable tears.

"Ye spalpeen!" bridled Maggie to the cook; "whiriver was ye fetched up—bahd luck to yez! Nivver moind, Jean, darlin'," she consoled in a tone quite audible to the half-nude dispenser of chops, "yez can't ex-

TO AVOID COMPLICATIONS

pect manners from thim as was nivver learned none. It's the divil he looks like behind his smokin' pots, an' the divil's ways he's got!" The culinary gentleman's response to this is unrepeatable, but Maggie, harboring her huge mound of food, went on, nothing daunted. Blindly, Jean followed her out to a landing and up a flight of iron steps.

"See, darlin', it's a roof-garden they give us in the summer-time," Maggie informed; "swell, I'm tellin' yez, not barrin' Madison Square."

Jean dimly saw a roof, if no garden, and two long oil-cloth-covered tables flanked by backless plank benches. The change of air temporarily refreshed her; though, between the tarred floor and the low awning, the roof was stifling enough. She laid down her tray, climbed over the bench, and sat silently beside her voluble friend. She made a brave try at eating, but the first bite sickened her, and a few seconds later she was hysterical. Maggie embraced her, fat and sweaty, but sympathetic, commiserating. "The pore darlin'—it's homesick she is. Come, dearie, don't be cryin' loik thot. Come, eat a bit, an' yez'll feel bether." To Maggie and her kind, an opportunity to eat is the panacea for most of the ills, as well as the highest compliment one can offer a neighbor. It is hard for them to comprehend how even homesickness can mar the joys of food, but all the women felt obvious pity for Jean, and tried, in their own coarse, but well-meaning, ways to "cheer her up."

"He—threw it at me!" she gasped at last; "*threw* it at me—like I was a dog!"

"Begora, an' pwhat d'ye care for the spalpeen, darlin'?" Maggie consoled, ineffecually, however. As vainly did the others barter their vulgar anecdotes for her benefit, and offer her their various dishes. Jean grew calmer, but nothing could dissipate her sense of despair. She could not stand it here. But getting out involved as much red tape as had getting in. Eventually she was paid her eighty-five cents, and, according to directions, turned a resignation card in to Mr. Smith.

"Oh, so it's *you* that are dissatisfied, is it?" he discovered, unpleasantly, his first impression from the explanation on the card being that the firm was dissatisfied with Jean.

"Yes," Jean murmured. "I—I—can't stand bein' treated—like a dog!"

He shrugged. "Oh, all right. From the way you spoke when you came in, I thought you'd be glad of *anything*."

CHAPTER IX.

RESPECTABILITY'S FLOTSAM

TILL the skyscrapers began to cast long mantles of early shadows over the city, Jean sat in Washington Square Park, trying to form some clear plan of procedure. But her maze only deepened with the deepening gloom. At last she arose wearily and walked along Fifth Avenue with no special goal in mind, only feeling the need of motion.

In the sense that it is always changing, New York is forever the same, and at that time there stood on East Twenty-third Street, opposite Madison Square, a long row of decrepit studio buildings, which sheltered the pursuers of devious and dubious arts. They presented uniform front doors led up to by high flights of crumbling, iron-banistered stone steps. On some of the railings posters were fastened advertising for help wanted. Jean drew near one of these, and, as she scanned it, her numbed interest stirred once more. "Artist's assistant," the board announced; "young girl to help in studio. Apply Bancroft, third floor." The double doors stood open, and this time there was no hesitancy in Jean's decision. Up the stone steps she climbed and then up two creaky, musty flights of stairs within. A faint illumination from the setting sun sifting through the dusty skylight aided her as she neared the third floor, yet she blundered around in the hall considerably before she came to the glass-paneled door labeled "Bancroft. Walk In." There was, however, no availing oneself of that invitation, for a turn of the knob proved the door to be locked. Jean knocked softly, then less softly. No response. Disappointment, unreasonable in its intensity, sickened her. Finally, with a resolve to come early next morning, she turned back. Half-way down the stairs, almost involuntarily, she yielded to the call of overwrought nerves and muscles for another interval of rest and sank upon a step. Outside, the city roared, rushing eternally, yet never passing, as though it were built on some huge, dizzy wheel revolving round and round her. Here, for all the dinginess, there was comparative peace and seclusion. Jean leaned her head in her hands, for it throbbed and ached. Far, far away she seemed to hear the Metropolitan clock chime half-past five. She felt weak, and the blood pulsed in her ears, drowning the thump, thump of ascending footsteps till they were nearly upon her. She started.

"Well, I say—you're not a spook?" The soft-voiced query ended in a nervous laugh.

"No," answered Jean, as quietly; "I was —just resting."

"Fatigued, are you, my dear? Been working hard to-day?" The full-bodied form of the woman in white loomed over her pleasantly. Something inviting emanated from it, something maternal, which Jean in her need could sense.

"I'm *looking* for work," she explained.

"Oh, you don't say! Were you looking here?"

"Yes. Bancroft, but there's no one there."

"My dear!"—it came in a sort of gasp which might have betokened surprise or relief—"I'm glad of that! Who sent you here?"

"No one. I just saw the sign downstairs."

"But really, you oughtn't to come to these places—unadvised—don't you know? I take it you're a stranger in the city?"

"Yes," Jean murmured. The ample woman in white touched her arm. "Then come along with me to my room for a bit," she urged. "We'll have a dish of tea and talk things over. Maybe I can aid you. My name is Nita Baily—of the *Evening Sun*."

A CHILD OF DIVORCE

Jean accepted gratefully. Miss Baily resided next to Bancroft's in a queer, cluttered-up, little studio. Every square foot of it seemed to be occupied, while the walls were lined with photographs, lithographs and pen-and-ink sketches, original cartoons, etc. At the far end, opposite the door, one large grated window over an asphalt court afforded a view of clotheslines, brick walls and similar grated windows, supporting their invariable milk-bottles on the sills. Miss Baily's own sill quite obviously served as pantry, and the gaslight which she struck revealed, beside her kindly, ruddy English face, the amazing multiplicity of uses to which she put everything.

"Sit down, my dear." She waved toward a gaily covered and bepillowed piece of furniture which was bed at night and lounge by day. "We'll have a bite in a jiffy."

Jean, at once too tired and fascinated to protest, watched her shed the jacket of her white linen suit, slip it on a hanger hooked over the gas-jet, hang her hat on the doorknob, extract a few dishes and some strange contrivance from a cretonne-covered box which did triple duty as dresser, cupboard and table, and proceed to use the otherwise wasted heat of the flame by fixing the little apparatus to the burner, so as to turn it into a miniature stove upon which she soon boiled water for the tea.

RESPECTABILITY'S FLOTSAM

'Dearie, I'm pleased that you found no one *there*,'' she broke out; *"if you could hear what I've heard in there—"*

"Why—what?" Jean asked, puzzled.

Miss Baily was pushing back the toilet articles on the box to clear a corner for the meal. She shrugged her thick shoulders. "Never go there again, dearie; it's just no place for you, upon my word." Jean's intuition helped her to divine the reason for this warning and silenced further questions, despite her curiosity. Miss Baily cut some thin slices of bread, spreading them from a dish of congealed white substance, and smiled. "My butter. Hope you'll like it. It's the suet from the meat. I let it harden, and eat it this way. Put a bit of salt on it and think you've a roast-beef sandwich. Have some tea, dearie; here's cheese, too, if you want it, and crackers. Don't mind 'em being broken a bit. They get damaged in transit, and I buy 'em that way for half-price. A lot of folks do it. It doesn't spoil the taste any."

This was but the overture to Miss Baily's confidence, and before long Jean heard all about why she lived so frugally. She was saving money to hunt and wreak legal vengeance upon a rogue who had abducted from London her very young sister, and to claim and support the little nephew whose whereabouts was still a mystery. The sister had been her sole remaining relative, and she, Nita, had followed to New York in answer to her last pathetic letter, only to find her prostrated, the brute having absconded with their child.

"We couldn't see whatever he wanted with the little chap," Miss Baily related, "but he must have had some scheme for making gain of it, for he wasn't the kind to want it otherwise. I always detested the fellow, but poor Ada! It was her first love affair and she was seeing everything through rosy glasses. Poor child! She died the same week I landed, and the last thing she did was to beg me to save her little boy."

Jean's heart swelled in sympathy. The world seemed indeed a tragic place. There was little more to be said on the matter, however, and finally the conversation veered to her own predicament.

"Say," Miss Baily exclaimed, as if suddenly inspired, "I've a friend who's manager of the ten-cent store on Sixth Avenue. I'll wager I can get him to take you on. It'll be a bit fatiguing at first, as you'll have to stand on your feet, but you'll get used to it, don't you know? And you'll have your Sundays and every evening after six. I'll take you down to see him to-morrow noon; shall I?"

This she did with fruitful results. The manager said he would have a vacancy, looked

Jean over and seemed satisfied with her as a prospect for it, though he regretted her lack of experience. Due to this, of course, she could not expect to start in at the same wages as her predecessor had been getting, but, out of deference to his friend, Miss Baily, he offered "five dollars to start." Gladly enough Jean agreed to begin Monday morning, when the other girl's week was up.

"Well, that's that," exulted Miss Baily, as they went out; "now for living quarters, for you can't stay at St. Barnabas', can you? I think I can get you in on Christopher Street. You'll have car fare, but you'll make it up on what you save for board. Down there they give you a room and meals for three-fifty a week. It's all girls, and if you're over twenty-five or earning more than ten a week, they won't take you, but *you're* eligible. Deedle-dee—come along."

Down the iron steps of the elevated station a human cataract was surging, but she breasted it in fine spirits, Jean following, a little envious of a heart which could take life's blows so philosophically. What a lot of self-confidence Miss Baily had! Jean now vaguely dreaded to part with her. At last they stood on the platform waiting for the downtown train, and, in open admiration, Jean surveyed the stalky, but trim, figure. "Your white suit looks so nice," she observed timidly, "I don't see how you keep it so fresh this hot weather."

"Like it?" Miss Baily grinned. "You'd laugh if you knew where it came from. It's all hand-made—by myself. Made it out of sheets. Yes. You know in my part of England we never use cotton sheets like you do here. They're all pure, heavy linen, spun from the family's own flax, and handed down for generations. They wear like iron. I had several in my trunk, but after I got here I decided cotton would do *me* for sheets, as I found I could make better use of the linen. This'll last forever and always look right. Don't you know, dearie, a spiffy appearance helps a lot in this world? This world values you at just about what you value yourself. Don't let people *know* how poor you are. If you haven't much, stuff your bag with something anyhow—like this— see?" Drawing close, with twinkling eyes, she unlatched her smart, prosperously bulging handbag enough to afford Jean a peek, and in amazement the girl saw more tissue paper than bank-notes. "Not *too* much," Miss Baily continued, "that's ostentatious. But never let it get too flat either. Over here in America the fat purse commands even more attention than it does in my country." Jean had already noticed the involuntary respect which Miss Baily seemed to inspire in clerks, guards, or any one else she happened to address. She thought it due to her unmistakable air of good breeding, but no doubt these earmarks of prosperity helped, and an astute philosophy underlaid her precepts.

At Christopher Street they descended to earth again, and presently approached a stone-fronted building cleaner than the horde of others crowding about and against it. On either side of the vestibule was a long, high-silled plate-glass window presenting a flower-box in which throve geraniums of pink, white and red. Jean read in gilt letters on the door, "The Minerva Sweet Institute and Home for Respectable Girls." She did not just like the "Respectable." It sounded like a challenge to decent society. But this was no time to be fastidious, and she had a swift supposition that it was necessary because most institutes and homes were—for the other sort of girls.

The wide-tiled hall with its stone staircase and fireplace, flanked on the left by the dining-room, on the right by the parlor and office, impressed one as neat, if not especially homelike. Two matrons were in charge who arranged their shifts to suit each others' convenience; thin, wrinkled, wistful Miss Moody, who had "seen better days," and phlegmatic Mrs. Toole, who bodily would have made three of her. The latter greeted them from behind the office desk. "We're pretty full all the time," she answered Miss Baily, easily, "but guess we can tuck in one more."

A number of formalities were required to enter this place. An application card must be signed and references furnished, but they knew Miss Baily, who vouched for Jean, paying her board for two weeks in advance plus the twenty-five cents deposit on the key to her room, with which Jean was given a little folder of "Rules" and requested to study same. Then, with grateful reluctance, Jean bade Miss Baily good-by, for the lunch hour was already up.

"I'll have to put you up on the fourth floor," Mrs. Toole informed. "I hope you ain't got many things."

"No," Jean replied.

"That's good." The matron deigned no further remarks just then, the stiff climb claiming her surplus breath. Their destination proved a surprising place. A great, asphalt-floored room stretched the width of the building, containing three long, bare tables, folding-chairs and overhead lights. On three sides, at a depth of some ten feet from the walls, ran a dark green, sheet-iron fence, perhaps nine feet high and punctured by even rows of numbered doors, or, more properly, gates; for these were also of sheet iron and came at least a foot short of touching the floor. They reminded Jean of the summer doors she had seen in corner saloons, except that they were much narrower. Mrs. Toole approached to door No. 316, unlocked it, and then Jean saw that partitions of the same hard material cut the long space between the walls and the fence into little six-by-ten, cage-like rooms, painted buff inside. Each room, as she later discovered, boasted, like this one, a window, a radiator, a very narrow clothes-locker, a cot, cheap dresser, chair and small grass rug. There was no variety. Curtains were prohibited as a nuisance, and likewise all pictures, except what might be placed on the dresser. Trunks must be kept in the basement, and Mrs. Toole explained that no individual lights were permitted, the illumination which flowed over the fence and under the doors from the "general sitting-room" being considered sufficient to undress by. It followed that at night all sewing, reading or writing must be done outside one's room. In short, there was semi-privacy for the body only.

"You'll see by the rules," Mrs. Toole further enlightened Jean, "that no one is allowed in her room from half-past nine to four on week-days. If you want to kind of get settled, I'll make an exception of you to-day, but to-morrow, and till you get started to work, I

A CHILD OF DIVORCE

guess you'll have to stay downstairs or somewheres else them hours. I'm sorry, but rules is rules," whereupon she left Jean sitting on the edge of the cot with its two-inch-thick mat that crunched as if stuffed with excelsior. In this posture she remained for some time, hardly aware that she was alone, probably alone on that whole bleak area of fourth floor. Half-heartedly, she scanned the two-page, printed pamphlet in her hand. It set forth twenty-five tersely worded "regulations," among which the following struck her most forcibly:

Board must be paid weekly in advance of each week. No reduction for absence. We require notice as early as possible when leaving.

Those in charge reserve the right to ask the occupant to surrender her room without giving any reason.

Rooms can only be used by the girls renting same. No overnight visitors allowed.

No trunks will be allowed in the rooms. No food, fruit, beverages or refreshments of any kind whatever.

Occupants must keep their own rooms in order and make their own beds.

Lights in the sitting-room will be turned out at 10:30. No individual lights are permitted in the rooms.

The Home will not be responsible for any theft or damage under any circumstances.

No room can be occupied, unless in case of real sickness, between the hours of 9:30 A. M. and 4 P. M., excepting Saturdays, Sundays and holidays.

And so on, till Jean wondered what *was* permissible in this satire of home. Still, what could one expect for three-fifty a week? She threw the folder aside, got up and went out again, curious to look around. After her the metal door shut with a clang that contracted her heart, for it sounded like the clashing of prison bars. She paused again near the long, wooden tables strewn with a few torn magazines months out of date, then moved toward the blank wall between this room and the lavatory to read three lonely little mottoes hanging in narrow black frames. They seemed almost lost in space, yet attracted attention by reason of their being the nearest approach to decorative effort about the place. But they were not mottoes! "Girls will please not use towels for dust-cloths or shoe-rags," admonished the first one; "Bathtubs must always be cleaned after using," informed the second one; and the third one commanded brusquely, "Do not bang the doors." Jean sighed and passed on. There appeared nothing more of interest, however, and she was about to leave for St. Barnabas' to get her scant possessions when a faint moan reached her from under one of the doors. She listened. It came again—from 330. She advanced, and the metal resounded even to her gentle rap.

"Come in," bade a weak voice. Jean pushed the door open on a room just like her own, but badly messed with every evidence of unattended illness. Along the cot lay a girl, greenishly pale, her eyes only half opened.

"Y—you're sick?" Jean queried superficially.

"You bet I'm sick—blame this place!" But the words trembled: "Who're you?"

"Jean Laval. I'm just moving in. Can't I do something for you?" The other ignored the question. Her livid lips twisted into a cynical smile which made Jean shrink internally. "You're movin' in, huh? Hope you like it. You poor kid—you don't know what you're in for!"

"What d'you mean?"

"I knew the rotten meat here'd get me sometime. Sick? Gawd! I bet I'm poisoned! Last night it stunk somethin' fierce—but you got to eat somethin'!"

"Don't you want a drink? And hadn't I better ask Mrs. Toole to get a doctor?"

"*She* should worry! She ain't as much as come to the door all day, and I can't stand up. You got a lot to learn, kid. She's got a good name all right—she's nothin' but Rosie's tool; and if he knew this—he'd want me to get out—he'd as soon it'd be in my black box as any other way—"

"Oh, don't talk like that!" Jean cried, frightened. She went for a glass of water, but the girl only took a sip and turned over with another moan. Her suffering was evident. Jean made some attempts to straighten things up, smoothed the covers, and, having done all she could, hurried down to report to the matron.

"Three-thirty?" echoed Mrs. Toole; "that's Mamie Braden. Sick again, is she? Blamed it on the meat, did she? Well, she's got her nerve! It's her sprees that make her sick, that's what. If she'd behave herself decent, she'd be all right, but she's always got some kick comin'. The *other* girls ain't poisoned from the meat, and people want to be careful how they lay things on the Home. *I* eat here and do *I* look sick?" She tossed back her florid face, puffing out her expansive bosom in a way which made Jean smile in spite of her anxiety. "Don't you worry, Miss," she added, "we'll take care of *her.*"

Jean hoped so as she went out. She wondered which was right. Surely Miss Baily would not have brought her to a place where they served impure food, and it was reasonable to think that if that were the cause, the rest of the boarders would have been affected. Yet Mamie's ghastly appearance haunted her.

CHAPTER X.

FLEDGLING WINGS

"HERE comes a sale for you, honey. I think the party with the spinach wants the mouse-trap." Mary Dugan's words set all Jean's nerves to quivering. She reached mechanically across the counter for the article and the dime the bearded old gentleman presently held toward her in the mute way customers have of buying in stores where everything has but two pieces. Her fingers trembled so she could hardly manage the wrapping. However, she achieved an awkward package, and the gentleman sauntered off without seeming to notice anything unusual. She fumbled with the cash register, and, thanks to Mary's coaching, found the right key and "rang up." That was her first customer, it being early on Monday morning. She had been assigned to help Mary Dugan on the tin and wooden ware counter. "We mostly start green goils on that," the manager explained; "then they can't bust nothin'."

FLEDGLING WINGS

Just now business was slow, and their time had been largely devoted to replenishing stock and filling the scars on the counters left by the ravaging crowds of Saturday. Mary Dugan, copper-haired, saucy-eyed, seemed to possess two personalities. Toward the new girl she was all sympathy, chumminess and curiosity, while the approach of customers caused her to present a phase of serene nonchalance, spiced by a certain malicious enjoyment when they showed impatience. Before long, Jean discovered this attitude to be characteristic among all the girls. Comrades in toil, they instinctively regarded the public as a common enemy. Customers were indifferent to them. Why should they be interested in customers? Theoretically this ought not to be, actually it *is,* and, too gradually for her to realize it, Jean absorbed the sentiments of her new environment. With her next customer she was less nervous, with the third her excitement softened to eager courtesy. But even this latter concern soon wore away, and she began to shoulder her share of the "chip" as far as the public was concerned.

"Say, did you see that piece of cheese?" called Helen Gray across from the cracker counter, as a woman of the triple-chin type waddled out of earshot. "Looks like she can't afford to eat, don't she? I had to say it twice

A CHILD OF DIVORCE

—'No samples, madam'—before she *heard* me, and then she looked up—*so innocent!*"

"Didn't she buy any?" Jean asked.

"Like fun she did! What's the use buyin' when you got all you want for nothin'?"

"No doubt she's harda hearin'," Mary suggested ironically, "or thought you was speakin' to some one else."

"Oh, yeah; no doubt!"

A forty-five-minute lunch period was allowed for each shift, of which there were three, the bell announcing the first one at eleven-fifteen. Jean was released on this shift with several girls from other parts of the store. She had intended to go to some cafeteria, but Mary told her that upstairs in the restroom facilities were provided for light cooking, and the custom was to "chip in" for a common meal. At the Home only breakfasts and dinners were served, except on Sundays and holidays, and it relieved her to know that the fifteen cents per day to which she had limited herself for lunches was no less than what most of the girls contributed. Two were then detailed to purchase provisions while the rest set the table. Bologna, pickles, coffee, pie, or some French pastry, were the popular staples of these quick lunches, varied now and then by cold baked beans, or embellished with a cheap can of preserves or a bit of fresh fruit when the diners were flush. This, in combination with much jocularity, afforded a meal preferable to one eaten alone in some strange, teeming restaurant. The conversation was easy to follow, hovering mainly around the three central topics of customers, clothes and "gentleman friends."

"You shoulda seen the kid that tried to put one over on me this mornin'," related Hilda Schwabe, of the candy counter. "He come up an' says, 'Gimme fi' cen's wuth o' dem chawklets.' I weighed 'em out. He give me his nickel and then says, 'I'll take fi' cen's wuth o' dem jelly beans, too.' I give 'em to him and he starts walkin' off. 'Say,' I says, 'you forgot somethin'.' 'Huh?' he says. 'You ain't paid for the jelly beans,' I says. 'Sure I paid,' he says; 'ain't you got th' nickel?' 'That's for the chawklets,' I says. 'No,' he says, trying to ball me up; 'I paid for *them* before.' 'Say, come off!' I says, 'you can't pull that stuff around here!' I seen he was sneakin' to the door, but just then Barker come down the aisle, and I hit my bell. Say, you shoulda seen Barker light into him. He told him where to get off, and I got the jelly beans back all right! I bet he won't be tryin' *them* stunts no more—not on me anyhow!"

"There was a guy come up to my counter this mornin'," contributed Sadie Robinsky of department 27, ladies' lingerie, "to buy his wife one o' them nifty camisoles we got special, you know, ten cents for the silk, ten for the lace, ten for the ribbon, thirty cents all together, and he was givin' me a dime for the whole business. I explained to him the way it was. 'Oh, all right,' he says, and fished outa couple more dimes. 'What bust?' I says. He looked awful queer, and then he says, 'I didn't hear nothin'!'" This provoked shrieks of choking laughter, and some seconds passed ere the girls could resume their eating. Even then it would break out now and again, as one of them repeated slyly, "I didn't hear nothin'."

"Ain't you got one to tell, Jean?" asked Sadie. Jean recited the incident of the elephantine lady and the crackers.

"Say, I'll bet that's the same egg I got!" exclaimed Agnes Mueller, who presided over the hosiery; "I had my stockin's all stacked up nice by sizes, and she comes along and starts to pull out the bottom ones—the top ain't good enough! 'Each pile's the same, madam,' I says: 'what size d'you want?' 'Eight-and-a-half,' she says. 'For yourself?' I says. She looked like she was insulted and says, '*Cert'n'y!*' Say, did you see her feet, Jean? Eight-and-a-half for them canal-boats; oh, mamma!"—more laughter. "Well, I just happened to be outa that size, but I says I could give'r nine. Did she believe me? Like fun she did! She upsets my whole blessed counter lookin' for what wasn't there, and then she walks off without buyin' nothin'; 'cause she says *nine was too big!*"

"I got you all beat!" sang out pretty Alice Farley, queen of the jewelry section; "a wop come up to me to buy a weddin' ring and asks me how much it was. I told him, and he says, 'Tena cen'? You no gota for five?' " By now the hilarity bordered on hysteria.

"Did he sacrifice the exter nickel?" some one asked, when her voice returned.

"Oh, sure; I told him it cost more to get married in the U. S.—but it was cheap at the price."

"A ten-cent weddin' ring—oh, mamma!" groaned another.

"Say, you oughta see how many I sell," Alice boasted; "ingagement rings too. I'll bet if it wasn't for me the marriage bureau'd go outa commission."

"Better get your diamond examined," Hilda warned Sadie impishly.

"Say, d'ye think I'd go with a cheap skate like that? This ring cost twenty-five dollars; Max told me so hisself!"

"D'you go with a fella, Jean?" Alice queried sweetly. But before Jean could answer, Sadie popped in, "Doncha tell'er, Jean; she's just lookin' for business!" Laughter

A CHILD OF DIVORCE

again, and Jean, caught in the spirit of it, affected a tantalizing secrecy regarding the affairs of her heart.

The mental stimulus of the lunch hour helped her to forget the soreness of her feet from standing all morning, the climbing ache in her limbs; but consciousness of this returned painfully afterwards. She dared not sit down, for Mary informed her that the manager did not like it—it looked lazy. "Then, what's that stool behind the counter for?" Jean asked wearily.

"Because the law makes 'em put them in for us," Mary enlightened her; "but they hate to have you use 'em, and they keep their eye peeled on new goils more'n old ones, so you better look out, hon. Cheer up. It's only at first you feel that way."

Sometime later Mr. Barker, who manifested in his person enough dudishness to make him the incarnation of all floorwalkers, sauntered up to the tinware counter, a little notebook open in his hand, and leaned over to Jean, asking, "What's your name?" Thinking this official, Jean told him, and he wrote it down. "Live with your parents?" he wanted to know next.

"No; I board."

"Oh, yes. Where?" She gave him the address. Then, leaning closer, Mr. Barker queried in a low, confidential tone, "Do you go home alone nights?"

"Why—" Jean stammered, suddenly turning hot inside.

"Won't you meet me some night—to take in a show and eats—"

"Is there some one here to wait on me?" cut in a nasal voice. Jean started. Mary was busy, and the lady customer had appealed to Barker. "Forward!" he commanded gruffly, spun on his heel and walked away.

Jean finished wrapping the clumsy dishpan at about the same time Mary disposed of her own customers. She came over to Jean. "What's the matter, honey?" she questioned. "You're red as a beet. I seen Barker talkin' to you. What'd he say?"

"He—he—asked me to meet him," Jean muttered.

Mary widened her eyes and thrust her tongue into one cheek. "Fast woik," she observed; "leave it to Barker! He tries that on every new goil we get, but we're all wise to him. You've got a right to be mad, only I hope you didn't let on to him you really was."

"I don't know," Jean said miserably.

"If you did, he might get you sacked. You don't need to go out with him, though. Just kid him along—nice—that's all you got to do. They say he's married and has two kids. I don't know if that's true, but we got his number all right. If he comes back, just tell him thanks, you'll think about it, and if he tries to make a date, just say you already got a date for that night, see?"

"I see," Jean murmured.

"You shoulda said you lived with your folks, but if he thinks you got a steady, he won't bother you long; he's too much of a coward, and he can easy find some one else that ain't got no protection."

"Thanks, Mary; I'd never get along here without you."

"That's all right, kid. We goils've got to stick together, that's all—believe *me!*"

Barker did renew his attentions several days later, but Jean had learned the value of the shopgirl's crude diplomacy. She repressed her indignation and even smiled her excuses. As Mary had predicted, he was shortly discouraged, and Jean kept her "job." To Barker each new, comely girl held possibilities of prospective diversion. One was as good as another, but none was worth risking too much for. There are far too many Barkers in all our cities. From her unlettered comrades Jean soon gleamed much worldly wisdom. She learned that in numerous little matters they held the truth as something too precious for common use. Yet they were big-hearted, generous, and their glib fabrications were largely resorted to as shields for a still more precious virtue. What else could they do? One *had* to live, which necessitated a job; and *wanted* to "go straight." Thus the need of a compromise was evident. It must be a choice of the lesser evil. Few of them had ever heard the old adage about fighting the devil with his own weapons, yet most of them lived according to its theory, by intuition rather than reason.

For many nights Jean suffered agonizing pains in her feet, limbs, hips and back. She had but little appetite, and the fare at the Home was not calculated to tempt even that. True, she had not been offered any rancid meat, but—

"Nobody can say they're not economical here," claimed Myrtle Dixon, a pert little, dark-eyed telephone girl. "I bet they *never* throw anything out! What you're too ungrateful to eat one meal, faces you the next like the sins of your past—or what some one else's too ungrateful to eat."

"I used to wonder about reincarnation," mused Stella Bain, an amateur stenographer, who had delved a bit into such subjects. "I guess I know what it means now. The remains are always returning to us—*in a different form*—but still familiar."

A CHILD OF DIVORCE

"Well, we had real chicken Sunday anyhow," May Allen put in cheerfully; *"I know, because I found a feather in it!"* The others tittered. They did not dare do anything very loud. They were grouped in the fourth-floor sitting-room after the evening meal. A kind of hushed awe had pervaded that place ever since the officers had borne a lifeless burden from Room 330. An autopsy on Mamie Braden had revealed ptomaine poisoning—due probably, Mrs. Toole said, to the lobster she had eaten on one of her sprees. She had bragged a lot about her lobster dinners. It always seemed to Jean that a more thorough investigation should have been made of the case, but nobody heard much about it afterward.

The girls had a natural aversion to being sick there, especially since that incident, so they did their best to keep fit. Illness, however slight, ceased to be a luxury when you had to lie alone in a bare, iron casket of a room, with every outside noise and the aggravating light reaching you from under and over the door. There was never enough light in any of the rooms for a well person, and always too much for a sick one, and it must be borne each night till ten-thirty. It bothered Jean a good deal during those first evenings, when she retired early to rest her painful muscles. But she became inured to it, as she did to her work at the store, and was finally able to join the nightly gatherings around the naked wooden tables. So much talking made it difficult for any one to read, so she usually shared in the general gossip, while mending clothes or lolling limply in one of the folding-chairs. She heard much about "Rosie," and had seen him twice. He was Albert Rosenthal, the trustee whom Minerva Sweet, the endower, growing blind with age, had chosen to administer the funds and oversee the Home. The girls, especially the ones who had been there longest, mistrusted him. They recalled Miss Sweet as a dear old lady, and said the Home had been a much better place when she was able to visit it. They whispered among themselves a suspicion that "Rosie" was taking advantage of her infirmity—providing them inferior service in order to appropriate certain moneys. Miss Sweet lived now in a sanitarium at Syracuse. She had absolute faith in Rosenthal, who, for years, had acted as her business manager. But no one dared make any accusations, for no one could "get anything on him." Jean did not like him either. With Miss Sweet he was, no doubt, the pink of affability. He struck her like one who could assume such a manner if he chose. But with them he was domineering and bold. One would gather in-

A CHILD OF DIVORCE

deed from his bearing that having to live at an "Institute and Home" in some way minimized a girl's right to chivalry.

"We ain't supposed to be livin' on charity," complained Maude Scherman, a nervous, sallow girl, who did piecework in a corset factory; "but they treat us like we was!"

So passed the days, each one much like its predecessor. From eight to six, Saturday till ten o'clock, Jean was on her feet, helping Mary stock up, clean and rearrange their ever-disordered counters; wrapping cumbersome packages of pots and pans; breathing the exhalations of motley throngs; acting as a sort of shock absorber for the impatience and sarcasms of touchy customers. Even her dreams were haunted by "Will you wait on me's?"; by the hissings of Italians, who used that method to claim attention, or the pompous demands of some jet female from "Hell's Kitchen"*— "Ain't yo' all heah fo' to wait on us?"

Oh, there were some nice people too; some who, if they did not buy things, put them carefully back into place; some who made kindly remarks and did not act as if they were afraid of not getting their money's worth by bothering to thank a shopgirl whose

---

*Popular name for a rough section of New York city west of Sixth Avenue, above Thirtieth Street, thickly settled by negroes.

services were already remunerated, and, therefore, only their proper due. *Every one* was not making a train either; every one did not request double wrapping because they lived "out of town." There were even some who tipped. The latter were mostly men, and sometimes words meant to be flattering, but not always delicate, accompanied the coins. Here again, however, one could resort to diplomacy. It was worth the slight embarrassment to have the tip. Jean saved hers for a more comfortable pair of shoes, as otherwise she saw no prospect of getting any.

One of those annual heat waves from which there seems to be no relief, at least for the poor and laboring, had engulfed the city. Days burned away; nights stifled themselves. New York's speedy pace was slackened, and people, who could not get out to the country or down to the shore, went about their tasks on half-energy, sweltering, almost bodily melting. There was not enough vegetation left to absorb the humidity, and thousands of plate-glass windows, paved streets, mountains of bricks, served but as reflectors to the harshly glowing sun. The papers reported numerous deaths. Toward the end of August, every one looked for a climax, but it tarried distressingly, and under each hazy, sultry moon the rabble of the riversides crawled to their tenement roofs, or swarmed like insects to the Battery in quest of a chance to breathe. At night one could hardly walk across the patch of grass there for prostrate forms.

Twenty cents on the elevated cars covered a round trip to Brighton Beach or Coney Island, where most of Jean's associates spent Sundays bathing, dancing, dining royally with their respective admirers. Late one afternoon, Mary Dugan suggested such an excursion to Jean, even offering to provide the escort. "Bill Myers," she explained, "that was in here last week, 'member? He's woikin' down to 'Merican Can Comp'ny with my man, and he's stuck on you, kid, all right—wants to meetcha. We can get up a swell bunch, him an' you an' me an' Joe."

Jean hesitated. She did not want to offend Mary, but her impression of Bill had not generated a responsive desire for an introduction. She recalled him as a hollow-chested fellow, all the normal color of whose rather bold face appeared to be concentrated in certain unwholesome eruptions—the type one naturally associates with saloon corners and too many cheap cigarets. He had winked at her, causing an instinctive recoil on her part.

"I'm mostly tired Sundays," she evaded. From her stock list Mary glanced up in surprise. "Gee, kid, you wouldn't rather snooze

FLEDGLING WINGS

all day than go to the Island!" she exclaimed. "You don't know what you're missin'. Them fellas make all kindsa money, and they're good sports with it—take in everything goin'. Besides, you can sleep on the beach after we take a swim, if you want. Can you swim?"

"No," Jean confessed.

"Well, Bill's a peach at it; he'll learn you. You'll have the time o' your life, kiddo. Bill ain't no Maurice Costello to look at, but he's sure a good sport."

"I never went out—with any—fellows—" Jean was still fencing. Mary looked frankly as if this was something beyond her comprehension. True, she had never seen Jean meet any beau at closing-hours like most of the girls, but it was the first time she had definitely admitted the lack of one.

"Well, it's about time you was startin' in, then," Mary advised. "How the dickens d'you ever expect to get married without knowin' any fellas?" Jean crimsoned. Certainly Bill did not appeal to her as a matrimonial prospect, and she vaguely felt that in shop vocabulary there must have been some way of expressing this sentiment, if she only knew it, without seeming ungrateful for a proposal made in kindness. Mary, still watching her, laughed. "You're a funny kid. You make me think o' them goils in the movies from 'way down on the farm.''

"Why?" Jean's flush deepened.

"Oh, there's such a lota things you ain't wise to yet."

"Maybe I'm wiser'n you think," Jean blurted out; "I've heard the girls talking, and I know—those fellows they go with—they want to kiss you—"

"Oh, gosh, honey! Life ain't no Sunday school! There's worse things than kissin'—if that's all they want. Say, you can't expect everything for nothin', you know. If the fellas are good sports, we got to be, too—so long as they don't get *too* fresh. What's a little kiss hurt anybody anyhow?"

"Well, mine aren't for sale, Mary, that's all." Something bigger than Jean herself seemed speaking through her then. "I—I'd rather not go—if you have to do it. I don't want to take—what I can't pay for—it would just spoil the fun—" She finished with an inward shudder at the mental image of an embrace from Bill. It nauseated her. Mary shrugged her shoulders. "Oh, all right, kid, it's up to you; but gee! I think you're foolish, and if you get to be a hairy-faced old maid, you got nobody to blame but yourself—" The welcome shriek of the closing-bell drowned further argument, and, with the long day's first symptom of alacrity, the girls sprang to their various registers to bag the cash they had received. In another five minutes bags and stock orders were collected, counters covered, and the second bell released every one in a rustle to the street.

Long, lurid streaks behind the western skyscrapers evidenced a sinking sun, but the sidewalks held the heat like thermos, radiating it with dusty, heavy, sour smells. Jean hastened for a surface car. Had she ever paused to analyze why she was in such a hurry to get to her room each night, there might have been difficulty in naming any special reason, but, nevertheless, this was so. Several cars passed by her, however, too crowded even to slow down, their interiors solid with rush-hour humanity; men hanging, three deep, to the platforms and running-boards as barnacles to a sea-washed bark. So she climbed to the elevated, her burning, tired feet swollen till their worn casings threatened to burst. Conditions there were little better, but the cars *had* to stop. Whether you boarded then was largely a question of brute propulsion. With the rest of the city's teeming denizens, Jean was growing used to this morning and evening, though, combined with the temperature, it would have made an angel cross. Perhaps she wasted as much energy getting to and from her work as she spent upon it throughout the entire day. She reached one train just in time to have the gate slammed in her face, but the next absorbed her by the help of carnal suction, and she found herself nicely dovetailed into a group of gum-chewing Jews whose conversation was obviously hampered by gesticulatory restrictions. It always seemed to her on these rides that she somehow lost her identity as a person. No one was a person, except in the sense of being one tiny particle or a loaf of hash. With every jerk and lunge of the cars, the whole mass lurched or swayed in unison, and Jean often wondered, if they could stand like that long enough, whether they would not really all grow together, as they stuck together now, perspiring like a lot of squeezed sponges. And not many hours distant—out where the dew might christen leaves and grasses, where night came down like fanning, caressing, star-set wings instead of a smothering pall—unrolled acres and acres of meadows, mountains and forests! Why did people have to do it—*this* the people God made in His image? Foul breaths, fumes of sweat, garlic, tobacco, pepsin, thickened the humid air till Jean's senses reeled. She clung desperately to enough consciousness to save her from fainting, though, had she fainted, she could not have fallen, there being nowhere to fall.

FLEDGLING WINGS

Mercifully, in time she was belched out at her station, and, with the ability to expand her muscles, recovered strength, actual casualties being two lost buttons.

Dinner had usually just started by the time Jean came in. She glanced over the spread of envelopes on the mail-table, found a letter from her mother and went to her seat. In common with every one else and her floral namesake, Violet, the cook, had been shriveled by the weather, so that the meal was even less than ordinarily appetizing. Something like resentment of an outrage swelled in Jean's breast when she regarded a charred strip of pork and the dessert of canned apricots for the fourth time that week. Apricots she detested, and no arguments apropos of their wholesomeness could have softened her toward this modest dish. Between slow bites, she read the letter. She had learned to expect no cheer from her mother's missives. They seemed the rather to be penned as a means of morbid relief to the writer, and this one was no exception, unless on the side of gloominess:

"Jean [it closed after a long, pessimistic recital of real or imaginary abuses], could you send me a dollar? Just a dollar, that's all. It would help so much. Your father's so close, Jean, I can't bear to ask him. But you are independent; you don't need to ask any one. I only wish I'd had your spirit and opportunities when I was young. I might have been better off to-day. But my poor spirit was broken long ago. . . .

"Sometimes I think I just can't stand it any longer. Jean, I don't want to worry you, but I've had an awful temptation lately to end it all. . . ."

In 1917 a dollar was half the price of a fairly good pair of shoes and at any rate a fifth of Jean's weekly wage. She refolded the letter nervously, arose and dragged herself up to her room, an oppressive ache in the top of her head, which she noticed more now than before. She was hurt and irritated. It might have been selfish to want it, but there was little in her mother's missive to indicate a concern as to her welfare. Her way of taking that for granted made Jean feel reckless.

From the dresser drawer, she extracted absently a little pasteboard box to count her accumulated tips. They came to nearly three dollars. Again, perhaps it was wrong to wish she had bought the shoes yesterday, so she would have an excuse for not sending that ill-spared dollar, but she could not help remembering Trixie and like indulgences of her mother's. Mrs. Hasbrook had always shown a faculty for getting, in some way, most things she wanted very much; and now, with one less to support in the family, why was she so hard put to it? Did she need the dollar as much as Jean needed—? Here, however, the girl's conscience pricked, for was she not hoarding the surplus over the shoe fund for a luxury? Yes. Sometime before Mary's suggestion of this afternoon, Jean had secretly planned a trip to Coney with Myrtle Dixon. She wanted another two dollars for that, with which to rent a bathing-suit and cover other amusements, and anticipated wearing the new shoes first on that happy occasion. The season was too far advanced for time to start another fund. Yet, now, if she withheld the money, could she really enjoy the trip? A knock on the tin door made her jump. Myrtle entered. "Say, Jean," she proposed, sinking on the cot, "let's go for a sail."

"Where?" Jean asked.

"Ferry—Christopher Street. Didn't you ever do it? You could ride all night on a three-cent ticket—if you didn't get caught. Better take some money, though, in case they get wise, so's we can get back."

"You mean—not get off on the other side?" Jean grasped the idea; "but s'pose the guard, or some one, sees you?"

"Jolly him. 'Taint likely he will, though. Nights like this there's always a crowd, and then it's dark. Make believe you're gettin' off, then turn back and mix up with the ones gettin' on. Even if they do get wise, all they can do is make you pay another fare. It's a cinch. Me an' my girl friend in Jersey done it often. Come on. I'll die stickin' around here.''

For just a moment Jean demurred, not quite confident as to the ethics of this program; then her eyes caught the letter on the dresser, and she sprang up with a little harsh laugh. "All right, Dix, just as soon as I address something to mail." Automatically, she folded in a sheet of paper one of the precious dollar bills, slipped it, without writing, into an envelope and sealed it. "It's all she wants from me anyhow, I guess," came the bitter thought, as she scrawled in pencil her mother's address.

Myrtle's strategy worked to perfection. Under the murky shroud of a late August night, what was there about this pair of small, dark-clad, rather threadbare girls that the keenest guard might ferret them out from the hundreds of other passengers? Indeed, it is to be suspected that they were not the ferry's only clandestine excursionists.

After an hour or so on deck, they decided to invest another three cents each in return tickets for the pleasure of exploring Hoboken. Myrtle's temperament was gay and shallow; as for Jean, a peculiar abandon possessed her. She did not care to-night what happened. Powerful arc-lamps, electric signs, theater vestibules and the radiance from many late-open shops all blended mistily to render Washington Street a tempting lane of light, and, arm in arm, the girls tripped along it, chatting, giggling, a bit too conspicuously, halting every few yards to survey some window full of tawdry clothes or trinkets.

"Say," Myrtle broke out, "look at that gold bracelet for one-ninety-eight! Gee whiz! that's just what I want to wear with my dance dress!"

"Are you goin' to buy it!" queried Jean.

"I don't know if I ought, but I'd sure like to. Maybe I'll never get a chance like that again. Let's go in anyhow—and look around."

Jean was nothing loath to comply. Alertly enough, the suave proprietress drew the bracelet from the window for Myrtle, who, the instant she saw it on her slim arm, forgot whatever good resolutions she had made concerning economy. Her cheeks turned pink with excitement. "Jean," she panted, "ain't it perfectly grand?"

"It's sure a bargain, Miss," the proprietress inserted. "You couldn't get nodding like it noveres else for the money. It's the best value ve got—guaranteed for twenty years."

"I'll take it," Myrtle decided huskily; "I'll keep it on." Her fingers fumbled shakily with the latch of her worn handbag. "Jean, don't you want somethin' too?" Did she want something? What did she not want? But out of all the gewgaws her eyes lingered longest on a generous string of ruby-colored glass beads. She touched it reverently. "How much?"

"Seventy-five cents, Miss, reduced from one-and-a-quarter—another value you couldn't beat noveres. Vouldn't you like try 'em on?"

"Oh, Jean," Myrtle encouraged, "go ahead. That's just what you need with your best dress, that black serge one—a dash of color. Say, ain't that swell-lookin'?" as Jean, yielding, stepped back to be approved. "Look at yourself in the glass; don't you think so now?" Jean was not really thinking. She was having impressions and intense desires. Only about half of her seemed to be there, and that not the wonted sensible half which included her judgment. Anything worth more than the highest price of the Five-and-Ten took on really treasurable proportions, and the beads were well molded, truly good-looking. No one could deny their beautifying effect. Suffice it to say that they kept their new place around her neck, and, beside Myrtle, she went out with her little purse seventy-five cents lighter—not daring to think of the shoes.

FLEDGLING WINGS

"Gee," Myrtle informed ruefully, "that was almost all my lunch money, and I'll have to walk to work—but I wouldn't 'a' missed a chance like that for nothin'."

As they sauntered on, the reckless detached feeling waxed in Jean. She was superficially buoyant. She even offered to treat to sodas, over which they both flirted shamelessly with the fountain clerk. Then they indulged in an hour of "trying on things" at several different clothing-stores, coveting about all they touched, but pretending dissatisfaction as an excuse for not buying, and, despite many proffered concessions or invitations to "mek a leetle deposit," leaving with nothing but the ill will of tired shopkeepers.

"Gee, ain't it tough to be poor!" complained Myrtle, the light of her bracelet already dimmed by other unappeased longings.

"You bet," Jean agreed fervently. "I hate it—I *hate* it, Dixie! What's the use of just livin' if you can't ever have *anything* pretty? What's the use of it, anyhow—just workin' to keep alive, if you only keep alive to work —to keep alive to work—to keep—"

"Oh, gosh, Jean!"—Myrtle was less of a philosopher—"don't make it out no worse. Well, we on'y live once and *I'm* gonna have some fun yet—and if I can't pay for it, somebody else can, that's all! Say, for Pete's sake,

A CHILD OF DIVORCE

there goes ten o'clock! Hurry up, we'll be late for breakfast"—this with a snicker.

"Such a lot to miss," derided Jean, as they quickened their pace, for the Home doors were locked at eleven.

"Which half of the egg will you have, Jean?" mocked Myrtle, referring to a circumstance which was no joke, however. Only for Sunday breakfast were the girls served a whole egg apiece. Other mornings, eggs, when forthcoming, were fried "over," and then each cut in two.

As frequently happens when people are pressed for time, they just missed a ferry, and after ten the boats only ran every half-hour. "And it takes fifteen minutes to cross!" Jean lamented.

"Yes, and all of that to walk up Christopher, unless we get a car, and maybe there won't be none waitin'."

"You didn't tell Mrs. Toole anything, did you?"

"Nope; I thought we'd get back on time."

Impatiently resigned, they sat down in the waiting-room, realizing with relaxation how tired they were, and all but succumbing to the sleepy atmosphere.

Five minutes late, the next ferry churned and bumped into the slip with much clanking of chains. Ten minutes after the scheduled time, they landed again on the New York side. No trolley was visible on the horseshoe curve of tracks, or even in the distance. "We won't save any time by waiting," Jean said; "let's go on."

"All right," and Myrtle matched her stride.

But they lost the race against time, being still four blocks from home when the city clocks boomed out eleven. "If they'd only be late!" gasped Myrtle, hopefully.

"No such luck," mumbled Jean; "they never are."

Nor were they. Even the protective iron gratings over the big front doors had been locked; lights were out. Under Jean's pressure the door-bell emitted a clang which startled them both, and must surely have awakened the inmates. There was no other response, however. Jean rang again, longer. Still silence and darkness.

"Keep it up," Myrtle whispered nervously; *"they got to leave us in!"*

At last a light glimmered in the hall, hazily revealing the person of Mrs. Toole, bulkier than usual in a flapping kimono and the absence of corsage restrictions, her face a bulletin of ill temper. She opened the door a bare crack to whisper harshly through the bars, "Who's there?"

A CHILD OF DIVORCE

"Miss Laval and Miss Dixon. We—"

"Well, this's a pretty time o' night to be comin' in! I don't seem to remember you're notifyin' me you'd be out after hours."

"No," Myrtle began; "we was delayed. We're sorry. We—"

"Delayed, was you? Well, rules is rules, and you know 'em well enough. If you thought you was to be delayed, you had a right to leave word in the office. How much respect d'you think the rules 'ud get if we let the girls in any old time they want?"

"We're sorry. We'll try an' not do it again—"

"You'll be lucky if you get a chance to do it again! Rules is rules, and my orders is not to let *no* one in after eleven, unless they leave notice. The night's half gone now, and since you're so fond o' skylarkin' round, you can just spend the rest of it somewheres else. Maybe that'll teach you some respect for rules, and if you got any complaint to make you can see Mr. Rosenthal when he comes back. Nobody can say *I* didn't do *my* duty!" The lock clicked a period to this, and the girls were presented with a broad rear view of Mrs. Toole laboring back up the three vestibule steps and across the hall, till she snapped out the light. For an interval they stood stunned, then Myrtle exploded, "Well, can you beat that?"

FLEDGLING WINGS

"Where'll we go?" Jean worried.

"To the devil, for all *they* care, I guess!" Myrtle's voice vibrated sharply; "and *they're* supposed to be Christians—*some* Christians!"

"They aren't Christians," Jean defended, she would not have known why; "they're only hypocrites!"

"Well, they go to church, don't they? *She* does, anyhow. I never did have no use for church people. Well, my flop's paid for inside this dump, and I ain't gonna budge 'nother step. I'll stick right here till mornin', and' if I'm dead, the world can see whose fault it is!" She slumped down on the single damp stone step, leaning back against the bars. Jean still gazed between them and through the glass panel incredulously. Against the blackness of the interior, the fitful light from the corner caught the gilt "Respectable Girls," making the letters scintillate like so many mocking eyes. Slowly, she sank beside Myrtle, complaining, "Anybody'd think we weren't respectable."

"They can think whatever they please!" challenged Myrtle. "We're just as respectable as *they* are, and don't you forget it! You just wait!"

"But, Dix, we can't stay here all night. Hadn't we better go to the park, or somewheres? We could hide in the bushes."

"Go on if you want to," crossly; "*I'm* gonna stay here."

Jean sighed. They were both fagged out. They had no money for a hotel room, even if any hotel would have taken them in unescorted. Conversation dwindled to occasional monosyllables in lengthening lapses of silence.

Again the clock struck—twelve times. Drowsy, cramped, and, despite the hot night, a little chilled from the dampness, they did not notice the stealthy approach of a shadow, till a deep voice startled them, "What's the idea?" Both pairs of eyes flashed upward to a blue-clad, brass-buttoned form. To the girls, each crouched in her corner of the doorway, it looked gigantic. Consternation paralyzed them.

"Come," urged the officer, offhandedly prodding Myrtle with his night stick, "what d'ye think this is—a dormitory?"

"No, sir," Myrtle husked; "but it's as near as we can get to our rooms. We was ten minutes late gettin' home, and they wouldn't leave us in."

"D'ye live here, then?"

"Yes," both chorused, and Jean added, "we didn't know what to do."

"What kinda funny business is this?" But good humor savored the ejaculation, for the man's experienced eye and instinct told him these were not the sort of females he was accustomed to discovering on doorsteps during his small-hour beats. He sought the button with a thick thumb and pushed it strongly. Shrilly, once more the bell pealed out, but in vain, for there appeared no answering Mrs. Toole. Again and again he rang it, then knocked sharply with his stick. Once Jean had the feeling that some one was watching from a second-story window, but no face met her upward glance.

"Well, Miss," the officer turned at last to Myrtle, "sorry, but I guess you'll both have to come along with me."

"Where?" Myrtle choked.

"To the station, and tell your story to the judge. It's just around the corner. Ye can't camp here all night, y' know."

To resist was futile, so dumbly they accompanied him, holding tightly to each others' arms.

The technical charge, for there always has to be a technical charge, was "vagrancy." However, contrary to their conception of police judges, the official to whose mercies they were committed proved a decidedly human person. Perhaps he had a daughter of their own age; at any rate, he was more fatherly than judicial, albeit in a brusque, hurried way. He smiled slightly at the tears his sympathy called forth, as he told them: "You're nice little girls—too nice to be running around so late nights. Don't you know how dangerous that is? Don't cry. We aren't going to lock you up. We'll send you to Grace House, where you'll be safe for the night. Come back here to-morrow at ten o'clock. We'll send out a summons for Mrs. Toole."

The night matron took them to Grace House, a kind of detention place for girls of every degree of waywardness. There they were assigned to a little bare room, dimly lighted by gas. Though it was better than the cell which had loomed so fearfully in Jean's imagination, yes, and better than the doorstep, she felt badly stigmatized. Only their complete physical exhaustion brought them any sleep.

"Oh, gee!" muttered Myrtle, upon awaking, "some bed! I feel 'sif I'd been sleepin' on the soft side of a pine board!"

"What time is it?" wondered Jean. Her head ached.

"I heard the clock strike eight."

"Eight! We'll be late—" Then Jean remembered there would be no going to work this morning, for they must appear in court at ten.

But ten o'clock had long passed ere their case was called. Mrs. Toole was present, shaken out of her usual phlegmatism, but clinging stubbornly to her defense—that she had only enforced the discipline she was paid to keep. The ethical and moral question involved in her shutting two young girls out on a city street at midnight, and that from a house supposed to protect such girls and from lodgings honestly paid for, seemed not to disturb her in the least, or even occur to her. Rosenthal was on one of his frequent trips out of town, no one knew just where, so he could not be summoned. Neither is the law concerned very much with ethical and moral questions, strange paradox as this may seem. Another judge presided this morning, gruffer than the night judge, and, after all this fuss and suspense, he dismissed the case in a few minutes with a short, sharp reprimand to the girls, charging them to obey rules hereafter, if they wished the benefits of those interested in their welfare.

Mrs. Toole fairly swelled with relieved complacency. "I guess *that'll* teach you a lesson," she exulted on the way out, "and the others, too, that try and be so smart!"

"She'll prob'ly recommend herself to Rosie for a raise," surmised Myrtle, when they left her gloating presence for lunch and work.

This episode, of course, made Jean feel less at home than ever on Christopher Street, and no doubt the consciousness of strain reacted on her overwrought body, for she was weak and tired all the rest of that week.

Saturday came once more, as exacting at the store as ever, yet she always welcomed Saturday, for it meant a pay-envelope and a following day of rest. After the ten o'clock bell, in a long, tired, but eager, line, the girls filed by the cashier's stand, grasping as usual for their respective wages. Most of them would unseal and count the money before leaving, and this had been Jean's habit. Having drawn aside, she extracted from its paper sack the weekly five dollar bill. But to-night there was something pinned to it, a narrow, pale-blue paper strip, bearing typewritten words. Curious, she held it closer in the partial light, to read, "Your services are no longer required."

Something sprang to Jean's throat, leaving a hollowness at the pit of her stomach. Then she began to burn all over, every nerve a-quiver.

"C'mon, Jean! You'll get locked in!" But Mary's call fell unheeded. Jean looked toward the manager's cage in the rear of the store. Yes, he was still there, smoking. Dazedly she approached him, holding forth the blue slip.

"Wh—what does this mean?" she pleaded hoarsely; "why am I—*fired?*"

FLEDGLING WINGS

The manager frowned, drew long at his cigar and blew out a cloud of smoke with his answer: "Sorry, Miss Laval, but we have it on good authority that you were arrested the other night for vagrancy. Of course, I don't know the particulars, but we simply can't afford to keep any one in our employ whose name is on the police books."

"But—I—I—" Jean stammered gropingly.

"Sorry," repeated the manager with evident distaste, "but—that's final." Another burst of smoke through the wicket nearly choked her. She turned away slowly. Every one else had gone now but the janitor, who awaited her exit impatiently that he might lock the doors and leave himself.

Only instinct guided her home, for panic possessed her active consciousness. She still trembled. Oh, if Miss Baily were only here! But several days ago she had received a clue as to the location of her little nephew, and had gone to follow it. To-night she was far on her way South. In all New York, Jean could think of no other friend to whom she might turn. Underneath her panic, like sinister black waters rising to engulf her soul, gathered swiftly the deadening sense of absolute despair.

CHAPTER XI.

AN OPENING CHRYSALIS

"BUT, Uncle Paul, you hardly even know him, so how can you tell what he's really like? You're just prejudiced against him, and is—is—that Christian?"

"It's a good deal more than prejudice, Adele. I know him better than you think. I don't want you working under his influence, and I certainly will not permit him to call on you. That thing is absurd. Why, the man is as old as myself!"

"I like older people, uncle. Haven't I always lived with you and Kingsy? I don't think it's years that count—between people—half as much as—mutual interests."

Across the breakfast table Paul Manson threw his niece an anxious, searching look. Mrs. Kingston, formerly the girl's wet nurse, who to his satisfaction had all these years remained with them as chaperon and general housekeeper, was in the kitchen frying more wheat cakes.

AN OPENING CHRYSALIS

"Adele, what mutual interest can there be between you and Bascomb?"

Adele's large eyes dropped. In her fluffy, blue crepe kimono and lace morning-cap, with gold-bronze hair rippling freely from under it around her face and behind her shoulders, she looked very sweet and very, very young. An ascending blush intensified the wonted color in her cheeks. "Well, it's hard—to put it in words, uncle, but he—he's—not like the boys at school. He knows just how to treat—a lady. He can see that, even if I *am* young in years, my mind is developed, and—he treats me like a—companion. He even said he needed my friendship more than I knew—and the other day he asked if he could read one of his briefs out loud to me—for my opinion—"

Manson ceased eating, as deliberately under the tablecloth his big hand clenched on his knee. "Did you let him do it?"

"Not yet. That's what he's coming up for."

"Adele, I forbid it!" At that, her glance flashed up again. "Oh, Uncle Paul! You can't—when I've invited him!"

"But I can, and I do—*decidedly!* Bascomb is no fit companion for you, or any young girl. Let him seek women of his own age. All this talk of his needing you is non-

A CHILD OF DIVORCE

sense, and his wanting you to work for him—it's nothing but an excuse to come here and spite *me!* Let me tell you frankly, Adele, he is one of my worst enemies, a foe of all that I'm striving for in the way of decent living. There are lots of stenographers; why, you haven't even finished school yet! There's plenty of time for that sort of thing; but if you want practice, come down to the study with me. I wouldn't have you exposed, even in a business way, to the philosophy of a man like Bascomb. He has no genuine respect for the convictions and principles which form the very fabric of Christ's teaching and safeguard civilization. To him they are 'sentimental fictions,' and he thinks it smart to ridicule them. So he's set himself about a mission of freeing humanity from what he probably calls the 'bondage of stupid scruples'—if his motives savor even that much of altruism. More likely it's because he finds it a good source of revenue, and a chance to air his cynical wit!"

"I'm sure that isn't fair, Uncle Paul," Adele's voice quivered with hurt impatience; "he never said such things to me, and his influence hasn't made me feel that way at all. How do you *know?* What right have you to judge him?"

"He draws the largest clientele of would-be divorcees in the State, and does all he can

AN OPENING CHRYSALIS

to encourage divorce. He has a genius for proving the unstability of marriage and most of the other conventions—or trying to. That's the real reason why he maintains his New Jersey practice."

She began to pout. "I don't see what difference it makes where he practices."

"Only, dear, that the divorce laws of New Jersey are more lax than those of New York."

"But if married people will fall out and want divorces, is that *his* fault? They'd have to get *some* laywer, and that's only his business. He—he—has to earn his living. Is it so awful to be a lawyer?"

"Nonsense, child, that isn't the point. It's not his profession, but the way he uses—or *abuses*—it. The legal profession is one of the oldest and finest there is. It ought to be used to supplement and defend divine laws, not contradict—" Suddenly Adele flung her napkin aside to spring up, interrupting shrilly: "I won't listen to you, Uncle Paul! It isn't fair—what you say about him—I *know* it! He's a gentleman, I tell you! He never put such thoughts in my head as you're putting in it now! And he's been kind to me—when *you* went and left me! You don't care how lonesome I am—you even break your promises to take me places on account of your old sermons and funerals and weddings! Every time

A CHILD OF DIVORCE

I want you, there's some old speech or committee meeting. *They* come first! And now, just because I have a friend who *does* care—and can help me and *inspire* me—you want to drive him away—just because you're *prejudiced!* That's all! Do you think I want to sit in the house with old Kingsy *all* the time—or go around with those *cubs* in school who don't know any more than I do? They can't hold a candle to Mr. Bascomb, and he—*he's* got enough sense anyway to see that I'm a *woman*—when you keep on treating me like a baby, and—o-oh—hoo—hoo!" In a bad break of sobbing, she fled from the room.

After a paralyzed minute, Manson resumed the use of his knife and fork, but the process was plainly mechanical. His set face betrayed a blending of impatience, anxiety and pain.

"Why, where's 'Dele?" exclaimed Mrs. Kingston, entering behind a steaming stack of fresh flapjacks.

"She seems to be upset, Mrs. Kingston. She's gone upstairs. When she cools off, I'll go up to her. Sit down, please; there's enough on the table, and I want to talk with you."

"She's not sick, Mr. Paul?" Alarm swept over the housekeeper's kind old features.

"No, just temper, I'm afraid, Mrs. Kingston"—his look sought hers directly—"has Jerome Bascomb been coming here?" She

AN OPENING CHRYSALIS

started slightly and reflected. "Bascomb? The lawyer, you mean? That sort of elderly gentleman—compared to her, I mean? Yes, he's come two or three times as I can remember, but he never stayed long. He came twice last July before we went to Maine, and once again last week, when you were at that Stony Brook convention."

"Did he ever ask Adele to go out with him?"

"I don't know all what he asked her, Mr. Paul, but I remember he took her auto-riding once. That was all of two months ago."

"And that's the only time he took her out?"

"Yes. He might have asked her, but if he did I guess she didn't go. 'Dele 'most always tells me when she's goin' out, and I guess she would if it was with him. I was just wonderin' the other day if you knew about this one, Mr. Paul. He seems sort of old for her, but I guess she likes him. It's funny he isn't married already, a man his age and that good-lookin'—unless he's a widower—I don't know. They do say he's awfully smart, though, and I heard him tellin' her one time how he'd never lost a case yet."

"Maybe not. He has the devil on his side!"

She stared in surprise. "You don't like him, then?"

A CHILD OF DIVORCE

"Worse than that, Mrs. Kingston, and my reasons are much more than personal. He is not at all a suitable associate for our little girl, and I wish to heaven it hadn't gotten this far! I don't want you to spy on Adele, but please keep a prudent outlook hereafter, will you? And, don't, under any circumstances, admit that man to the house again when I'm not here. I know him, Mrs. Kingston, and—he's the wrong kind!"

"You don't say!" She was used to Manson's rather strong assertions on some occasions, but this intelligence caused her to bristle much after the fashion of an indignant mother tabby; *"the nerve of him!"*

"There's nothing weak about his nerve, but if he thinks I'm blind to his little scheme, he'd better wake up!"

"Scheme, Mr. Paul?"

"Yes, it's pretty plain. You know my ideals, Mrs. Kingston, and they're not welcome to certain people who like the easy road. But, as I announced last Sunday, I'm going to fight with all that's in me, and get every citizen I can influence through preaching or otherwise, to fight for a decent amendment to our Constitution—a Federal law regulating marriage and divorce, with a good deal higher standard set than most of the States have at present. Our differing laws on this important

AN OPENING CHRYSALIS

question are a scandal to the nation. The fact is, that unless some unusual situation comes up, a couple moving from one State to another don't know when they're properly married and when they're not. They may think they are, and the first thing they know, if property is involved, they find themselves branded as adulterers or bigamists with a lot of illegitimate children who have no rights. Several such cases have occurred lately and great injustice has resulted from it."

"Why, I didn't know that, Mr. Paul. I've always thought that a marriage was a marriage anywhere. I don't understand—in a Christian country like ours—I should think *that* would have been in the Constitution before this."

"It wasn't, because back in 1787, at the time the Constitution was adopted, divorce was so rare it was almost unknown, but it's growing over this country like a black cloud, and, believe me, it will bring the wreck of a storm! Think of it—our proud, Christian, civilized America leading all the countries of the world in divorce! I like America to lead, but not in such things as that. It's a case of liberty running to license. Our imperative need is for a uniform law in keeping with the best American traditions that will make definite what marital rights exist here, and I mean a Federal law by Congressional amendment; for even if every State but one agreed to adopt uniform State laws, that one would become a divorce Mecca—the rotten apple that pollutes the whole barrelful—and we can't afford it. The situation affects the whole nation, and so, grounds for divorce ought to be reduced to a minimum, dictated by the people of the whole nation. We have federal laws for less important things. Marriage, which is the foundation of our whole social order, we leave to the regulation of the widely divergent whims of individual States. And more than all, this question is one which falls within the province of the church. Marriage is a sacrament, not an economic arrangement, and the church itself has no greater stake in the future than the welfare of the home. For that reason, all the various church organizations should take an active interest in it, and I feel that there *is* in the church a growing conscience on this subject. The question is whether it will grow to worth-while dimensions. I mean to do all in one man's power to stimulate and cultivate it. But you can see the opposition that will come from people of Bascomb's type and following. For one thing, the present conditions afford them a profitable means of income, easy loopholes out of responsibility, chances to exploit a sacred relation for

AN OPENING CHRYSALIS

ignoble ends. Then they seem to find a certain pleasure in overturning the moral sanctions which inhere in religion, picking flaws in the church and its ideals. Mrs. Kingston, if I'm wrong, God forgive me, but I don't think I am. Bascomb resents my stand. He's afraid of its influence—thank heaven for that! I wish he had more reason to be!—and''—his voice hoarsened, but the words came grimly—''he's ingratiating himself with Adele—in order to—turn misery and humiliation to the 'prophet's' own door! Good God! When I think of it—'' He finished almost in a groan, his fist again doubled on the board till the skin drew white across its hairy joints, face rigid, eyes fixed in space as though upon some enemy visible only to himself. So fierce was the light in them that the old nurse shrank with fear.

"Mr. Paul," she husked, "you look—like murder!" He came to himself. His expression softened, and, in a sad tone, he replied: "No, Mrs. Kingston, let us hope there'll never be cause for that. Thank God, I've discovered things in time. Now I must go up to her."

Adele, the worst of her tantrum exhausted, was lying with her face forlornly buried in the pillow when her uncle's staunch arms drew her up to his breast. "'Dele—little 'Dele!" His tone vibrated with tenderness, and after

A CHILD OF DIVORCE

awhile, crushing her to him, he repeated it chokingly, "*'Dele—little 'Dele!*" Her head came barely to his armpit; she could hear the quickened beating of his heart, and felt intuitively that he was in the grip of some unusual emotion, the power of which vaguely frightened her. A shy upward glance at his face increased her alarm. They were near the window, and his eyes, uplifted, gazed through it and far away to the fleecy summer clouds, some yearning, infinite, fathomless, in their rich brown depths. Slowly tears gathered there, brimmed over and ran down, via the strong lines around his mouth, to splash upon her hair. She clung tighter, not knowing why, nor did she know that just then it was not herself he felt there, but another Adele whom he had loved—and lost. At last he sobbed, not out loud, but she could hear it in his bosom, and his eyes came down to her. He took her face between his hands and searched it earnestly, then, as solemnly as if it were some religious rite, he kissed her forehead. The simple act seemed to free his tongue: "*'Dele, little 'Dele—she gave her life for you!* Have I seemed indifferent? *Have* I left you alone too much? Have I been too busy to see the beautiful miracle unfolding under my eyes—her little girl become a woman? Forgive me, little 'Dele. I'm afraid I have been selfish, but I understand now.

AN OPENING CHRYSALIS

I would have kept you always—mine—my little girl. But oh, 'Dele, now that you are a woman, know this: I'm a lonely, lonely man! For some reason which I can't understand, God saw fit to deny me the love which makes a man's life complete. I've filled my life with work, 'Dele, work for the Master—feverish work at times. I've tried to drown that cry in my heart, to close the place forever which only one woman could fill. That was your mother, little 'Dele, and it might still have been—if she had not died for you. And I've almost succeeded, only sometimes—sometimes—in the quiet of night, in the solitudes of nature—oh, 'Dele—*I want her so!*"

In the young girl this unusual confession set her heart to swelling and every nerve a-tingle. "Dear Uncle Paul," she repented, "and I've been so mean to you! I wouldn't if I'd known! And, oh, uncle—how you must hate me—to have taken her from you!"

"No, no, my darling! You mustn't think such things! I only told you that you might realize, 'Dele, how great was the price of your life, and—because some day I want you to mean to a good and worthy man what your mother meant to me—I want you to know, 'Dele, how sacred and beautiful—yes, and sacrificial—a thing is love. Don't cheapen it, 'Dele, or ever let any one cheapen it for you."

A CHILD OF DIVORCE

"No, uncle," she murmured, "I—I don't want to, and—can't you understand now—that's just why I like—him? There's nothing rough about him—like the boys. He's so refined, and—" But Manson's look cut off further eulogy. The warm feeling in his face had congealed again to firmness.

"Adele, will you not trust me as a man who knows men? I wasn't referring so much to the outward manner. An unpolished, shy young fellow may bear in his heart a love as true as that of the most sophisticated. There are surface refinements in courtship, though, which you have a right to expect, but I'm sorry to say there are also such things as wolves in sheep's clothing. You must learn to distinguish between the real and the false, and you have not lived long enough yet to do it alone, so you must let me help you, 'Dele. I have definitely forbidden Bascomb the house, and, of course, my child, you will respect my wishes. I would like you to cultivate more friends of your own age—several of them— and to promise me you'll not think seriously of marrying anybody till you are twenty-one, will you? Now, now, 'Dele"—as he read the disappointment in her countenance—"some day you'll see how it was all for your own good."

AN OPENING CHRYSALIS

"Nearly four years!" she whimpered tragically. "You want me to be an *old maid?*"

For all his seriousness, he could not repress a smile. "No, dear, of course not, though I'd rather see you that than wasted on an unworthy man."

"But, uncle—I don't believe *he's*—unworthy. Something tells me so. Professor Barton said once there's nothing truer in this world than a woman's instinct—he said it was sure, like chemical attraction—and he said it was often right where the *reasoning* of men was wrong, so, perhaps, even if I'm not so old, I'm right because—because—oh! Don't you think you ought to know him better before you—judge him?"

"I couldn't know him much better than I do, Adele. As for your instinct, I'm afraid, dear, it's more likely romanticism. Adele, my child, I'm sorry, *sorry*, that this has grown to mean so much to you. I wish I'd known of it before. But, Adele, the pain my advice may be giving you now is nothing to what you and all of us will suffer if you do not heed it. In your mother's name, little girl, promise me no more than this: that you will respect my wishes, and *wait*. Now, dear, it's getting late; time for me to be at the study."

She kissed him good-by, but she was really far from reconciled. In her aroused soul

A CHILD OF DIVORCE

there seemed to be fermenting all sorts of conflicting emotions. In fact, it had never experienced such cross-currents of feeling. There was still the glow of a new sense of sympathy with her uncle because of his revelation, but fervent faith in and defense of Bascomb, stirred up with a bitter resentment of Manson's attitude toward the lawyer. It seemed to her that since she so well understood her uncle's heart-hunger, he might at least have appreciated her—love. Love! If only she had known her attachment by its right name—infatuation. For that is what it was, the dangerous infatuation of a girl under eighteen for a man in the forties. Youth can enter with a certain sentimental interest into the bygone disappointments of its elders, but the present is ever with it, and the thing of major importance is its own big affection.

Irritably, Adele threw off her cap and kimono, wound up her hair and donned a smart little street frock. As she was descending the stairs the telephone rang on the landing. Nothing unusual about that, yet the sharp sound caught at her heart. She answered it, and Bascomb's voice responded, cautiously at first. An instant's excitement, then she was happily calm. There were suave, otherwise meaningless, preliminaries. "Big

AN OPENING CHRYSALIS

case coming off to-day," he presently informed her; "Straub versus Straub. No doubt you've read of it in all the city papers."

"Yes—that is, I've seen the headlines. Uncle won't let me—"

"My dear young lady, do you suppose 'uncle' will permit you to grow up? Or will he endeavor to control that natural process as he is trying to control the progress of the world?" The fact that this aroused no resentment in Adele proved the present extent of Bascomb's influence over her. Indeed, in her prevailing mood, she intuitively caught and shared some of his hinted commiseration for herself.

"I—I—don't know," she mumbled blindly into the telephone receiver.

"Well, you must shake your wings, and let them all know it's time to break the chrysalis. Parents—and uncles—have a way of overlooking that event, Miss Manson, which has to come in every life. I suppose, just because they're so used to seeing a chrysalis, they don't expect anything else, and then they're so busy. So you must give uncle a pleasant surprise pretty soon. A butterfly's better than a grub. He'll like it himself when he sees it. Ha! ha! not to imply that you ever were like a grub, but you know what I mean, don't you? I'm giving you advice that's worth something—know it? What are you doing to amuse yourself? Anybody else there?"

"Yes—Kingsy," in a warning stage whisper.

"Oh, another well-intentioned suppresser of youth. Poor little pal, you're up against it, aren't you? Too bad they don't understand you better, but that sometimes happens in a person's own family. Uncle still trying to keep an honest man from earning a living?" The well-assumed jocularity of his tone purged these words of offense.

"Oh, I'm afraid uncle don't—just understand. I tried to make him—but—"

"Did you? Bless your heart! Well, we all have a right to our opinions, but it's a big world, so I don't see why they need cross. Home to-morrow night?"

"Oh—you mustn't come!" Her impulsive admonition was prompted as much by fear for Bascomb as for herself. "Uncle—he found out—I—he—I guess we'll have to—"

"Oh, I see! Well, don't worry, little girl; we'll fix things up. All the more fun, eh? Inquire sometime at the general delivery."

"Y—yes," breathlessly. "Oh, here comes Kingsy. I—I'll have to say good-by—I hope you win the case!"

"Thank you, Miss Manson. I've one little champion in that quarter, anyway, haven't

AN OPENING CHRYSALIS

I? And, anyhow, I guess you know, *I always win my case!*"

Young as Adele was, she was woman enough to thrill with a pleasant sense of daring at the significance of those words. Mrs. Kingston had come out to the hall, and was running the carpet-sweeper close to the foot of the stairs. Adele felt glad of its concealing clatter. She skipped lightly down the remaining steps, and stopped before the mirror to put on her hat.

"Goin' out?" the old nurse asked.

"Yes, for a walk and to the post-office to mail some letters. Want anything?"

Meanwhile Manson had reached the church, and was fitting the key to the lock when the door opened from within. "Oh, good morning there, Borland! Thank you!" he greeted the sexton.

"Mornin', sir; you're welcome. There's a young lady waitin' to see you, sir—that li'l Miss Frances—"

"Frances?" Manson's forehead puckered. He passed into the study. "Why, it's Jean," he exclaimed in warm surprise, proffering a cordial hand, "after all this long time! I'm glad to see you. Where have you been?"

Jean's lips parted, quivered, but gave forth no response. She looked both paler and thinner than on the last day she had come to him,

A CHILD OF DIVORCE

and in the big hazel eyes, lifted for a moment to his face, lurked a hunted, desperate expression. It made him retain the small hand to keep it from sudden trembling. But his warmth melted the last barrier of her reserve. She began to cry. She was dizzy, and no wonder, not having eaten for three days. This was one of the things she finally admitted during a disjointed recital of the last three months' events. Weakly, but frankly, she told him all, even to the episode in the police station. "I remembered what you said," she ended, "but I didn't want to come and bother you—till I just had to—"

"You did just right to come, Jean, just right. I often wondered why you hadn't been in before. I enjoyed your two letters so much. They were sweet, brave letters, Jean, and I knew a girl with that spirit would make good. We've struck a boulder in the road, but it's only temporary. We'll climb over it. You know, it's been my experience that we hardly ever lose anything unless something better is waiting for us. Now, the first thing to do is to get your strength back. I'm going to call up Mrs. Dennison. She's one of our finest women—loves girls. I know she'll be glad to have you visit her for a couple of days."

"If I could help—" Jean conditioned faintly.

AN OPENING CHRYSALIS

He nodded, smiling, "Perhaps you can, perhaps you can," and reached for the telephone.

Not long after that, from the open windows of the study, they saw a runabout stop before the church and lightly discharge a slim youth. Manson took Jean's arm and led her out. Exertion sent sharp pains jabbing through her stomach; her head felt like an aching, empty shell, and her ears rang so that her introduction to Freddie Dennison was hardly more than a confusing mumble. Dully she heard him explain something about his mother being too busy to come. Then the air rushed coolingly against her face, and, when her power of consecutive observation returned, she was lying on a couch in some one's sunny living-room, being slowly fed from a bowl of hot broth by a long, thin, knotty hand. From the hand her eyes wandered up a bony forearm till they reached a correspondingly long, lean face. But what a kindly face! Its lines did not mar it; the rather they seemed the registration marks of tender, deep emotions and responsibilities nobly met. It smiled, and Jean smiled faintly back—smiled before she could speak.

"Good?" asked Mrs. Dennison.

Jean nodded, then managed a little hoarsely: "Yes, thank you."

"Suppose you've been eating in restaurants, you poor child! That stuff's cooked till there's absolutely no nourishment in it for one."

"We—were supposed to get the best—at the Home—only I—"

"Well, never mind, dear. Plenty of time to talk later. Now, you've finished the bowl. That's good work. I think you'd better take a nap, and before long you'll be ready for a real meal."

Jean was nothing loath to comply, for relaxation had brought on drowsiness. With her stomach warmed by soup and her heart by kindness, she felt unusually comfortable. She did not want to stir. She turned her head away slightly, and once more closed her eyes. Mrs. Dennison arose, glided away, and quickly returned to spread a cover over her. At this tender action, from under Jean's eyelids crept a few more silent, grateful tears.

CHAPTER XII.

STRIPES

FOR a whole month now, there had raged over all America a suddenly rekindled fire of patriotism. It burned in the breast and glowed through the eyes of every loyal citizen. On her last day in New York, Jean, hungry, friendless, exhausted in her vain search for work, and stalked by the consciousness of her "police record," which in her mind had grown out of all proportion to its importance, had taken a brief refuge in the shadowy, mystic, soothing atmosphere of the old Fifth Avenue Presbyterian Church. From a half-swoon on one of its padded pews, she was aroused by a ring of martial music and the rhythmic, thunderous tramping of many thousand feet. With a strangely inflated heart, she crept to the vestibule doors to look out upon the long, grim, earth-colored line of infantry moving, like some swift, resolute dragon, down the avenue, cheered on its way by home-staying crowds which she hardly saw. A sense of reckless excitement quivered in the air. Shouted ap-

A CHILD OF DIVORCE

plause, shot with threats against some distant enemy, enhanced the swelling challenge of the band. Now and then, a woman would dart from the curb to grasp and kiss abandonly some portion of the dragon's body, cling to it for a moment in hysterical devotion, drop back and be left behind. But the huge reptile, with bayonet-bristling vertebrae, smileless, unwavering, rumbled on—and on.

Later she heard the weird shrieks of many whistles, the clamorous tongues of the city bells—like a long-repressed cry of farewell anguish bursting at last from the nation's lips—as the big, laden army transports steamed away from the East River piers. Even then, however, she could not digest the meaning of all this. *War?* In 1917? It could not be real! Wars belonged to history—*we were civilized!* Jean's bewilderment was only part of an entire country's which, despite all official proclamations, and with troops being torn daily from under its nose, could not yet believe itself at war.

But, by the end of a month, America's mind was thoroughly adjusted to the spirit of combat. Many there must be, as in all wars, to "tarry by the stuff," to provide the food for soldiers and guns, to build the craft, produce the clothing, bandages, medicines—and sad, but also inevitable, a few to reap personal harvests of gold from numerous other men's

STRIPES

sacrifices. Then began the wheatless, meatless, heatless, sweetless days, the days of thrift stamps and Liberty bonds, of unselfish heroism and flagrant profiteering, with all the degrees of emotional excitement a people under such conditions can experience in between. Things that had always mattered greatly, suddenly shed their importance; nothing seemed permanent, and all were suffused with a sense of being poised for some stupendous crisis. All felt that the crisis must come soon, yet no one thought beyond it—unless, perhaps, the profiteers.

It was this contagious patriotism, alloyed with a human desire for gain, which sucked young women from offices, schoolrooms, stores and kitchens into the expansive, slap-stick munition plants erupting over the State. Never in their short professional careers had such wages been offered to girls. At least, Jean heard, there were schoolteachers. She had never worked in a factory, and vaguely supposed that to do so one had to be stalwart, not to say tough. Her strength now fairly recovered, she talked things over with Mrs. Dennison, considering: "You see, if I could make that much money, just for awhile, I could save up for my business course and be doing my bit besides. That's one place they'll take you without experience."

"Yes, I know," her new friend conceded; "I guess that's all right, if you can stand it ten hours a day."

"Just for awhile," Jean repeated. "It's Friday. I could start in Monday. They're still advertising. I'll go over now and apply; then, if they take me, I'll stop at Harland's on the way back. Maybe I can get my old room again, and I could move over to-morrow."

"No hurry about that, child, only I suppose you want to get settled. Well, good luck, dearie, you're a brave girl, and better days will come." Mrs. Dennison emphasized her prophecy with a motherly squeeze, as they arose and moved toward the hall, Jean to take down her hat.

About half an hour's walk away, the Blumfelt Arms and Fuse Company spread its low main building and numerous detached sheds over several acres within the concealing walls of a very high board fence. At each entrance and man-door was stationed a uniformed guard, and a sort of lean-to shack had been hastily constructed for an "employment office," divided by a partition into two sections, labeled respectively "Male" and "Female." In the women's compartment some long board benches were already occupied by various types of potential "hands," each awaiting her moment to approach a sallow man behind a desk,

STRIPES

whose alert manner of dispatching them, black wall-eyes and receding chin somehow reminded Jean of a Central Park squirrel. Even his hair was consistently bushy, standing up as though he were in a perpetual state of alarm.

"Well," he yapped out when Jean's turn came, more indifferent than unpleasant, "what's *your* excuse for livin'?" By this time friction with the world had generated over Jean's sensitiveness a sort of metaphorical shell which enabled her to resist with less wincing such receptions from prospective employers. She actually managed a smile and responded cleverly: "No excuse—but I want a reason." He darted her a closer look, then shook his head: "Sorry, not a clerical place left."

"Then I'd like to work in the factory." His swift appraisal registered doubt. " 'Fraid you ain't strong enough. We need hands on the turret machines—heavy work. Maybe, t h o u g h—yes—assembly-room—piecework—name?" He was already manipulating his fountain pen, and, without further inquiry as to any preference of hers, proceeded with the details of "taking on." Very shortly she had signed something, she was not quite clear as to what, been passed to another department where she swore an oath of allegiance to the United States of America, and given a conspicuous, square, tin-framed badge, against whose blue

A CHILD OF DIVORCE

celluloid background shone the black figures 9746. Several times on the way to Harland's, she took this insignia from her jumper pocket to study it curiously, though it bore on its surface nothing but what could be seen at the first glance. To her, however, it was the assurance of a job. Wages, she had been told, would depend upon her own dexterity. Some girls in the assembly-room made forty a week!

Mrs. Harland greeted her with pleasant recognition. All her rooms, including Jean's old one, were full, but she referred the girl to one Mrs. Nicolson, down Park Road near the Newark line. Jean was happily surprised to find this almost opposite Manson's church. Mrs. Nicolson, an angular, white-haired, high-cheek-boned woman, whose finely wrinkled face betrayed an age for which she was marvelously agile, scanned her with unveiled suspicion, softening a little, though, when she mentioned Mrs. Harland. "A room? For yourself and husband?" she queried. Jean shook her head, "Just myself."

"You ain't married, then? Sure enough? Nobody can tell now'days—with all the girls gettin' married to soldiers and what not, so they can get exempt from the draft and all like that! Slackers! D'you keep comp'ny?" Her tone condemned this also to the category of misdemeanors.

STRIPES

"No; I'm strange here."

" 'Cause I can't have no one takin' up the parlor every night from the other boarders, and spoonin' on my front steps—*that's* somethin' I *don't* allow! Fact is, I don't generally take in girls. They're too much trouble that way, but since you're out all day and don't have no men friends—I've got a small room on the third floor. Come in; you can see it." She widened the crack at which she had opened the door and admitted Jean to the rather bare hall of what had once been a spacious private home, but was now degenerated into one of the numerous boardinghouses of the neighborhood, accommodating the influx of business and factory people inevitable as rapidly expanding Newark overflowed upon East Elair. Only four blocks away stood the thriving magneto works, of which Manson had spoken on Jean's first visit.

"Furnished Rooms" might be termed the convenient and profitable receptacles of all the junk a landlady has no personal use for, eked out by a few begrudged necessities scraped up from second-hand stores. If they had any other object besides that vulgarly flaunting one of revenue, it might be to demonstrate just how far one can carry artistic incongruity.

Much too large a proportion of Mrs. Nicolson's available third-floor room was monopolized by a dresser of obvious antiquity, a massive thing with a double-decker, cracked marble top, many knobs and curlicues and much dust-clogged scrollwork. It boasted a beveled mirror, but bad scars in the quicksilver, as well as warps in the last few coats of varnish, further testified to its longevity. The owner concentrated upon it: "Look at that dresser. You don't often see one like that *these* days."

"No," Jean murmured, wondering why any one should want to, for it did not harmonize with the ten-by-twelve area, the kitchen table, camp cot and dining-room chair. There was also a small "catch-all" amateurishly mended and smeared with cheap stain. Here the landlady's attempts at economy were more commendable than her skill, as some spots had gotten left, while in others the stain had run over to double thickness and dried that way. Two pieces of threadbare carpet, cut down into rugs, were spread in such outlandish places that they were plainly meant to cover holes in the matting. The wallpaper, no longer of nameable shade or traceable design, was blistered in some parts, scraped and sagging in others, while its smoke stains gave evidence of former "light-housekeeping" endeavors.

"Is this all you have?" Jean asked tentatively. Mrs. Nicolson nodded, "It's all I have now. Ain't it big enough for one girl?"

STRIPES

"Oh, it's big enough." To give it another thorough survey, Jean stepped back and leaned against the table, as it happened over the shortest leg, so that it wobbled. In her mind, growing daily more adaptable to conditions as she found them, yet clinging to its innate love of beauty, she saw the room as she might make it were she to stay here—and Mrs. Nicolson to co-operate. For it did have possibilities, being of southwestern exposure, with a wide window catching full drafts of afternoon sunlight and framing a pleasant partial view of Park Road. She could even glimpse that half of the church in which the study was located, and close by rustled the branches of a tree that reminded her of her robin friends at the Twoways Inn. With new paper, cretonne curtains and—"How much do you ask?" she queried.

"Well, two dollars, if you want to get your own meals. But if you board here, I'll make it one-fifty; that's six-fifty a week for board and room. Several people have been lookin' at it, so I'd like for you to decide."

Jean decided at once and paid Mrs. Nicolson six dollars and a half out of the ten-dollar bill which Paul Manson had advanced her from the benevolent fund.

Thus it was that she became numbered among the Mollies, Minnies and Sadies of a vast munition plant, learned the trick of punching a time-clock and the divine rights of foremen. Hours were from seven to six, longer if need be, this being wartime. She did not meet any schoolteachers there, nor realize forty dollars a week. Indeed, the highest wage she ever achieved was $11.72. So the business-school budget did not grow very fast in proportion to the effort expended. In the assembly-rooms, certain small brass shells were analined, filled with powder, the caps screwed on, and then riveted in place by machine, thousands of racks of the product being passed from one table to another in these various stages of evolution. In the dearth of better men, a young ex-janitor foreman, with flat feet exempting him from the draft, and a flat head turned by his sudden elevation, went to brutish limits of linguistic abuse in keeping the female hands at high pressure—the more work his department turned out resulting in greater credit for himself.

"Shake it up there, kid!" he had growled to Jean the first day. "No—*cut that!* Screw it *this* way. Say, you ain't much good around the place nohow. What the heck *can* you do?"

"I think I could analine faster," Jean advanced hoarsely, her throat almost too hot for speech.

"All right, then, gwan down there to the analine bench, and shake it up, I say!" Jean went to where he pointed, filled an agate dish with the stenching, crimson liquid, found a brush, and began carefully to paint the insides of a new trayful of shell plugs, as she had observed the others doing. He followed her to watch critically for several seconds. "Say, no fancy business," he admonished; "you ain't paintin' roses, kid. Them's bullets fer the Huns. Shake it up!" Jean's hands trembled, but she found the task easier after he had gone, notwithstanding her awareness of the stares of many coworkers.

"Douse the water-works, kid," advised one of the girls just opposite, who had seen a hurt tear drop from Jean's bowed face. "It won't get you nowhere's with that geezer."

"She should worry like any onion and weep," came blithely from another. Unresponsive, because she could not trust her voice, Jean went on with her work, not realizing that they might resent her silence, and gradually gaining enough speed to be permanently assigned to analining. She was glad of this, as some of the powder contained poison and she had already heard of certain girls who in handling it had later sacrificed their beauty, if not their lives, on freedom's altar. Perhaps it was vain, yet Jean really would rather have died than to have been so horribly scarred. Even as it was, the brass

A CHILD OF DIVORCE

turned her fingers a greenish black till she dared not touch her face with them, and the monotony, combined with the mingled fumes of analine and gunpowder, the incessant roar of machinery and explosions of tested arms, sufficiently racked her nerves. Then the talk—no pressure of haste or authority could force verbal silence. To soften it all at first Jean tried stuffing cotton in her ears, but this shut out the air and made them sore; also it brought upon her much undisguised ridicule, for, rushed though they might be, these were the sort of females who always find time to notice the petty doings of their mates and feel her to be without the pale who is not similarly concerned. The fact that she owned up to having no man "over there" removed her another point from the ground of common interest. Most of the women bragged of anywhere from two to ten.

"Jer fella give ye his pitcher in uniform?" asked Sarah Polasky of Angelina Malatesta, who sat in sweaty proximity to Jean. Being farthest from the foreman's desk made the analining table one of the liveliest conversationally.

"Betcha. Got it hangin' right over me bed."

"Good way to keep the mice away," smirked one Hulda Steinhauser, who had just finished relating how her name had nearly barred her from employment. Instead of appreciating this humor, Angelina flared: "Oh, yeah! Say, how d'ye *get* that way? He's good-lookin' as any of yer squarehead Fritzies! Say, I'm glad I ain't got no *Huns* for relations!" Hulda discreetly subsided.

It was queer what a mixture of nationalities you could find there, how many blood representatives of both enemy and allies. A more intelligent general concern as to international politics might have given rise to impetuous argumentation, but, for the most part, these women, American subjects, had so vague a conception of what it was all about that their occasional tiffs were limited to such personal differences. Besides, there were topics more mutually absorbing, such topics as resulted in discussions far from elevating. War, itself the most primitive method of settling disputes, always unleashes other primal passions. Then the elemental impulses, however long trained in channels of conventionality, suddenly burst their dikes and overflow. Self-preservation and reproduction are humanity's two strongest instincts; and while the men at the front fought for the former, doubtless it was inevitable that the women, creators of life, urged by some natural law of compensation, felt, if not wholly understood, should have their thoughts more than normally colored by the second subject. Jean, like most modern girls, had somehow learned without being taught the biological process of birth, yet to her this knowledge never robbed it of a sweet and holy mystery. She felt no call to sit in judgment on her sisters of the plant, but, because it is the best in life which by coarse minds can ever be travestied to the worst, there were many times a day when her cheeks tingled with shame for those types of her sex which surrounded her. A number of girls in that very room were soon to be mothers by men now in camps, or supposed to be. Some wore wedding-rings, some did not, though this in no way appeared to affect the social status of either group at that erratic time. That some very questionable deportment went on within the walls of the plant itself, especially during the night shifts, became generally rumored throughout the neighboring towns. The authorities, however, refused to interfere "with the personal affairs of employees so long as they delivered the goods." This was war! No time for reforms, or even an insistence on peacetime standards. We could not afford to run the risk of irritating sorely needed labor. But it is to be feared that the vast profits of this spasmodic commerce in munitions blinded those at the head of it to one of patriotism's chief essentials, altruism. Any day might bring an armistice, an ebb in the golden tide, so they were loath to invest money in improvements to be shortly scrapped and wasted, improvements which at least would have offset open invitations to license. Only after a stiff moral battle did the Young Women's Christian Association succeed in so pressing home its threats of public exposure that the company was forced to co-operate in the erection of a flimsy cafeteria where girls so inclined might eat their lunches out of earshot of ribald talk and profanity, away from the scent of rank tobacco with its accompanying expectorations, and the dangers of flirtation. Up to that time the Blumfelt Arms and Fuse Company had provided for its workers barely the accommodations of ordinary decency, leaving both men and women to live for ten and more hours daily, and as many nightly, thrown together on a plane little above that of the higher animals —all in the name of a war which was to "make the world safe for democracy!" True, they were busy, yet nature will out, and how often Jean witnessed, with recoiling heart, girls promiscuously fling themselves into the arms of the olive-drab guards for night and morning kisses! How often she was nauseated by the sight of groups of young, perhaps pretty, faces leaning, with wide, eager eyes and tensely grinning lips, toward some older female disseminator of smutty information, drinking it in as though it were the elixir of life! And those faces—those future-mother faces which should have looked like the Madonna's— obviously as curious as any to share in this morbid mental diet.

Of course, there were women in the assembly-room who took no initiative in this sort of thing, and a few who never had aught to contribute; decent, if ignorant, daughters or wives doing their "bit" by the nation and an absent man's part by their families, yet they sanctioned it by compromising smiles, plainly fearing to be thought priggish if they openly disapproved. This type, observing Jean's solemn, automatically shocked expressions, told her she took things too seriously; she "would only make the other girls mad, and that wouldn't do no good." If she was so particular, why did she work here? "You better look out," warned a Mrs. Ricks, "some night they'll lay for ye."

"Why?" Jean asked, amazed.

"Well, that's the way they do with stuck-ups. Maybe you ain't one, but when you look so mad at what they say, they think you are."

The others apparently did resent her lack of participation in this favorite pastime as a kind of silent criticism, and in their way of

STRIPES

retaliating took particular pains to exchange the shadiest remarks they could think of in her presence, suspected her audibly of being a "spy," and even went so far as to turn against her, like a boomerang, the maxim "Evil to him who evil thinks." Yet, may it not have been the struggling divinity said to dwell in every human soul which, as much as Jean's manner, chagrined them by some dim self-accusation of her justification?

Those were hard days for Jean—hard on her body, hard on her soul—though later she was to realize the value of their discipline. Just as she thought she could bear things no longer, Sunday would come. She would rest till almost churchtime, when Manson's messages would inoculate her with fresh courage, and afterwards mingle with the new friends she was making, occasionally being invited out to dinner. Sunday indeed became to Jean's spirit as a vernal oasis to a desert-parched Arab. Then, for a little while, her real self would come forth, shaking off its sordid daily fetters, to walk in green pastures of congenial fellowship, to breathe the air of inspiration, and drink deeply of the water of life. She did not know she was religious, only she felt more and more deeply the intuitive urge to worship something, that lifelong yearning for a definite and worthy object of devotion. She thought of herself as working for bread, the while she was gaining far, far more. The battle of life is the crucible of character. None can pass through it and emerge the same. We are seared by its blaze or we are purified, according to the fiber of our souls. For some of us the fire burns slowly, evenly tempered through many years; for others it leaps in sudden scorching flames, accomplishing in shorter time its formulative end. No words are truer than those which say growth should be measured by epochs, not by years. From a sensitive, somewhat plastic victim of parental selfishness Jean was developing into a woman who in lonely hours began to think much on the problems of life, to weigh evidence, form independent opinions and make decisions, gropingly, yes, erringly, but ever more ably; a woman also, alas! with that tragic shadow over her of one who has missed the laughter-lightened heritage of *youth*.

On a memorable Lord's Day morning she had responded to the wooing tones of "Just as I am, without one plea," and the searching hunger in Manson's brown eyes for converts as he stood expectantly at the foot of the aisle during the invitation which invariably followed his sermons, and joined the church. Never would she forget the glowing welcome in his face, the strong closing of his

STRIPES

fingers over hers as she trembled with the feeling of that moment, for to Jean this step meant much more than a formality. It was what it might well oftener be to those acknowledging their faith, the manifestation of an inner revelation dawning slowly, but with transfiguring power. She had been a little frightened, too, till her fluttering hand came to rest in the pastor's like a stray bird finding its nest. Even in recollection that saving touch would warm her. The finest of feminine natures craves some personification of love, even the love of God. Jean had indeed found God, yet she little realized how inextricably her new consciousness of Him was interwoven with that of Paul Manson. This man answered some need in her soul never met before, he challenged her deepest womanhood, he stimulated by his very influence her inborn desire for the finer things of life. He was not an artist, yet it was strange how every beautiful picture she had a chance to see in some way suggested him. He was not a musician, yet in music, especially sacred music, though it might only be that of a phonograph record, she felt him mystically near. He was not an author, yet for her his spirit hallowed all libraries. In this esteem was doubtless a large percentage of the filial. What of encouragement and guidance her parents had not given her Manson

A CHILD OF DIVORCE

supplied, as much by the life he lived as by preaching or advice, commanding in return a daughterly respect. She trusted him utterly and still in his presence would frequently feel a sense of awe akin to that which stole over her in the nave of a cathedral. Inspiration involves such sensitiveness to atmosphere, such natural recoiling from those devoid of æsthetic appreciation and instinctive drawing to those possessing it. Then, all unconsciously, out of our imaginings we take certain attributes with which to further embellish the one who inspires us, till he becomes in a great measure the responsive mirror of our own best self. But why attempt to analyze this so long as it brings us naught but good? The noblest human relations can not be thus dissected and explained.

The country blossomed with service flags and patriotic posters. Wives, till lately more familiar with washboards, found themselves sitting on relief boards and developing unexpected executive talents. The spacious annex of First Church afforded a headquarters for one of East Elair's largest Red Cross units, drawing together in a common cause members of many neighboring denominations. There, day and night, against a background of long, blue-oilcloth-covered tables, 'midst foamy clouds of surgical gauze, the white-gowned, white-veiled women worked like true angels of mercy, living symbols of the unity born of service. Whenever her ten-hour stretch at the plant left her strength enough, Jean was among them, and there she saw a good deal of Adele Manson, over whom had come a noticeable change. With a seriousness worthy of the pastor's niece, the latter had risen to her part of the national obligation, perhaps more than her part, for she worked constantly, almost feverishly, as if America's victory depended upon her efforts. It made her seem more mature. Forgotten now, apparently, was the grievance anent her uncle's disapproval of Bascomb and his insistence upon her association with the despised "cubs." Indeed, the induction of several such "cubs" had caused them, as if by magic, to assume adult proportions in her mind, and, when her slim fingers were not rolling bandages and flattening pads, they were usually instrumental in the rapid growth of dirt-colored socks or sweaters. Adele, throughout the period of the war, must have made enough sweaters for a regiment.

Manson shared with his fellow-ministers the spiritual strain of that time. His sermons took their hue from it, were powerful as usual and fuller than ever of sympathy. He preached much from Isaiah, reminding his people of the promised Sun of righteousness with healing in His wings, of the swords to be beaten into plowshares, and the deserts which would blossom as the rose. In the prophesied sacrifice of Calvary, he found a parallel for their sufferings and a challenge to their heroism. He loved especially the fifty-third chapter, and on the morning of Thanksgiving Day quoted with stirring fervor: "He was wounded for our transgressions; he was bruised for our iniquities; the chastisement of our peace was upon him; and with his stripes we are healed." "My friends," his voice rang out at the climax, "make no mistake by interpreting this war as a failure of Christianity. Our God is a sacrificial God! Brethren, we are *healed with stripes!*"

Healed with stripes! Like stripes themselves, those words sank into the heart of Jean Laval—sank and throbbed, pained and quickened. Had she not felt stripes, the stripes of a sword which had cut all the love ties of her life? Could it be for healing them? Perhaps, in some distant time, she would understand. There was so much suffering now, from different causes than hers, perhaps, but suffering. There must be some reason for it, or would a kind God let it be so? Jean was beginning to conceive of how a loving hand may sometimes be stern, and from her breast

STRIPES

went up an involuntary prayer for greater faith, for a breadth of vision that would make her cling to that Hand of all hands, even when it seemed to strike.

Despite that petition, however, on this day of family reunions, the hunger pangs in her heart were more than usually persistent. In the afternoon, no longer able to stifle them, she took from her trunk two carefully cherished photographs, propped them up on the table, sat down, and, leaning her chin in her palm, studied them earnestly, wistfully, questioningly. They were of Verne Laval and her mother, taken when she was a baby. Unwitting tears suffused her eyes at length, and, through their mist, the pictures swam, seeming to blend together. Then something happened. She felt an intense depression with a prescience of stealthy disaster. Some impulse drew her eyes upward, and she shrank back, terrified. A form stood by her, airy, but distinct; grinning, yet mirthless. It was royally clad, with a sheath at its side, but the clothes were transparent, betraying naught but a hideous skeleton, no flesh, no heart, and as she met its eyes with hers, a hoarse voice fell upon her ears: "You've never seen me, or you would know me, yet I am always near you. Death is my master and I help him in his work. I

A CHILD OF DIVORCE

make widows and orphans, but I flatter myself that I do it less crudely, so I am preferred to him. It is only lately that I have been generally recognized here as a respectable member of society, but people seem to like my methods better than my master's, so they open their doors to me, more and more. This proves the value of diplomacy, for it gives me an entrance and enables me to take for my master, quite easily, homes which his sudden methods of attack would only drive them to fortifying. Yes, we have to destroy homes, for as long as they stand, closing their doors to us, we can not thrive, especially myself and cousins, Ignorance, War, Crime and Disease. *My* name is Divorce." Slyly, he pulled his sword from his scabbard and Jean heard his bony arm squeak in its socket with the movement. "I have read in your heart desires to thwart me. Know, Jean Laval, that this is impossible. Your parents, your home, your youth, and ours—by right of capture!" Swift, silent, the sword descended on the table, the blending pictures fell apart, and through Jean's body pierced a keen agony, as though she were being physically severed. It brought her up startled. She was alone! Before her stood the pictures, which her cleared vision no longer joined. The breath tore sharply from

STRIPES

her bosom and lips. In a panic of uncanny fear, her spirit was crying for help to God, to the church across the way—to Manson. Automatically, she caught up her coat and hastened from that lonely room.

By good fortune, the study door had been left unlocked. She stole through the hall, into the auditorium, to the blessed rain of tinted light and the cloistered, strengthening peace which ever enfolded her there. For long minutes, christened by the iridescent mist, she knelt in a pew near the pulpit, till her heart calmed to normal and her nerves ceased their quivering. She knew the whole weird episode had been fanciful, but Jean sometimes felt a need of deliverance from her painfully vivid imagination.

The main doors being locked, the only way out was the same by which she had entered, and, as she reapproached the study, she heard a low whistling—"When you come to the end of a perfect day." She tiptoed, but a creaking board betrayed her nearness. A moment later, Manson had invited her into his little, book-lined haven. On the desk stood a vase of fresh, red, hothouse roses, cheering the November day with a bright blaze of color and sweetening the air with their emanations. It was the frequent habit of loving parish-

A CHILD OF DIVORCE

ioners to leave such offerings there. Manson seldom knew to whom he owed them. They charmed Jean at once; he could see it in her eyes. He touched them reverently. "Some kind friend's remembrance. Isn't it good in these sordid times, Jean, to know that God still cares for beauty?" Jean could not answer. Slipping a half-opened flower from the vase, Manson held it toward her with that benign smile she knew so well. She hesitated, then took it timidly, barely breathing her thanks.

"What is it, my child'?' he asked. "Are you cold? What makes you tremble so?" Jean had bowed her face to the blossom's chiseled petals, inhaling thirstily of its perfume. She looked up. "It's just the flowers," she explained; "I don't see many now, and somehow—they always make me feel—like praying." Another silence, while Manson, still smiling gently, looked down at her, saying:

" 'In all places then, and in all seasons,
  Flowers expand their light and soul-like wings,
 Teaching us, by most persuasive reasons,
  How akin they are to human things.' "

Again Jean raised her eyes, delightedly. "Isn't that beautiful? Is there more of it?"

He nodded, and his mellow voice continued:

STRIPES

"'And with childlike, credulous affection
  We behold their tender buds expand,
Emblems of our great resurrection,
  Emblems of the bright and better land.'"

A rapt look came to Jean's face. Unconsciously, she pressed the rose to her breast. "Emblems of resurrection—and better things. It'll help me to remember. There *is* a better land, I *know*. I never used to think of it—somehow, I didn't care; but lately—everything's changed. Oh, Dr. Manson, I can't ever thank you for all you've done for me! You've saved my life—and my soul too."

He shook his head slowly. "I'm only God's instrument, Jean. I feel that He would have brought you to Him under any circumstances; but if it's true that He's done it through me, I feel it a privilege and am grateful. Always try to live up to your best self, Jean, the one which loves the flowers. I know better than you think how hard it is right now, but I'm watching to see you win."

Neither had heeded the peremptory summons of an automobile horn without, and, just as he stepped into the hall with her, a conspicuously stylish lady pussy-footed in. "Oh, Dr. Manson," she effused, "I beg your pardon—how-do-you-do, Miss—ah—I didn't know whether I'd find you here or not—" Through the study door her eyes glimpsed the

A CHILD OF DIVORCE

bouquet of roses and instantly stole back to the one in Jean's hand. Quicker than the tact she was sedulously cultivating, and upon which she secretly prided herself, a slight frown ruffled the brow of Mrs. S. Walter Walton. She was a widow of reported means who, though not a member of First Church, had settled upon it for her "spiritual home and workshop." Being at that age most profitable to beauty parlors, she wore her widowhood more lightly than its resultant wealth.

Jean bade a confused "Good-by," hearing the widow coax as she descended the steps: "Oh, Dr. Manson, *do* come for a ride and refresh your poor brain. This is a holiday and it's clearing off beautifully. All work and no play—" Jean went back to her room to give her rose the place of honor on the antique dresser. Thereafter, she snipped a mite from the stem each evening when she changed the water, thus holding as long as she could to its little life. When, at the end of three days, it began to droop, it was to her almost like losing a friend. Arranging the leaves with tender grace, she interred it in her Bible, at the fifty-third chapter of Isaiah.

Manson, who had done a good deal of work in addition to preaching hard that day, finally succumbed to Mrs. Walton's invitation. "Who is that little girl?" the widow asked, as the chauffeur started away with them comfortably ensconsed in the rear seat of her monogrammed touring-car. Her tone just grazed on patronage.

"That is Miss Jean Laval."

"Laval? An odd name. I met some Lavals on Vernon Place—divorced people, I believe."

"Indeed?" Manson said, noncommittally.

"Hasn't she relatives?"

"None who are able to help her. She is making her way alone, poor child."

Mrs. Walton turned to him, smiling. "Kind heart," she accused with well-assumed naivete, "you are too good to every one. But beware of pity for a pretty girl, sir—it has a dangerous kin." She had a way of using adages, having discovered long ago their value in bridging gaps where one's mind was not alert with something original, and little intimacies with men she took by right of age and rank. Manson was a single-hearted man, devoted to his calling, and sincere to the point of bluntness. While he could defend a principle with scathing cleverness, he was not quick at the frothy repartee of social intercourse. There are feminine vagaries of which the male mind seldom acquires comprehension. A few married men achieve it, bachelors never, however sincere their sympathies and pure their theories of human relations. This was why Manson, though he did not know it, could meet intrepidly big national and religious problems and yet feel in his heart, at times, an utter helplessness where the guidance of his niece was concerned.

"Do you think she's pretty?" he asked so guilelessly that Mrs. Walton glanced away to hide the sudden biting of her under lip.

"Oh, yes, as girls go. Young and undeveloped, of course. Don't *you* think so?"

"Why, I never thought much about her looks. She's a sweet, brave little girl with a hard battle to fight, and I'll be glad if I can help her win it."

"Of course, you are her pastor—old enough to be her father, or nearly. I often think of what a great privilege and opportunity you have in shaping such young lives." The subject not proving quite to her relish, she skillfully switched it to generalities, evincing an ardent interest in his work, and from thence to his much-mooted views on matrimony. She had absorbed late worldly advantages with genuine native intelligence and could talk well, when it suited her to do so. "I've been following your ideas on modern social problems with so much interest," she exclaimed. "They certainly make one *think,* especially the question of divorce. I suppose that will be universally interesting as long as the race lasts. There are certainly a lot of foolish marriages, and I wonder more isn't done to regulate it, but, then, this is a free country, and it's largely a personal matter."

"Yes, the real solution is back of all legislation and lies only in the recognition of marriage as a sacrament."

"I've heard you say that before. You speak of it as a sacrament—as if there was no marriage before the Christian church, when as a matter of fact marriage is centuries older than the church."

"Yes, but not in its ideal state. Christ recognized the importance of it, uplifted it, dignified it—made it a sacrament. But even in this I believe he was only emphasizing what God had always meant should be so, and human nature was not equal to interpreting. Remember our Lord's words: 'Because of the hardness of your hearts, Moses suffered you to put away your wives, but *in the beginning it was not so.*' Our lack of understanding has caused us to fall far short in many ways of the divine intentions of the *beginning*. This is, no doubt, the reason Christ came with His new revelation, to re-establish the sanctity of marriage as well as to put other relations once more in their true light. Life is progress. We are working toward an ideal conceived by the mind of our Creator. That's why I say marriage is a sacrament and should be honored as such." With the fervor of a true prophet Manson now talked to the woman at his side just as he might have addressed an eager audience.

"What other relations?" she asked.

"Well, for instance, that of man to his Maker and his fellows, that of parents and children, master and servant, and the elevation of womanhood."

"You think, then, that the monogamous marriage—the being hopelessly bound to one man with only death as a means of escape, if escape becomes desirable—really makes for the elevation of womanhood?"

"Yes, I do, in spite of many abuses. The ideal of the monogamous marriage was to place woman on an equal footing with man as helpmate and comrade, and troubles arise, not from any fault of the plan, but from its violation by either the man or the woman."

"Ah, there you have it. The theory is all right, no doubt, but there have always been violations, more often by men, and what is there to prevent that? It seems to me that the monogamous marriage is of real protection to only one of the parties—the man. Of our own country, would you say that the fact that the last century had so few divorces, as compared with the present day, indicated a wholesomer state of society? How about the double moral code so generally accepted—the 'wild oats' creed for men, absolute chastity for women? Isn't it more likely that the unbroken marriage only glossed over a multitude of sins on the man's side and much silent suffering on the woman's—that the apparent 'faith' of many wives was really not so much faith as fear of economic dependence and public condemnation if they asserted themselves? Is a disease less insidious that confines itself to eating out the vitals and doesn't erupt on the skin? For my part, I believe that all this matrimonial upheaval to-day is nothing less than an eruption of repressed evils which we have inherited from the so-called saner generations!"

"There you may be right, but that just goes to prove my statement that violation of divine intentions, by either man or woman, will bring disaster in its wake. A man can not be untrue to those vows without dragging some woman down with him."

"But, then, where do you get your 'elevation of womanhood,' if monogamous marriage makes the woman, however true she is, a victim of such things? That seems to me unfair."

"Women can do much by demanding as good as they give."

"Not when a man has her hard and fast, and knows it. But if there is an alternative, such as divorce, then she might *do* it."

"No, I don't think that. I don't think the solution lies in degrading the fine power of woman's influence to the level of a threat to keep men in order. I still have more faith in my own sex than that. The need of both is more inspiration and a higher conception of their relations to one another. I have so much faith in womanhood, perhaps too much—perhaps I do her an injustice by forgetting the humanity of her—yet I wouldn't by any means throw the responsibility all on her. That has been done too much already. Man must face up to *his* part of the contract. To fret over the injustice of the double moral code is futile. It was unjust, we all know it, but the results can not remain forever hidden. Doubtless, as you say, we are reaping them now, for 'be not deceived, God is not mocked, and whatsoever a man shall sow, that shall he also reap.' Ugly as eruptions are, it is better that the disease should come out. Then, at least, we will know it is there and can make some definite effort toward its cure."

"And do you think this Federal amendment you are preaching will be its cure?"

"Not entirely; in fact, only in a small degree. As I said before, we can never make men good by legislation. We hear a lot now of the divorce evil, when divorce is really not an evil, but the *result of an evil*. However, we can by legal control lessen the bad influence of violation and thus get a chance to inject the serum of a finer idealism—the things that *will* cure. Naturally, too, when young people realize more difficulties in the way of getting married, and when they *are* married it must be for life, they will think more before taking this step. I see the inculcation of these ideals as the peculiar duty of the Christian church and one of the greatest challenges she faces to-day, for behind all laws, all conventions, that which will determine destiny is the *human conscience.*"

The ride, the conversation, plus her companion's magnetism, quite stimulated Mrs. Walton. She maneuvered to make it as long as possible, but the end was inevitable. At supper-time she dropped him before the manse with profuse thanks for a "new vision."

"My!" she reflected later; "how thrillingly prophetic he is—or delightfully *passe!*" Then she remembered the roses and a pair of big, appealing hazel eyes, and for some reason, in the liberty of her own apartment, the pucker returned to her forehead to complete itself in a full-fledged frown.

CHAPTER XIII.

YOUNG WINGS WILL STRENGTHEN

IT was now dark in the mornings when Jean tore her shivering, never fully rested self from between the covers of her cot. Even the radiator had not begun to work at that hour. She had brought all her will-power to bear toward hardening herself against the increasing cold, and, what with the numerous heatless days observed both at home and at the plant, she had sufficient external discipline to help her. The winter of 1917-18 will be recalled as one of the severest in history, adding, as it did, the torturing sting of its incessant blizzards to the other miseries of wartime. Conservation, the watchword of the hour, was applied to coal as well as food. The long assembly-room, with its concrete floor, blotched wooden benches, roughly beamed, unfinished walls and ceiling, iron machinery and loose windows, was at best a bleak place, swept by drafts, and frequently the women worked throughout the day bundled in coats, hats and whatever else they could appropriate as wraps.

YOUNG WINGS WILL STRENGTHEN

Some of the older ones tied their feet in burlap bags which the vicinity yielded, though the latter precaution was scorned by those of the new generation, who, though the thermometer might drop below zero, though they piled cheap furs about their shoulders and their food was as chaff that soldiers might have flour, still, by some strange incongruity, would sally forth in spool-heeled, papery pumps and silk-fiber hose through whose transparent tissues showed many a chapped ankle. It seemed that neither Jack Frost nor common sense could have induced these girls to protect that portion of their anatomies, although, had high shoes been in vogue, they would doubtless have worn them, since one touch of fashion makes all women kin. But, then, conservation extended also to leather. On the other hand, from local indications, one might have deduced a great reduction in the prices of tawdry trinkets. Certainly what unwonted financial inflation the war afforded munition workers was not wholly absorbed by Liberty Bonds. Luxuries, long coveted and now rendered secondary to the prosaic needs of life, they saw at last within reach—and grasped for them. Fate is ironical, and perhaps this was her way of evening things up. While the work was fatiguing to Jean, and would have been to any girl unaccustomed to it, it was not so to the experienced factory hands and menials who made up the bulk of her mates, and many women, especially those of foreign extraction, with physiques stronger than intellects, did approach in their earnings the fabulous wages of which Jean had heard. Yet it is questionable how much of this they laid by. It was at once their inducement and recompense for transferring to munitions, since none of the "glory" allotted the uniformed heroes of the trenches was accorded them, notwithstanding that their employers worked "patriotism" for all it was worth in the exaction of labor and stimulation of output. After several scores of drafted men had left the plant, the company officials concluded that it would be quite a proper thing to raise a service flag for them beneath the "Stars and Stripes." They had decided upon the order when to one came the kindly idea of letting the employees share in the privilege of donating this flag. Subscriptions were solicited, to which, of course, the several thousands of men and women responded, some enthusiastically, more from a sense of duty; most, alas! so grudgingly that only fear of current sentiment kept them from curtly refusing, for they failed to appreciate the "privilege." In their opinion, the company should have supplied this memorial, and the "graft" provoked much undertoned grum-

YOUNG WINGS WILL STRENGTHEN

bling. In due time, however, the big service flag was delivered, as handsome a thing as ever corporation flew, and it was then announced that the raising would be held next day in the factory yards. Those who were not now curious to attend felt obliged to. The service lasted an hour. The officials and their guests sat upon a bunting-draped platform near the flagpole, looking, in their thick fur coats, against the snowy perspective, like an exhibition of grizzly bears, and, huddled below in a great, shivering, goose-fleshed mass, the employees warmed up somewhat to "The Star-Spangled Banner." Several speeches followed, by the superintendent, the mayor and an officer of the Ordnance Department, all in frosty breaths, all dwelling upon "our splendid boys who are laying down their lives for the sake of democracy" and "our duty as fellow-citizens welded in affections and interests under this glorious ensign." Though not all could hear, every one clapped loudly. Then came the raising, and a borrowed army chaplain prayed that this flag might ever be the emblem of the common cause which bound all present together, that peace might soon be restored and brotherly love rule in every human heart. Another song ("America"), a benediction, and the toilers dispersed to their various tasks. On pay-day *all were docked for that one lost hour!* Another privilege, doubtless!

According to the State labor laws, however, even in that time of emergency, Sunday work was awarded extra pay. Jean had known all along that the plant never shut down on Sundays, but when, one Saturday evening, the foreman ordered her to report with the rest for work next day, she felt it a sort of tragedy. Yet it was true that the Huns were no respecters of the Lord's Day, that fighting in Europe went on just the same, and munitions must be had. Who was she more than the others to be exempt because it was Sunday? She asked this of herself quite honestly, bravely trying to gulp down her bitterness as, by the gaslight and with stiff, numb fingers, she hooked on her old working-dress instead of her best one, and pinned in place the badge, that symbol of her bondage which was beginning to give her the feeling of a convict. At the last moment she snatched up a small New Testament ere plunging, breakfastless, into the dark and snow-chilled morning. Mrs. Nicolson would not serve breakfast before eight o'clock on Sundays, though she had consented to put up a lunch on the previous evening as usual, which Jean found in her place at the table. Throughout the night it had been storming, and still the wind howled angrily, pierced Jean's body,

YOUNG WINGS WILL STRENGTHEN

spat icy particles into her face, did its evil best to push her back, but she bowed her head and breasted it grimly. Over the bulletin-board on the church the single night lamp drew her glance suddenly upward and flashed the morning topic to her mind: "The Healing of the Nations." Healing! Yes, Manson on that sacred day would preach of healing—while she spent it making shells to rip apart flesh and bones! A wave of nausea swept Jean, a sickening realization of the horror of war. Her heart went faint, and she could have dropped. But her feet trudged on, on through drifts sometimes knee-deep, past blocks of houses with windows dark and closed like the eyes of those who still slept warm within, her pocketed fingers clutching the little book as if it were some talisman of strength. All that morning, while her forced hands aided in the means of destruction, her spirit was in the church, crying out to God, with Manson's, for healing —the healing of the nations! and she saw no longer merely red analine, but stains of human blood upon her shells. During the short lunch period she sought a surreptitious comfort from the little Testament, but was quickly detected. Some one threw a defective primer at her. This was followed by other rejected parts and remnants of shells, a few of which struck her lightly, the rest flying afoul.

She looked up, manning a flare of resentment, but there was nothing to betray the source of these missiles. Indeed, every face within her range appeared unconscious of her presence, and the girls were only bantering each other:
"Gee, kid, it's Sunday. You got to be good, or you won't get to heaven. Look at *me*, how good I am."

"Say, you ain't got nothin' on me! Can't yez lamp the wings a-sproutin' on me back?"

"Sure, an' it's on'y me suspenders that keeps mine from growin'!"

But one stitch does not make a pattern, nor one day a life. It takes both many stitches and many days of patient perseverance. By January Jean had repaid the ten dollars to Dr. Manson, and saved the tuition fee for her course in stenography. Due to the lure of munitions, a large badge factory in Newark had gone begging for women hands. She found it willing to give her afternoon hours in the inspection-room at the rate of "eight dollars per," or four dollars for this half-time employment, with fifty cents extra for Saturday mornings. The work was light and comparatively neat. All the girls did day after day was to inspect, count and box a great variety of badges, buttons and small celluloid novelties. The building was quite new, permanent, therefore substantial and

YOUNG WINGS WILL STRENGTHEN

warm, and, because the goods must not be soiled, the inspection-room was kept clean, so that her surroundings were both pleasanter and more comfortable, nor were her neighbors so heterogeneous. A number of them were old stand-bys, who had begun with the firm in its downtown plant and never worked for any other. One middle-aged woman at Jean's table had a service record of twenty-two years, and, as a recognition of her fidelity, had just been "raised to ten a week"! She was older than the forelady, who had started in the even humbler capacity of an errand-girl, but by her initiative won swift advancement. "A'nt Molly" Lindberg was simply a good inspection hand; never would be, and probably had no desire to be, anything more. Jean might have put in full time here, but she found the day course to be shorter than that offered by the night school, and she was very anxious to get through. In this way she could attend classes each of the five mornings a week and study in the evenings. She decided to keep her room and board herself for the term on the remaining two dollars and a half. She had yet to learn how poor is that economy which is achieved by stinting on food. Having been always quick to absorb and digest knowledge, before long she began to wonder what caused certain queer and embarrassing periods of mental vacancy, times when she simply *could not* grasp things which her fellow-students seemed to manage so easily. Desperately she wrestled with dashes, circles, hooks and word-signs. Her reward was a headache more often than a clear understanding. Frequently the letters on the typewriter chart would blur together in an almost hopeless maze and her hands feel nerveless. She did not realize that, while canned beans, stale crackers (she remembered Miss Baily's expedient) and diluted milk might keep her alive, they were insufficient, in such small quantities at least, to properly nourish her brain, and, due to the wartime practice of substitution, even these cheap rations were poorer than usual. Then, of course, she had to skimp on carfare. The badge factory stood about halfway between East Elair and the school in Newark. She would walk to the school in the mornings; attend classes from nine to twelve; eat or skip lunch, according to her finances; walk back to the factory, where she toiled from one to six, and then home to a solitary meal in her room, if meal it might be called, a matter of some six miles daily. Perhaps it was no wonder that she kept on losing weight, grew intensely nervous and unsteady as to her emotions. The slightest offense, real or imaginary, would start the tears. But worst of

YOUNG WINGS WILL STRENGTHEN

all were those dizzy spells, which increased both in frequency and length of duration and rendered concentration impossible. She fell considerably behind the rest of the class, and could sense that her teacher was much disappointed in her. Miss Ray was indeed puzzled by the seeming stupidity of a pupil who had started out as one of the brightest in her class.

But in March a crisis came, for Jean's overworked mind and body went on a sympathetic strike. She was just leaving school when she swayed against the wall, and slid down in a heap on the tiled floor of the entrance-way.

An ambulance came, and, after hours of feverish oblivion, Jean regained consciousness in the City Hospital. Some one was near her with broth, just as Mrs. Dennison had been on that day last November, only this time it was a nurse. She swallowed the hot liquid mechanically. It was not until Dr. Manson came that her interest in living revived. For a long time he sat beside her, holding her thin hand as her father might, and should, have done. A dimness veiled his kind eyes; his quiet, deep voice wavered slightly: "My dear child, why didn't you tell me how things were? I had no idea what you were trying to do."

A CHILD OF DIVORCE

"I don't know what's the matter with me," Jean answered, weakly petulant; "I just feel disgusted with myself—I—I'm the—*dumbest* thing—" She broke off in a sob. Manson caressed her hand at this and smiled: "No one can beat nature and come out on top, Jean. The candle burned at both ends lives only half its normal life and has nothing left to stand on. You must never do such things again. Don't you know how you've scared us all?"

"I—I—know I'm a useless thing, that's all—falling around on people's charity—no matter how hard I try—to be independent. I'm not worth being scared about!" Nevertheless, she was gaining strength. It seemed to circulate from Manson's hand. When, at last, he had to go, he left for Jean a sort of radiance behind him as if—as if the Saviour had been there. Not long afterwards Mrs. Dennison came also, and the next day Mrs. Nicolson and two more ladies from the neighborhood. Others sent flowers and fruit. Within the week she was out again, recovered in spirits, if not fully so in health, for Manson told her of some friends who insisted upon "seeing her through" to the end of the course. They looked upon this as an "investment," he explained, were well able to make it and only required that she devote her best energies to

YOUNG WINGS WILL STRENGTHEN

study and justify their faith in her ability. Her board would be paid for the remaining two months of the term, change for carfare and other incidentals supplied her. He was acting as their agent, and some day she could repay the money if she wished to. Jean naturally longed to know the identity of her benefactors; but could not ask for information he had promised to withhold. It was a great incentive to her and she did make the most of this unexpected opportunity. She left the badge factory and spent the afternoons practicing on one of the schoolroom typewriters. As she had no machine of her own, and the mornings were largely devoted to shorthand and text-book work, the typing had been one of her main difficulties. Now, with square meals at regular hours, more rest and freedom from anxiety, she soon made up for lost time, overtook the other students, and, in her eagerness, could have passed them. Final examinations occurred the last of May, when she graduated with an average grade of 98.

That was just before the second draft, and the East Elair Exemption Board found itself needing another stenographer. In some way the chief clerk heard of Jean, and called her one day on the telephone. Would she like the place? Headquarters being in the local high school made the office within walking distance, and the pay was—$15 a week! Of course, it was just a war position, but it would give her experience. Jean accepted, highly elated. Later on, however, there came a reaction, a nervous fear that she might not be equal to the work. In this respect she was like all newly fledged stenographers.

CHAPTER XIV.

A CLEAR, IMPERIOUS CALL

"But this one golden moment, hold it fast!"

"MAWNIN', Missy, reckon we's done approximated ouah destination at de scheduled houah." With a grin which seemed to separate his black face into upper and lower portions, Admiral Dewey Jones handed a sheet of paper across the gate of the exemption office to Jean, who happened to be the nearest clerk. He was the "personal response" to the peremptory summons typed thereon. Jean took it and shot a glance past him to the small, but broad-cheeked, negress who had followed in close at his back, seeing which he stepped aside to blandly introduce the lady, "Dis am mah wife, Mis' Pearl Opal Jones, whom yo' designate in dat lettah."

"Yes," smiled Jean. "Just sit down over there where the others are and your name will be called. Mr. Rollins is a little late this morning." Admiral Dewey looked slightly crestfallen at this rather nonchalant reception, the official letter having puffed him up with a

A CHILD OF DIVORCE

feeling of individual importance, but quickly recovered his affability, nodded and grinned once more. "Yas, Missy, thank yo' kin'ly, dat sho' am an appreciation—come on, niggah," turning back to Pearl Opal, who remained blankly motionless, 'si' down an' make yo'se'f mis'ble.'' She obeyed in a dazed manner and the couple formed a dusky end to the fast-growing line of applicants for exemption.

Jean sifted the files, found the Jones questionnaire and laid it, with the letter, on the pile already waiting for the Draft Board to assemble. The actual transcription of correspondence, that art to which she had applied such especial devotion, had proven to be the least of Jean's duties. She received just enough dictation to keep her in practice, but all the other doings in the Exemption Office were so absorbing that she had no time to even think of failure. It was an immense room. It had once been a classroom, but now a hastily constructed fence divided off that section of it near the door for registrants, while behind this stood the desks of the chief clerk and employees, the filing cabinets along the walls, and, in the corner farthest from the entrance, the lengthy polished table about which the board met daily at eleven o'clock to hear the pleas of men who wished to be excluded from the draft and confirm

A CLEAR, IMPERIOUS CALL

their classifications. Louis Rollins, the town clerk, was chairman, and most of the other members came from offices of their own, this being emergency work.

The fact that, out of all the millions of people born under the sun, no two are quite alike, makes human nature of exhaustless interest, and Jean was now seeing human nature as she had never seen it, even from behind a counter. What intimate secrets were hidden by those plain-looking rows of questionnaire drawer-fronts! Men supposed by all their friends to be quite alone in the world unexpectedly revealed some one dependent upon them for support. Childless couples acquired ready-made children. There was a startling jump in the marriage rate, and a sudden reawakening of consciences on the part of delinquent young husbands. There were widows, claiming dependence on eligible sons, who came dressed in their weeds and wept before the Draft Board, wrote pathetic letters to the Governor or President, did everything the instinct of self-preservation could impel them to do in order to keep their offspring from service, and when the Government compromised with allotments, bought themselves blue-starred service pins and were always most conspicuous at all meetings and benefits for the mothers of soldiers. Once two evaders were forced in by a policeman and created considerable excitement before the same blue arm propelled them outward in the direction of the courthouse.

On the other hand, there were boys who had achieved the remarkable feat of being eighteen within sixteen years after birth, so eager were they to rush over the sea and "over the top"; there were brave old parents who concealed aching hearts and boasted larger incomes than they had in order to release their sons for duty. Jean was kept busy all over the room, but her desk was so near the Board table that she could not help hearing many of the interviews, and her professional indifference to them was only an outward assumption. Surely there could have been no better representation of democracy than that afforded daily by the flanks of waiting registrants. Jean had filed, and sent in duplicate to the office of the Adjutant General at Trenton, the record cards of managers, engineers, plumbers, actors, hod-carriers, students, florists, bartenders, even one young minister, ordained after the first draft; and still they came in their respective turns, mechanics, teachers, chauffeurs, reporters, salesmen, motormen, carpenters, blacksmiths, cobblers, men of all the trades and professions which it takes to make a world—and a war. Hundreds of them had still to receive their blanks, while question-

A CLEAR, IMPERIOUS CALL

naires given out earlier were already returning, filled in and sworn to, by the sackload.

Jean liked to follow certain cases from the moment of registration down to the interview, if exemption was claimed. Odd names aroused her interest, and she would watch for the inevitable appearance, with his testifying dependents, of some bearer of such a cognomen whose summons she herself had written. It was thus with Admiral Dewey Jones. His jungle type of face and painfully suave mannerisms were about as incongruous as himself and his name. Jean managed to be at her desk when the chocolate-dyed couple were called. Admiral's loquacity surpassed that of the entire Board's, but Pearl barely parted her thick, sullen lips. Even when Chairman Rollins addressed her directly, she only rolled an apprehensive look toward Admiral Dewey and mumbled a half-breathed "Yas, sah," or "No, sah." Presently the chairman, in frank impatience, dismissed Admiral. "Wait outside," he suggested; "we want a word with your wife alone." The effect of his going upon Pearl was something like the loosening of a brake.

"Now, Mrs. Jones," repeated the chairman, "how much *is* it your husband contributes to your support?"

"Mah—sup—pawt?" vaguely.

A CHILD OF DIVORCE

"Yes, how much money does he give you to live on?"

"Money? dat niggah?" The mental process of identifying Admiral with the source of her livelihood was obviously too much for Pearl.

"Yes, now look here, Mrs. Jones. If your husband goes to war and the Government sends you fifteen dollars a month, could you get along without him till it's over?" Pearl's eyes began to bulge. She leaned forward, incredulous. "What dat?" she demanded; "yo' mean fo' to tell me dat if dat niggah done gone to de wah—*ah'll git fifteen dollars a munt?*"

"Yes, Mrs. Jones, that's it." Suddenly Pearl Opal shoved back her chair and jumped up like a broken spring. "Lawd a'moughty!" she cried, "bress de Lawd! Dat de fust good news ah ebah hearn tell 'bout dat niggah since ah done marry him!" Everybody laughed. Admiral was doomed. He must go to war, but Pearl's step quickened magically. She departed, still audibly exulting, "Hally-looya—hally-looya!" Through the open window Jean could see her descending the wide stone steps like an African queen from her throne, with scarcely a glance for her waiting spouse. He caught her arm, but she shook off his grasp, tossed up her flat nose and strode ahead, leaving him in dull amazement, to follow when he pleased.

A CLEAR, IMPERIOUS CALL

The next case also had its humorous side, at least for those who could see humor in so tragic a thing as a harmless lunatic. The man, Victor Phelps, of a well-to-do East Elair family, but eligible only in point of age, was led in by his male nurse as an explanation of the blankness of his questionnaire. He denied being a Phelps, claiming in a rambling way that his name was Constantine Josuez and that he was a king of the Fiji Islands now traveling incognito. With expansive friendliness, he confided to the Board that his father had caused an operation to be performed upon his head to make him forget who he was, but he had fooled him by remembering it after all. He now had a number of detectives rounding up the people who were trying to disinherit him. In Fiji over a hundred wives were his and so many children he had long since run out of names for them. He wanted to join the army if the Government would be sure to put him where he could win the war. He further explained, however, that as soon as he recovered his kingdom, he intended, himself, to declare war and then it would be "all over with the Kaiser!" Of course there was no hope of his making out a questionnaire.

Those were strenuous times and Jean never knew what might happen next. One young fellow who had left his card during her lunch hour, described himself, in the space reserved for personal appearance, as possessing "bright golden" hair and "deep violet" eyes. Jean kept on the lookout for this angelic combination. When eventually the gentleman returned for induction, she could hardly decide whether he was color-blind, or merely trying to be witty. His hair was about the shade of a tangerine and the only part of a violet his eyes resembled in hue was its foliage!

The month of June had almost breathed its tender last when the Burnetts came. They were a prematurely aged little mother and her tall, wiry, studious-looking son. Jean remembered typing their summons, but the name awakened no recollections in her mind. Indeed, there were many Burnetts, even right there in town. One of the principal streets had been named for some of them. It was the low, quavering pathos of the mother's voice as she talked to Chairman Rollins that seeped into her soul and drew her attention. That mother's plea was so different from most.

"I don't want to stand in the way of my son's duty, sir," she insisted; "yes, he's all I have—but so many others are giving all they have too. I'm getting old and America must live long after me. If I kept him from defending his country, the time might come—when he couldn't forgive me. I want you to let him

A CLEAR, IMPERIOUS CALL

go. I do sewing—I can get along—'' Her utter lack of affectation made the noble words sound nobler still. Jean could feel that the Board members were touched, also that the young man was torn between two duties and desires. Affection unashamed shone through every look he gave his mother, but his blood leaped too at the call of patriotism.

"You're in your third year," the chairman reflected, addressing him; "you could be discharged from immediate service under the draft by enlisting in the Reserve Corps of the Medical Department."

"I know I could, but I want to get across with the regulars—the Medics if I can. When I wrote for exemption, I didn't know Mommy mother—was going to be such a sport."

"Miss Laval," called Rollins, "please get me our correspondence with Truman Burnett."

As Jean laid the folder of letters before the chairman she was conscious of Mrs. Burnett's gaze upon her. A little later, on their way out, the couple stopped before her desk. Looking up suddenly, her eyes met the blue-gray, long-lashed ones of the young man and somehow she was reminded of the way the sun sparkles through the dark fringes of forest trees. "Pardon me," came the low voice of the mother, "but did I hear Mr. Rollins call your name Laval?"

"Yes, ma'am," answered the girl.

"Could it be Jean Laval?"

"Why, yes," she arose, wondering.

"It's an unusual name, that's why I've never forgotten it—or your face either, even if you've grown so. Didn't you live in Chenango Valley once?"

"Why, yes, when I was little!"

"Then I'm right and you *are* the girl who used to play with Truman—to help him eat apple pies?" Smiling, she turned from Jean to her son. In candid, puzzled delight the two young people searched each others' faces. Truman spoke first: "Well, what d'you know about that? Say, do you remember it? I'd nearly forgotten, myself. There was a fight once in your yard, wasn't there? about apples, or something, and you were my nurse—" Dim reminiscences reawoke in Jean of a yard that seemed immense, an apple-tree, a fence over which lolled two dirty, jeering boys, of another little boy jumping down from the branches, of arguments, blows and blood, of a spacious kitchen, a wet dishtowel and badly battered young face, then of an endless road down which a small figure melted dizzily to dissolve at last in her own tears; of such disconnected, trivial incidents which, looming big in childhood, had stamped themselves on her memory without her realization. She smiled

A CLEAR, IMPERIOUS CALL

back at Truman timidly. Somehow she could not quite associate this self-reliant young man with that forlorn little boy of other days. Even Mrs. Burnett had aged so much that her time-blurred impression of the "goodest mother in the world," who made dresses on dummies and delicious apple pies, bore little resemblance to the old lady standing before her. For one thing, that Mrs. Burnett had seemed very tall. This one was a trifle shorter than Jean herself.

"Well, isn't that—funny?" she finally stammered, "and for you to remember me all this time!"

"How'd you happen to come to East Elair? Are your parents here too—your mother and stepfather, wasn't it?" Mrs. Burnett asked. Jean bit her lip. "No," she answered, "I—I'm alone. It's a long story. I hope I'll see you again—"

"Well, you bet!" exclaimed Truman; "give us your address, Jean. I'm coming to see you —to-night if you'll let me. Can I?"

"Yes, and you must come to see us," his mother added. "We live near here, Jean; you must come often and get acquainted again."

Jean promised to come, and after they had gone, broken recollections, thus aroused in her mind, kept multiplying all morning, subconsciously adjusting themselves to one another like the various parts of a picture puzzle. But hadn't there been something unpleasant relative to the Burnetts? Some taint upon their name? Ah! another scene flashed back—her mother's face and voice as she turned to James Hasbrook, "Consider the source, Jim—and we mustn't keep him near *our* children!" and then the shrill denunciation of the angry youngster whom Truman had beaten, "—that *bastard!* Everybody knows his mother wasn't never married!" Jean's heart swelled, flushing her face with a gush of hot blood. Little had she known in those days the meaning of that indictment, but she knew it now. When the Board had dispersed, and, alone in the back of the room, she was replacing the questionnaires, those confidential documents supposed never to lie, a pained curiosity led her to commit a breach of ethics by opening Truman's. Opposite "Birthplace" had been written, "Florence Crittenden Home, Newark, N. J." She closed it quickly with the guilty feeling of having surprised a secret. Never had an afternoon in the office seemed so long. She could not think clearly about her work, for questions kept intruding themselves upon her, big questions of life and relationships. Perhaps if Jean had known the even-tenored happiness of a conventional home life, this might not have been; she would have accepted, like thousands of other young women, the

A CLEAR, IMPERIOUS CALL

ready-made criterion of civilized conduct and let it go at that. She would have recognized the "legitimate" and shunned the "illegitimate" with no thought for anything below the surface of either. But she had seen conformation to the so-called legitimate customs result in as much misery for other lives as ever had been threatened by disregard of them, and since human happiness was the real test of all culture, wherein, then, lay the superiority of the conventional over the unconventional? Truman's mother may, unfortunately, never have been married; her own had been married twice, and yet—

"I'd give anything if my mother loved me like his!" in sudden defiance her heart beat out the words. "I don't care what the world thinks! *Society!* What has it ever done for me? Truman Burnett's as good as I am. I'm glad he's coming and I'll be his friend!"

But the association of Jean and Truman was destined not to stop at friendship, although friendship constituted one of its sweetest elements. The soul of a womanly woman is like a many-stringed harp whereon love plays with skillful fingers. There is the thrilling treble of admiration, of hero-worship; there are the alto and tenor of esteem and reverence; but not until the deep bass chords of the maternal have been stirred, is the harmony complete. Those are the tones which sustain. The challenge of Truman's position awakened a responsive vibration of those mother chords in Jean. Not that he ever knew of her awareness of the shadow over his birth. His own attitude toward the matter was apparently one of happy unconsciousness. This surprised Jean at first, then she was glad. He came that night, just after dinner, and, remembering Mrs. Nicolson's warning about the parlor, Jean acquiesced to his suggestion of a walk with his own home as the goal.

The evening was ideal, and, sauntering close beside her under Park Road's arching trees, he talked freely about his own affairs, evincing, as well, a deep interest in hers. An almost inordinate happiness had seized upon Jean, especially so since any day might see him inducted, to return—God knew when! But her thoughts just then afforded no room for their impending separation. Strangely, it seemed as if she and Truman never *could* be separated, and, moreover, never had been. Their spirits had only bridged those twelve years to an inevitable meeting again. Their initial strangeness with each other swiftly wore away, and the more they talked and laughed together, the more each recognized in the other the comrade who had been, yet with something added to each nature, something

A CLEAR, IMPERIOUS CALL

intangible, beautiful, baffling, still to be revealed. Things they had played at once, they now discussed seriously.

"So, you *are* going to be a doctor after all," Jean reflected, "and I suppose you'll have that hospital."

"And you? You were going to be a nurse, don't you remember?"

"Yes, and I never thought about it again—till the war came, then I wished I'd taken training."

"You were going to work in my hospital," he recalled; "there's time yet, Jean." She laughed. "It would be funny—to work for *you!*"

"Yes, I guess so. I'll be working for some one else for awhile yet myself. Only one year more, though, till I graduate!"

"I think it's wonderful, Truman, honest I do, the way you've gotten ahead all by yourself."

"It's Mom, Jean; give Mom the credit for anything worth while I do. She's a brick. Kept on sewing to support herself so I could plug through college. Mom has it on all the financiers I know of for managing things. She even owns the house now. And you're wonderful yourself, Jean. You haven't had any one to help you like I've had her." A rush to Jean's eyes of unaccountable tears made her grateful for the darkness. "I'm going to borrow her after you go," she threatened when she could steady her voice.

"Say, I wish you would, Jean! Mom'll be lonesome."

"So'll I. I've been lonesome a long time."

"Have you, Jean?"—his voice softened with sympathy—"I wish I'd known. Well, Mom'll be glad to have you come down any time, I can tell you that. Here we are." They were now on Greenwood Avenue, where stood a row of old-fashioned, small frame cottages, and he turned into one of these.

Mrs. Burnett welcomed Jean with a kiss so warm that she again felt like crying. She had some refreshment ready for them—cold milk and home-made apple pie!

"Well, if this isn't like old times!" exulted Truman with a meaning smile for Jean as they all sat down. Between luscious bites more questions were asked and answered and many things discussed. Jean had never felt so naturally at home, even at the Two Ways Inn. She forgot the years which had elapsed, became a little girl again, and Truman a little boy. Only when she was leaving did some letters lying loose on a writing-desk bring to her mind the *shadow*. They were addressed to "*Mrs.* Laura Burnett," and, looking furtively at the old lady's left hand, she noticed

A CLEAR, IMPERIOUS CALL

that Truman's mother, like most other mothers, wore a wedding ring. This puzzled her. She felt somewhat ashamed of her earlier thoughts. Perhaps—what could have happened? Then she remembered the questionnaire, glanced at Truman, and her intuition pierced to the heart of that mystery. But she kept all these things to herself. Truman went home with her, which meant another delightful walk.

It was on the following Saturday that he called her on the office telephone to inform her of his induction. "I leave for camp Monday," he said; "maybe you know about it already. Gee whiz! I'm all excited, and, Jean, I want a long talk with you before I go. Let's go up to Eagle Rock to-morrow, shall we?"

"Yes, Truman—I'll be ready right after dinner." Jean managed the words thickly, her heart had sunk so low. But she set her lips as she hung up the receiver and went resolutely back to work. This was the price of war and she was not alone in the paying. For Truman's mother it must be infinitely worse and her breast filled with pity toward the brave old lady.

Early in the afternoon of the next day, she and Truman rode on an open trolley to Eagle Rock in comparative silence. Too impressed by the seriousness of things for levity, they had nothing to say for the crowds around them to hear. But Eagle Rock has room for every one. Avoiding the stairs, for which most of the people made a rush, they started slowly up the mountainside by way of a secluded, sun-flecked, winding lane, still wordless till, when they were quite alone, Truman turned impulsively and reached out his hand to her. At this simple movement there recurred to Jean, with startling distinctness, the memory of another day on another lonely road when they two had clasped hands and realized a new sense of comfort from some common bond of sympathy. With instinctive trustfulness she gave him hers. His fingers closed over it until they hurt. She supposed she should have resisted, but she could not, nor did she want to. What was happening to her—to them both? Were they being caught in that mad tidal wave of romanticism which at present seemed sweeping before it so much human discretion? Was she, who had wondered so soberly how other girls could give themselves to men they hardly knew because those men were soon to brave the fangs of death, herself a victim of the same primitive urge? But it was not as if she did not know Truman, even though her acquaintance with the man he had become was still so short.

"Jean," he was pleading huskily, "do you feel—the way I do?"

A CLEAR, IMPERIOUS CALL

She could not answer. They had now gained the place where the road wove through the forest. He led the way into a woodsy cloister and they sat down on a fallen trunk. No sounds reached them save those of nature, unless, perhaps, the thumping of their own hearts. She clung to his hand involuntarily, for she seemed to be slipping, she knew not where, though it no longer mattered much so that they went together. She had looked to Paul Manson as her pattern of manhood. Now, had there been room in her consciousness for any one but Truman, she would have known that Manson had struck but the hitherto untouched strings of gratitude, reverence and aspiration, while Truman awoke her soul's full melody. Manson was of a generation gone before, a spirit whose riper needs she could not have met, a benefactor—an *ideal*. She raised her eyes to Truman's and in their eager glow upon her read the call—the "clear imperious call of mate to mate"—and felt it in the throbbing of his blood. He was her equal, her own complement. He had not success already captured to offer her, only a yoke to share in the race toward a hope which beckoned them both. A far better thing for the strengthening of Jean's womanhood was such a tie as this, better than any paternal tenderness which would have sheltered her, even as a wife, from life's ennobling hardships.

"Remember"—his words fell incoherently—"you were going to be a nurse—and work for me—but that wasn't all—you and I—we were—" His look finished what his lips could not. Under it Jean's eyes dropped and her whole body tingled.

"Jean—" He leaned close, his voice quivering, "Jean—*Jean!*" Suddenly she turned, and with utter abandon yielded herself to his reaching arms, all the long-pent yearning for affection bursting from her in a flood of responsive passion, finding speechless outlet in an embrace as tense as his own. Moments passed, or perhaps hours.

"Jean," he soothed at last, a little brokenly, his lips against her hair, "I understand—don't cry—it's all right, Jean. I know what you've had to suffer—I—I've been through it too—the world's been sort of hard on you and me—only I've had Mom. But you're not alone now, Jean—oh! I love you—I love you!" Their arms tightened about each other. Both still trembled.

"Jean," he murmured on, "everything'll be different now, won't it? It's been hard to understand some things—why we both had parents and yet no real homes—we never did anything very bad, did we?—why your parents

A CLEAR, IMPERIOUS CALL

didn't love you—and my father ran away—'' Jean lifted her face and saw the frank tears on his cheeks. This was the first allusion he had made to his father.

"You were going to find him when you grew up," she recalled softly, feeling that now there was nothing of moment to either of them that might not be discussed.

"Jean, Mom don't want me to. She made me promise not to try. That's what I can't understand. Sometimes I believe she—*cares* yet, and why should she? Why should a woman keep on caring about a man who married her—made all those promises—and then deserted her before her baby was born? He left her to charity—that's what he did, without a cent or anything! I promised Mom—but yet—if I should ever run across him—" The youth's face darkened.

"No, Truman, whatever happens, don't ever do anything to spoil our happiness. We've had enough trouble and it wouldn't make things right—not now."

"But, Jean, he ruined my mother's life!"

"Maybe he tried to, Truman, but her life isn't ruined. She's risen above it. She's happier than mine with either of her husbands. Oh, she's so brave! Let's just think of what'll keep her happy, Truman, and do that and leave the rest—to God."

A CHILD OF DIVORCE

"Do you think God cares, Jean?"

"Yes, I do."

"I don't! I think He's served you a rotten deal—and Mom too! If He's fair and can do anything—why does He let the innocent suffer on account of the selfishness of others?"

"I don't know," Jean admitted simply, "but I believe He cares. I think He trusts people, Truman, and if they don't live up to the trust, then they make some one else suffer, but I think that *some* time He always makes it up to those innocent ones. Oh, Truman! Isn't this beautiful—what has come to us now? In spite of everything? And, Truman—maybe *we'll* be trusted and tried—for some one's happiness—some day—" She hid her warming face again on his shoulder. With the realization of a deep love expressed and requited, the first excitement gradually calmed. In Jean's heart uncertainty gave place to peace and her ingrained habit of thoughtfulness began even then to reassert itself.

But even life's sweetest hours must pass away. Were all the passions and affections of mankind concentrated into one tremendous force, it could not detain one second of the time allotted us with our dear ones. Jean and Truman came back to earth startled to discover that night had thrown its cloak around

A CLEAR, IMPERIOUS CALL

them. Cramped, but happy, they arose and smoothed out their rumpled clothing.

"Hungry?" Truman asked prosaically.

"Yes, I am," Jean confessed. They stopped for supper in a little cafe at the foot of the hill, then boarded a home-bound car.

Behind the hydrangea bushes in Nicolsons' back yard, just outside the radius of the arclight, they lingered another long while. Several times he said he must be going, his low voice halting on the words, while Jean's pulses stood still. There was his mother. This was his last night with her too. He would move a step or so, then return for one more farewell. At last he caught her to him almost roughly, kissed her blindly, whispering, "Good-by, Jean —*darling*—good-by! Don't worry—I'm coming back—I *know!* Take care of Mom—*goodby!*" and, with desperate resolution, tore himself away. Yet she stood there, as if she thought he might come back again; that her spirit, which followed him, would bring him back. Only when satisfied that he had gone indeed did she steal into the house and up to her room, like a sort of automaton. Without lighting the gas, and discarding only her hat, she sank on her knees beside the cot, not praying, however; that is, consciously. She could not think now. She could only feel. In one brief afternoon the crowning gift of life had been granted her and snatched away. The exaltation of the woman loved, the agony of the woman bereft, struggled together in her bosom, nearly bursting its walls.

Finally came the relieving tears, the inarticulate supplication, ''God—spare him! Send him back to me—he's all I have!'' and slowly, as if in answer to her plea, a new conviction warmed and consoled her. Of course he was coming back, or *this* would not have happened! Why need they have been brought together at all if this was to be the end? God was not so cruel!

CHAPTER XV.

"THE CHASTISEMENT OF OUR PEACE"

ALTHOUH she had done her "bit" in the munition works and on the staff of the exemption office, the actual catastrophe of war had remained to Jean somewhat remote. It was no longer so. Now, like thousands of other women, she had a vital interest in it, and this opened to her fellowships which she had hitherto felt "out of." Over and over she would review that wonderful Sunday afternoon at Eagle Rock, Truman's every word and look, the inflections of his voice, the thrill of physical contact. It was the food of her subconscious thought by day and of her dreams by night, a food that never staled. Such precious memories, with still more sacred anticipations, her visits to Truman's mother, her Red Cross work in the evenings, and the bulky, travel-worn letters bearing the red triangle of the Y. M. C. A. and the purple stamp of the censor, helped her to live cheerfully through those long, long weeks when a strife-torn world waited for the dawn of peace, to resist the monotony of routine tasks, the sordid annoyances of boarding-house life, even to laugh off good-naturedly the inoffensive but conspicuous advances of Tom Daly, a plain, young, limited-service man employed in the office. He had asked her repeatedly for a "date," and, without being bold, seemed nothing daunted by her consistent aloofness. At first her engagement to Truman was too dear to share with any one except his mother, but, as days wore by, the bigness of it made her want the world to know, so one morning she confided in Miss Haynes, whose desk was nearest her own. After lunch the whole office force had somehow learned of it, and, as she came in, her comrades surrounded her, congratulating and teasing, all but Tom, who kept in the background, trying to recover from the shock.

"Where's your ring?" the chief clerk asked.

"Oh," waived Jean, "we hadn't time for that, but I'll have it when he comes back. Nobody's bothering now about rings with so many things more important."

"I guess you're right all right," rejoined the voluble Miss Haynes; "the way they're killin' off the men, we all oughta be glad if we get *wedding*-rings—I'll tell the world."

"Look at poor old Tom, Jean; you've broken his heart," observed Mr. Vale, an

"CHASTISEMENT OF OUR PEACE"

ancient but twinkly-eyed professor who had come out of his retirement from addressing classes in rhetoric to address envelopes. Short and fat, with a round, florid face, white goatee and whiskers, he always made Jean think of the little nine-pin players in "Rip Van Winkle." The chief clerk laughed. "Pooh!" she scoffed directly at him, "as if you could break a man's heart! They're made out of rubber. All they ever do is stretch, and when you let go they spring right back in place!"

It was much the same at Nicolsons'. Matrimony has never yet grown quite so commonplace as to rob an engaged girl of a special kind of interest. Perhaps it is because the girl herself becomes so magnetically radiant. It is a time whose joy she can not hide and seldom desires to. In the room next to Jean's, a much larger one, dwelt a couple lately united, the "better two-thirds" of which had, from the day of her advent, all but smothered her with attentions and confidences. Mrs. Webber was forty-three, and, having so narrowly escaped the Spinsters' Retreat, seemed to live in a constant and ridiculous fear of becoming a widow; perhaps not without reason, though, for she weighed almost three hundred, while the poor male she had captured may possibly have tipped the scales at one-fifteen. He was, moreover, her junior (which tinged the fear with jealousy), callow and sunken-chested, with a chronic cough and a touchy temper. Notwithstanding these physical disadvantages, as if to remind the world of his masculine prerogatives, he frequently indulged in public spurts of verbal abuse, to which she bowed with the meekness of a martyred wife, thankful to *be* a wife, and went on brooding over him like a mother, entertaining all who would listen by explanations of the preferences, opinions, virtues and peculiarities of "Jack." With that unconscious complacency of most women who have recently achieved a "Mrs.," she never missed a chance of referring to "my husband"—lest perhaps, in her case, one might mistake the relation! Because of a prodigious appetite that made her cast yearning eyes upon his unemptied dishes at mealtimes, saying pensively, "Dear, if you don't want that, *I'll* eat it," Jean had secretly dubbed her "Mrs. Jack Spratt." Still, she was very sentimental, and, having little to do while Jack was at the Magneto Works but decorate the front veranda, this characteristic throve on novels, and she developed *penchants* for different mental vagaries, such, for instance, as "cyco-analysiss." If there was an engagement anywhere around, Mrs. Webber usually smelled and tracked it down. It was she who sensed Jean's, and, for the rest, it took but a teasing accusa-

"CHASTISEMENT OF OUR PEACE"

tion to bring out the truth, whereupon she gushed, "Oh, you darling, foxy little thing! and letting us think all the while that you hadn't any beau! But I *knew* you must have—a girl as pretty as you. Who *is* he, darling? What's his name?"

Jean appeased her curiosity by displaying Truman's picture, with information answering those questions, and if her eulogy of the young man was a bit exaggerated, understanding hearts will pardon her. For news-vending Mrs. Webber's talent more than equaled Miss Haynes'. The situation seemed to afford her as much delight as a "happily ever after" ending to one of her novels, and she gloated joyously over having been the first to "discover" it. But when it reached Mrs. Nicolson, she gasped, looking sharply at Jean: "Well, of all things! I thought you said you didn't keep no comp'ny!"

"I didn't," smiled Jean; "I met him since—"

"D'you mean to say you're *engaged* to a man you don't hardly know?"

"Oh, I know him"—Jean in her happiness could afford to be patient—"we used to be playmates—"

"Ain't it sweet?" oozed Mrs. Webber; but Mrs. Nicolson derided: "Playmates! Well, marriage ain't no play. What can you tell about a man after all them years? Can he support a wife?"

"He's a doctor," Jean explained, "or going to be."

"Doctor? Humph! Well, it's all right if them sick people pays their bills. It'll take him a long time to get started, though, and you'll have to grub like a slave. He'll never be on time to meals and he'll be out all hours of the night. I s'pose you're in love, so you think that won't matter. Well, you girls are welcome to them silly notions, but if I was a girl again, there's no man's love 'ud pay *me* for scrubbin' pots 'n' pans!" Jean by now had grown used to her landlady, so she laughed lightly at this gloomy prediction. Whenever people have such pessimistic views of life, investigation will generally prove them to be the outgrowth of personal disappointment. Mrs. Nicolson had, herself, married for material support, and when this prop failed there was little left to fall back upon. Just as they were getting along fairly well, her husband had been inconsiderate enough to die, creating funeral expenses in addition to those of the unexpected illness which had already eaten up his savings. None of her children, now grown, overwhelmed her with affection, though the youngest son was much attached to home. Once, after venturing away for several weeks,

"CHASTISEMENT OF OUR PEACE"

he had returned to present her with a daughter-in-law who, with himself, had been "visiting" ever since. The bride shortly acquired a toy dog named Zu-Zu, which resembled nothing so much as an animated dishmop, and spent hours embroidering a pillow for the little pest with pictures of his canine relations, this, to all appearances, being the extent of her industry. "Floyd" was in town a great deal, ostensibly looking for work, but it seemed that no one appreciated his abilities. Even the army rejected him, due to some physical defect which no one would have suspected from his looks. He was a heavy, phlegmatic fellow, and several times, in the heat of summer, Jean had seen him lounging on the front steps, fanning himself with the newspaper he had just finished perusing, while old Mrs. Nicolson, sweating from every pore, jerked the lawn-mower across the lumpy front yard. In winter-time, too, it was she who managed the furnace and lugged up scuttles of coal from the cellar for the kitchen range. Perhaps her cynicism anent the institution of the family was not surprising. And yet it was only this Floyd who could awaken what latent capacities she had for tenderness. Snappy and suspicious of every one else, under the pressure of his desires her will was as dough. Even though it might be reluctantly

A CHILD OF DIVORCE

and against her judgment, she invariably gave in to Floyd. That he played upon this circumstance to his own advantage was patent to all but his mother.

The bride liked to dance and play cards, and whimpered because the "old war" had put a damper on these amusements. She felt outraged by the limitation on sugar. Along toward September, when, as if things were not already bad enough, influenza came spreading its seeds of plague and reaping a harvest of human lives, she fretted because the theaters were ordered closed. Jean marveled at a disposition so impervious to the suffering all around it. Not that the bride was hard. She was simply shallow. It was as if the sympathetic element, without which no woman is complete, had been omitted in the making of her. Yet there were others of similar caliber, older ones too, for even experience can not build character where there is nothing to build on. Jean's letters from her mother bore the same petty strain of personal complaint against the prevailing turmoil: in answer to Jean's missive telling her of Truman, she wrote:

"I'm glad if you're happy, Jean, and I hope everything is *all right*. So many of these soldiers are bad, but I guess you know how to take care of yourself, and I hope your life will be happier than my poor life has been. It's terrible, Jean, the way things have gone up,

"CHASTISEMENT OF OUR PEACE"

and your father is so stingy, I can hardly make ends meet at all. I know it must be the same with you, so I didn't want to ask you for anything, as you have yourself to take care of, so I sold my wedding-ring. There were things I needed so much. My last pair of silk stockings were all worn out, and you know I simply can't bear the feel of cotton, and Trixie just *had* to have a new collar—"

Almost without realizing it, Jean was falling into the habit of contrasting her own mother with Truman's. Surely it is time we had outgrown the fallacy that filial love, or even respect, can be demanded merely on the ground of a physical relation; that the bare animal fact of parenthood should raise a man or woman to a pedestal in the eyes of their offspring, *unless they discharge conscientiously the obligations of that connection.*

"Who plants the seed should help the shoot to grow." Jean was too honest to dupe herself into the belief that she loved the two people whose selfishness had wrecked the life their passions had produced. This is not to say that her growing indifference to them did not worry her. She wondered, sometimes, if she were devoid of natural feeling. Her responsiveness to Manson and all he represented, her love for Truman and his mother, proved that she was capable of deep affection, yet the thought of her parents stirred no tenderness in her heart; the rather it seemed to cause a contraction of that organ, a shrinking as from those who would have caused her unnecessary pain. This was something involuntary, utterly independent of her reason. Nor does it mean that she did not crave parental fondness. She hungered for it with all the intensity of one who has never known it. But those from whom she had a right to expect it had failed her. She knew it now. For a long time she had loved the women to whom fate and the courts had awarded her, loved her for what her own speechless longings had made her believe her to be, because she was her mother. Now, disillusioned by bitter trials unshared by maternal sympathy, temptations unrelieved by maternal understanding, loneliness through which no mother-hand had ever come to caress her, or mother-voice to console, through a perspective of time and distance she saw Mrs. Hasbrook without that glamour of idealism—a pilot who had released the wheel at the first twinge of fatigue, let her ship run on the rocks—and then complained because the rocks were desolate! Could such a woman have wisely coached her daughter over the course to a fruitful harbor?

Her father, too, when the first shock of her disappointment in him had worn to a dull, hidden sorrow, Jean could not but see as cowardly, else why had he not acknowledged

"CHASTISEMENT OF OUR PEACE"

her and faced like a man the result of his earlier actions? Why had he been ashamed of her, the child of his true marriage, willing that her birthright should be sacrificed to "protect" those children of legalized adultery? What made him fear the opinion of a world to whose conditions he had so carefully conformed? That in itself was inconsistent. She had talked it all over with Manson. Some pastors might have harped on the trite old theme, "but after all, you know, *they are your parents.*" Manson understood better than that. He may have been an idealist, but he was not a sentimentalist. Time enough, he thought, to preach filial duty, when *parental* duty had been performed. He advised Jean not to distress herself over her feeling, or lack of feeling, toward the authors of her being, only to keep her heart free from malice and let its affections go out to those who inspired them.

Hence it happened that in three months Mrs. Burnett had become more like a mother to her than her own had ever been. Notwithstanding this intimacy, however, Jean discerned a certain restraint in the older woman's manner more or less noticeable at all times. It was characterized by a kind of uncertain fear, even a hint of apology toward herself, which she could not understand. She had never been reticent with Mrs. Burnett. But she was all too soon to learn the reason, for one afternoon in early fall when she stopped, on her way home, at the cottage on Greenwood Avenue, she found Mrs. Burnett sitting up in an arm-chair with a face that at first glance frightened her. Jean had never seen a human face look so. It was tense and pale as a plaster relief, the eyes staring vacant and fixed, like the eyes of one in *rigor mortis*. Only a slight movement at the sound of her approach assured Jean that she was alive. Tongue-tied by some ill foreboding, she slipped a gentle arm around the old lady's shoulders. At the touch a tremor ran over Mrs. Burnett. She groped with one palsied hand for Jean's fingers, murmuring hoarsely, "It's you?—the girl my Truman loved—"

Loved! Why that past tense? Everything suddenly stopped in Jean, then pulsed frantically. The chiseled lips of Mrs. Burnett had bent in a half-smile more terrible than any paroxysm of weeping; she was speaking again, huskily, "It's all over, Jean—the lie I've lived —for *his* sake—there's no need of it any more—" She unclenched the other hand from a crumpled slip of yellow paper, holding it mutely out. Its brief message struck Jean's eyes and a fearful blow her heart:

"Truman Burnett died July 23, Commune of Hamel, Somme, France—"

"CHASTISEMENT OF OUR PEACE"

For an interval she stared like the other woman, numbly trying to absorb the truth, but at last she got up to pace back and forth with her hands pressed to her mouth against the rising screams, her whole young soul bursting in a reaction of anguished protest. Truman dead! Her Truman! It could not be—*it could not be!* There must be some mistake! But she looked again at that figure in the chair, now drooping abjectly, and felt there was no mistake. She went to it, an overwhelming realization of the mother's greater sacrifice for the time lessening her own agony. Summoning all her will power, she prepared some spirits of ammonia for them both, loosened Mrs. Burnett's clothing and persuaded her to lie down, then sat beside her, firmly holding her hand. Still stunned, the old lady had relaxed enough to seem more normal.

"Mother—it may be a mistake—another Burnett—" Jean bravely voiced the hope which her faith did not echo. Mrs. Burnett shook her head: "No, Jean, I guess not. He's gone—they've killed him—but it won't be long before I go to him—I feel it. It's hard for you, Jean—you with your life to live—it's harder for you than me. It's my price—the price—of my sin—I've paid it at last, Jean—I've given back what I hadn't any right to.

A CHILD OF DIVORCE

He was all I had—yes, *all*—I've been punished—"

"Don't!" the girl choked.

"Yes—let me tell you now—I want to—oh! if you only knew how I wanted to—but when Truman told me how he loved you—I couldn't do it—yet I felt as if I was cheating you—but now that's over—and I want to confess how I've lied to you—and the world about—the *Mrs.*, Jean—and this—" She held up a trembling left hand, spreading the fingers to display the gold band on the third one. "I had no right to it, Jean—I bought it myself—and I called myself 'Mrs.'—I did it for *his* sake, Jean—I knew how they'd treat him—*people*—if they knew the truth—it was the only lie I ever told him—I had no right to it—I had no right to him—I—I wasn't married—" Jean only pressed her hand, the hot tears now overflowing her eyes to dash down upon it, but Mrs. Burnett had no tears. "I guess you noticed," she went on in the same hopeless monotone, "how we never had much company. That was why—only Truman never knew it—but I loved—his father, Jean. He promised to marry me—and I tried to keep true. I hoped and prayed that some day—his heart would be touched and he'd come back—to us. Truman never knew his name. I was afraid to tell him, for he couldn't under-

"CHASTISEMENT OF OUR PEACE"

stand, poor boy! I didn't want to force his father. I was to blame, too, and the worst was done. The law couldn't change that—and if he came—I wanted it to be—because he wanted to—''

That night Jean stayed with her, though even their emotional exhaustion brought them little sleep. The next day Mrs. Burnett seemed unable to move and Jean urged her not to try. She obtained a short leave from the office to nurse her and, in a desperate effort to escape from her own misery, plunged into household and sick-room tasks. That was the only thing to do. Neighbors soon heard of the tragedy and came to offer help and condolence, though Jean could hardly bear this. Sunday's edition of the *Call* carried Truman's picture over a short and flattering biography, largely the composition of a reporter. It was in a photographic strip of deceased heroes, which brought home to Jean how many other women were at present suffering with her on this mount of her spiritual Calvary. For Mrs. Burnett medical aid became necessary, but, despite this and Jean's constant care, she never left her bed. The severe nervous shock had brought on a form of paralysis, rendering useless the tired old limbs. She did not rebel against it. Had she had the spirit left to rebel, she might have been cured, but she had sunk into an apathetic state so far as life was concerned. She had never fully come back to it, but was like one already half over the threshold of that other world whence all her treasure had gone. She neither desired to live, nor tried to die. She ate mechanically, as much as she could at each meal, but with ever-lessening appetite. She liked best to have Jean sit by her on the edge of the bed and talk of Truman. She was the only one it did not hurt Jean to discuss Truman with, for to his mother her heart was bare. Yet Jean moved through it all as through a nightmare from which she must awaken. Her grief, her anxiety, was still repressed, denied the outlet of indulgence while she bent her active thought to material duties. She was dully grasping the idea that she must lose Truman's mother also, though the full meaning of it did not quite penetrate her mind.

Two or three times, in her sweet, weakening voice, Mrs. Burnett had alluded to the future. She mentioned it again one day toward evening when a beautiful October sunset sent red-gold shafts into her room. She seemed brighter than usual, so much so that a new hope quickened in Jean's bosom. "Jean, come here," she said mysteriously; "I don't know why—but I have such a queer feeling—about Truman—as if he was near me—alive—as if it *might* be a mistake after all—" Jean

"CHASTISEMENT OF OUR PEACE"

smiled dolefully. The old lady's apparent improvement then was only due to a wandering mind, an illusion born of her torturing desire for the lost one's presence. Jean could not but humor her, wishing she might share the belief. She perched on the bed in her accustomed place and took the feeble hand, now little more than the skeleton of a hand, covered with skin like crumpled tissue-paper through which she could see every vein. But the old lady's strange excitement soon passed and she murmured, leaning back in pathetic resignation, "But no—no—that's foolish—I don't know what made me think it—here's the telegram—" She drew from under her pillow the oft-read yellow slip with its pitifully meager information. No further details had reached them since its arrival. Jean had written three times to Washington, and in answer to her last letter received word that the case had been noted and would be "looked up as soon as possible." She had even sent a pleading inquiry to the chief of the Graves Registration Service, "S. O. S., France," by whom the telegram was signed, and each day of silence increased her conviction that the worst was true and deepened her despair.

"And yet"—Mrs. Burnett looked up once more—"things like that—*have* happened, Jean in the Civil War—my mother knew—"

"It was different then," Jean inserted, "they hadn't the system they have now."

"No—that's right"—again her face clouded, the hand with the paper dropping limply—"but yet, Jean—you'll think it's queer—but I had this feeling yesterday too—just about this time. I didn't tell you because I knew it was foolish, but to-day—I couldn't help it—and, Jean, I wrote him a letter—something I wanted him to know—of course he'll never see it—but, somehow, it made me feel better just to write it—Jean—if anything should happen." Her breath drew heavily; she paused to recover it, then continued: "Jean, will you look in my bottom drawer and get me a package? It's back in the left-hand corner—under those shirtwaists—" Jean complied, her thoughts returning to yesterday, when the old lady had asked for stationery with which to write "some friends." She found a small package and brought it to the bed. It had been securely tied and sealed with wax, evidently long ago, for the paper and cord were faded and the wax was beginning to crumble at the edges. As Mrs. Burnett took it, her face twitched and she closed her eyes an instant against some obvious pain. She held it to her breast, resuming presently: "Jean—if anything should happen—if I—I feel, it Jean—I'm not

"CHASTISEMENT OF OUR PEACE"

much longer for this world—and in here is—everything about Truman. Jean, if it's a mistake and he—should come back—give it to him—but if he don't—in a year after the war's over—take it to—Jerome Bascomb—"

"Jerome Bascomb!" echoed Jean, startled.

"Yes. He's the lawyer—who knows about Truman's father—he knows everything—and this"—from among the covers she produced a thick letter addressed to Truman—"Jean, I know it's foolish—but there *might* be a chance—will you—leave it on the little table where he always looked for his mail? Leave it a year—and then burn it. The house—I've left it to him—and after that year—to you. Do what you want with it—I wish you would live here—but that would be too lonesome—and remind you of the past. The deed is in the dining-room—back of the clock—and my insurance policy—a thousand dollars, Jean—I made you beneficiary—you've been so good to me—and Truman loved you—and you'll need it—what's left—for taxes and things. Yes, Jean—I had everything fixed. Remember the day the notary came and I wrote the insurance company? I thought about everything—lying here like this—I couldn't help it. I never told Truman, Jean—it would only have worried him—but I hadn't been strong for a long time anyway—and I knew—the way the doctor looked—I'd never get well—and there was nothing left to live for—and so—'' She sank back, panting, her unwonted flush of strength puffed out by the effort of the long speech like the final sputter of a candle's flame. The sunset had faded and the gloaming come, gray as the wan old face upon the bed. Jean sat motionless, too numbed by the sense of disaster for thought, feeling or tears. She had not clearly absorbed the import of all Mrs. Burnett had said. That would come back to her later.

Some time after dark she stirred, arose and went out mechanically to light the lamps. There were no modern improvements in the cheap little house, except water. She finished quietly the work she had been doing when Mrs. Burnett called her, took a lonely turn on the porch in the fresh evening air, and prepared for bed. In her kimono she reentered the sick-room to place the night lamp on the dresser and see that all was well. Mrs. Burnett opened her eyes and smiled. Jean kissed her. "Good night, mother—are you all right? Is there anything you want?"

"Nothing, dear—I think I'll be better tomorrow—just tired—you must be too—try and sleep—good night, dear—" Her voice trailed into nothingness.

It may have been two o'clock in the morning when Jean awoke from a doze, sure she

"CHASTISEMENT OF OUR PEACE"

heard Mrs. Burnett calling her. She put on her slippers and tiptoed to the old lady's door, but the faint illumination of the night lamp showed her sound asleep.

"That's funny," thought Jean. Fearing to disturb her, she went back to bed, and, after tossing wearily for some time, relapsed into slumber only to hear the voice again. She drew herself up and listened intently. Nothing but silence, a silence so heavy it oppressed her. But sleep became impossible. Nervously she reapproached the sick chamber. Mrs. Burnett had not moved, but now some weird fascination pulled Jean closer to her. She lay so very still. Jean spoke impulsively, "Mother," then more loudly, though her own voice frightened her, *"Mother!"* No response. With a strange sensation of timidity, she touched the pale forehead and drew back, terror-stricken. It was cold with that clammy coldness which marks the clinch of death! For a moment the girl stood petrified, then, groping for her coat, she flung it around her as she stumbled blindly across the street.

The Millards were kindly people who had shown a willingness to assist their neighbors in every possible way. Next day when the sun was high, they told Jean how she had fainted in Mrs. Millard's arms after her inarticulate story; how the authorities, Dr. Manson and

A CHILD OF DIVORCE

the undertaker had been notified and necessary arrangements already started for the funeral on the morrow. Jean mentioned the insurance, for practical needs must be met, however much we suffer. They begged her to rest, but she could not bear to lie idle, and with several other women, who shed tears though she could not, she assisted in bathing and dressing for burial the poor remains of that shipwrecked little woman whose brave struggle the waves of destiny had overcome at last. Mrs. Orr was there, commiserating and helping with Mrs. Stevens, about whom just yesterday she had expressed an acid opinion because the latter had neglected to return a pat of borrowed butter; and Miss White and Miss Payne, who had recently quarreled to the extent of "not speaking" over the attentions of a gentleman whom they mutually admired! There is nothing like a fellow-being's misfortune to melt the bars of disputation and fuse into one the hearts of neighbors. The doctor concluded that Mrs. Burnett had simply "slept away," had probably been dead five hours when Jean discovered her. For years she had been drawing on her reserve strength, both physical and mental.

Jean went through the funeral like a sleep-walker, and it took a long time for her to be-

"CHASTISEMENT OF OUR PEACE"

come adjusted to her double loss, days even before she could find the relief of tears.

It was all a fearful blow to her faith, and, but for the spiritual support of Paul Manson, she might have lost that too. Indeed, the first time he called she refused to see him. With tremendous effort she had hardened her heart and gone back to work, through praying, she swore, to a God who seemed as deaf as any Chinese idol! She would expose herself to nothing that might weaken this resolve and cause a relapse into "childish superstitions." But with his second coming, nearly a week later, the memory of all his kindness flooded back upon her; she saw that to keep on avoiding him would be discourteous, not to say ungrateful, so she went down to the parlor, determined, however, to brook no empty platitudes from him, or any one.

"Good evening—I s'pose you've come to preach to me—" It slipped from her lips with a harshness of voice and expression that surprised him at first.

But no preaching ensued. Manson arose and approached her quietly. "Poor little girl," he said simply, "do you think I don't know what this means to you? Believe me, Jean, I know —I've been through it—" The tone, the look he gave her, that Good Shepherd look of a Sabbath long gone, played havoc with Jean's

A CHILD OF DIVORCE

decision. She succumbed at last to the pressure of tears, and, because Manson could never resist the cry of such distress, he yielded to the impulse to take her into his arms and let her weep there. Till she was calmer they stood thus, Jean clinging to him out of the poignancy of her need, he gently patting her back as a mother soothes a heartsick child. When finally she raised her face she saw the mist of sympathy in his eyes, but he smiled down at her through it. "Jean," he repeated, "I know what it is to lose—one's love—I've been through it—and Jesus knows—He's been through it too, Jean—He died for it—a love all unrequited. Do my arms feel strong to you, Jean? I'm only a man and there are everlasting arms. They want to hold you up, my child—don't turn away from them."

Little more was said and soon he left, left Jean forlorn indeed, but with the ice of bitterness melted and a glimmer of the old faith rekindled in her heart.

In the hall she met Mrs. Nicolson, who had admitted Manson and was herself just going out. She shot Jean a quizzical look, but, too preoccupied to notice it, the girl went on upstairs. Still quietly crying, as much from relief as from pain, she sat in the dark by the window, till sounds of hilarity from the next room jarred incongruously upon her mood. A

"CHASTISEMENT OF OUR PEACE"

card game was in progress, the players' excitement waxing along with it and their voices rising discordantly: "It's your lead, Grace." "I'll boost 'er up another notch." "Too strong for me, I'm out!" and then the shrill complaint of the bride, "Well, of all the mean hands I been getting!"

Mean hands? Was life like that? A game —a chance? Was there no thought behind the cards dealt out, no higher plan behind the game? No object other than to pass apportioned time and perhaps afford amusement to some relentless Deity? No, no, Jean could not believe that. Even in that dark hour, something deep within her resented such a philosophy, and then from the dim recesses of her mind words once lightly stored there chimed again with welcome reassurance:

> "Yet love will dream and faith will trust,
> Since He who knows our need is just,
> That somewhere, somehow meet we must."

CHAPTER XVI.

BABBLING TONGUES

"Behold, how great a matter a little fire kindleth."

THERE are heights of faith and sacrifice to which the human soul may rise in unique moments, but our garb of flesh with its fleshly needs is not adapted to long dwelling in that rarified atmosphere. If it were, we could never bear to return to earth, to descend again to the pettiness, the sordidness, the limited understandings of mundane existence. One's visible body is not one's self; it is only the armor and vehicle of that self whose native air is paradise. It is the shield of sense and clay, made of earth stuff to suit the earth demand and, when it has served its purpose, crumbling back to its source once more. And those visions of heaven's mountain crests, those glimpses that "pierce beyond the grave," are vouchsafed to encourage us; to remind us, lest we sink under material pressure, of the goal which lies beyond, the waiting prize whose glory no man yet hath seen. But between that future and the present what tedious valleys wind! What narrow, dark and lonely gorges whose ugly walls obstruct the view and hide the sun!

Jean came to such again. Across her path had fallen the brief, transcendent beam of love. She had basked in it for a moment; she had tasted the bitter-sweet of service for its sake and then of self-abnegation, but, as weeks dragged past, by contrast her way appeared darker, more hopeless than before. Even the faith she had felt revive that evening after Manson's call she found it hard to nurture. With the sudden loss of Truman the mainspring of her life had snapped and now there was no longer even the care of his mother to provide an incentive for living. She began to shrink from all new contacts except the most perfunctory, to lament a cruel providence and pity herself.

Daily she visited the little house, at first spending hours there of sorrowful reminiscence. Every room, every piece of furniture, bore some painful association. But she was healthy and gradually her young spirit sickened of this morbid indulgence. There was something eerie about it all, something uncanny about the white letter on the writing-table waiting, because of a dead woman's whim, for a dead hand to open it. She found herself glancing toward it first thing each time with a fearful and foolish sense of expectancy. Though it would have saved her room rent, she could not have borne to live there, and each day she shortened the visits until they became mere tours of inspection made more out of loyalty to her promise to Mrs. Burnett than from any personal inclination. There was still Red Cross work to be done and the trenches kept calling for more human meat! Also Paul Manson, who was writing some short war articles for "The Survey," enlisted her Saturday afternoon services in the typewriting of his manuscripts, at which task she was quicker and more accurate than Adele. This naturally took her often to the study. She welcomed the activity. Though she had lost the dynamic of hope, it kept her from unwholesome brooding, and her room at Nicolsons' meant little more to her than a place wherein to sleep. About five o'clock on one of her few Sundays in it, she was interrupted while reading over some finished copy for Manson by steps ascending the stairs. She had heard the Webbers and other occupants of the third floor go out earlier and knew she was alone there. With the panic which fear of discovery in small misdemeanors sometimes causes, she pulled three damp articles from an improvised clothesline, ripped down the cord and stuffed all quickly into a drawer of the antique dresser. She had broken the house rules by washing them in the bathroom. Just as she resumed her seat some one knocked.

"Come in," responded Jean. Mrs. Nicolson opened the door, revealing a lady behind her. "A friend to see you, Miss Laval," she announced; "I brought her up." Jean arose as the landlady receded and the stranger stepped in. Astonished, she recognized Mrs. S. Walter Walton. "How do you do?" the latter greeted formally; "I hope you don't mind my coming up like this. I thought we could talk better here." Loosening the coat of her handsome brown suit, she sank coolly into the odd-lot rocker, laying on her lap a newspaper she had been carrying. Jean transferred her own seat to the cot, wondering what on earth Mrs. Walton wanted to talk to her about. She looked so affluent one instinctively associated her with a mansion and all its accessories of flunkies and motor cars. She made the room seem smaller, meaner and, somehow, colder.

"It's an errand," she began, "that I wish wasn't necessary, Miss Laval. I can assure you that I do not relish it, but I come as a committee of one, at the request of the ladies of our church, and I hope you'll take it in the right spirit. It is for your own good too."

Jean's puzzled face asked her unvoiced question.

A CHILD OF DIVORCE

"It's about our pastor, Dr. Manson," Mrs. Walton continued smoothly; "I'm sorry I must speak so plainly, Miss Laval, but you have made it necessary. You realize, I suppose, that he is a single man, and—well, to be frank, he has been embarrassed by your conspicuous and unwelcome attentions—"

Jean was shocked dumb. She felt stifled, her cheeks burned as though they had been slapped.

"Of course we realize," the other pricked on delicately, "that you haven't had the motherly advice a girl needs, and that's one reason we have been patient and said nothing before this, but really, Miss Laval, it's getting so—well, you're *not* a child, and it seems as if the natural sense of modesty that most young women have ought to keep you from throwing yourself at a man who doesn't want you; but you've made such a dead set at him that it's plain to every one and certainly embarrassing to him. For your own good you ought to understand that there isn't the slightest hope of Dr. Manson's returning the feeling of a girl like you—least of all after what happened."

"W-why," choked Jean, hotly, "I—I—don't understand you! I never even *thought* of him—*that way!*"

Mrs. Walton gave a short, tolerant laugh. "Oh, nonsense, Miss Laval; we may as well be plain. You're really not smart enough to fool any one but yourself like that. You've been seen constantly running to Dr. Manson's study, seeking him out in public places, and I have it on good authority that the other night when he stopped here merely on a pastoral call, you deliberately threw yourself into his arms and tried to force his attentions by working on his sympathies. Now, Miss Laval, girls these days aren't so innocent as you pose to be—least of all a girl with *your* connections—"

"My *connections!*" gasped Jean.

"Certainly; do you think we are blind to those? Of course you couldn't help your environment, but such things always affect one's social standing, and that's one reason why you should be all the more careful—" Mrs. Walton's kid-gloved fingers had been slowly unfolding the paper on her knees and she now passed it over, pointing calmly to a marked column on the suburban page. It was the latest edition of the *News*. As if in letters of fire, the heading burned into Jean's brain:

"ABSCONDING BANK CASHIER
MUST GO TO SING-SING

"Verne Laval, of East Elair, N. J., Confessed to Misappropriating over $25,000.00—"

A CHILD OF DIVORCE

In savage detail the item proceeded to flaunt her father's downfall—how, harassed by his inability to meet the increasing cost of maintaining his family "in their proper station," he had been goaded into periodically closing his hands over some of the cash which daily passed through them in the New York bank where he had been trusted so long; how, when apprehended, he had tried to escape and been captured; how the Vernon Place house had been foreclosed on; how Mrs. Laval was seeking a job at her old profession and the children were in charge of the charity organization, awaiting admittance to an industrial home! Worse than this, and with utter irrelevance it seemed to the girl's crazed mind, it dragged out and rattled for the entertainment of all who might read, the bones of his past misalliances—how he had been divorced and remarried, and his former wife had remarried also; how said former wife had a child by her second husband and he, Laval, had two by his second wife and one by the first, "the latter now employed on the Draft Board of East Elair!" *Where had they learned it all?* Ask any reporter the way to his fountain of information.

Mrs. Walton had played her trump card. Jean was too crushed by this latest blow to defend herself against the accusations relative to her designs on Manson. Helpless, she sat staring down at the evil print, now beginning to swim. The wealthy widow's parting words came to her like an arrow shot from some distant ambush: "I've always thought it queer that a girl with parents living should prefer to live alone. It looks bad, Miss Laval. You should have stayed with your parents where your duty was. Of course we are all sorry for your troubles, but you must show your worthiness of sympathy by acting in a lady-like way. You'll have all you can do to live this down and can't afford to do different. I've warned you quietly in order to save you and all of us the embarrassment of bringing the case before the Board of Elders, as some of the ladies wanted to do, and I warn you once again, *you will let Paul Manson alone—or be requested to withdraw from the church.* I'm sure you wouldn't find much comfort in doing otherwise under those circumstances. But if this doesn't improve matters, we intend to have you examined by an alienist to determine whether you are mentally and morally responsible for your actions—" Everything to which Jean had ever pinned the slightest trust was crashing down around her. Truman dead, her father a *convict,* and Manson—Manson, toward whom even now her instinct turned for refuge—*false!*

A CHILD OF DIVORCE

Then, his professed interest was not sincere after all! Only pretended because of his office! And his real feelings he had not been honest enough to tell her himself, but turned the matter over to gossiping women! And for him to think that she—Jean felt as if something white and beautiful had been dragged through the mud; her friendship, her idealism all splashed and stained by low insinuations. She reeled over on the cot, sick in body, sick in soul. Mrs. Walton had gone. The dingy walls of the little room seemed to be drawing together around her—smothering her. Suddenly she flung out her hands against them. Air—*air!* She struggled up and hastened out into the gloaming.

On and on she tramped, till the cold November twilight deepened into colder night. She had no knowledge of direction, only a desperate urge to run from her pain and *breathe!* She wished she might leap over the distant horizon and fall down, down—into the fathomless space between the stars. But presently even the stars closed their cloudy eyelids and the penetrating dampness which threatens snow intensified her desolation. Returning consciousness found her almost at the foot of the Orange Mountains. Not that she had swooned; she had kept on walking, walking while her mind was virtually blank. It was her only means of anything like relief. She turned back to Nicolsons'. There was nowhere else to go. The season's first snow had begun to fall and the big, sailing flakes melted before her on the pavement, as if contact with its hard substance struck them dead, leaving only their blood. When still many blocks from home, she saw the warm light shining through the windows of the church, and with increasing volume there reached her, as she drew nearer, the strains of the final hymn—"Rescue the perishing—care for the dying!" Never in all her barren life had she so craved, so needed, the church's consolation as at that moment, but she passed by bitterly. She was not wanted there!

From sleep induced through bodily fatigue she was jarred awake in the early morning by sounds resembling the crack of doom. Screech whistles, horns, bells, crashings and rumblings of nameless colliding implements, combined in a racket which seemed to rock the earth. Some one was vigorously rattling her door.

"Who's there?" she cried, frightened; "what's the matter?"

"*Peace*, Jean!" shrieked Mrs. Webber. "Peace—*peace!* The war's over! Come on and celebrate!"

A CHILD OF DIVORCE

Peace! Could anything be further from it? This was the first thought which struck Jean with a rather humorous tinge; then the serious significance of the jubilee, and the backwash of her own late anguish was lost in the torrent of universal human joy. Her first impulse was to fall on her knees in gratitude, but at that instant the door surrendered to the three hundred pounds of female against it, and the moon-shaped face of Mrs. Webber, framed in hair-curlers, grinned excitedly at her. "Come on—don't bother dressin'—nobody's dressin'—anything'll do—everybody's out! Oh, glory —*peace!*"

The respectable city of East Elair could scarcely have been recognized. The way its sanest citizens all at once relinquished their sanity, ranted, panted, stampeded, swelled the general bedlam with hilarious screams and howls, was the most astounding thing. Surely the world had gone crazy and all the lunatic asylums been thrown open! Half-dressed strangers hugged and kissed each other, swung off together on grotesque dances, reckless of age or sex, or galloped along in wild "parades" by the fantastic light of bonfires flaring to meet the dawn. Mrs. Webber and the bride dragged Jean along between them in one of these, and, caught in the giddy madness of it all, she screeched out cheers with every-

BABBLING TONGUES

body else till her throat nearly burst, and yet aware the whole time of feeling like a fool.

Nobody worked that day. In a few more hours things settled back into at least a semblance of system and all over the land celebrations were in order, rejoicings as divers in their manifestations as the temperaments of those who participated in them. The thoughtful remembered the "Author of Liberty" and met in the churches to praise Him; the shallow danced and gorged on rich food and sweetmeats long denied; the base got drunker than usual, wallowed in vice and challenged with abandoned bravado their only deterrent, the law.

For Jean, as for all, the novelty wore away. Consciousness of self returned, bringing the question of what the armistice meant to her as an individual. *Nothing*—but loss of employment! Hourly she was stabbed by the happiness of those whose dear ones would now soon return from service. She tried to share in it, but it only accentuated her own loss, tore open afresh the wound that had scarcely begun to heal. Back to torture her came thoughts of her father's disgrace and her own strange position in the eyes of the church, according to Mrs. Walton.

The office could use her until December first on clean-up work. The chief clerk

A CHILD OF DIVORCE

warned her to "look around" and she began at once to answer advertisements. She had mailed Dr. Manson's manuscript and received no acknowledgment, but when, on the following Saturday, she did not report at the study, to her surprise he telephoned her. His voice was as kindly as ever. "There's something I'm anxious to get out, Jean. If you could spare the time, it would oblige me. What's that?" Jean had made an incoherent sound. With considerable effort at cold restraint, she answered: "I'm sorry, Dr. Manson—but—there are reasons why I can't come any more—I—I'm sorry—"

"Why, what's the matter, Jean? You don't sound like yourself. Is anything wrong?" There were tears in Jean's eyes and a chill at her heart. She thought: "How can he be such a hypocrite? I'm all right when it comes to extra work!" Out loud she managed another reply: "It's only what you probably know already, Dr. Manson. I guess you understand—Mrs. Walton was here—"

"Mrs. Walton? What has that to do with your work? Why, Jean, I don't know what you're driving at, really I don't. Come on over here and let's have an understanding, even if you can't stay, won't you?"

"All right!" Suddenly Jean decided that she *would* have an understanding—she would make *him* understand that she knew all about his insincerity! Jean was essentially honest. Nothing hurt or angered her more than misrepresentation, or what she felt to be such. Her blood throbbed painfully on the way to the church.

But just as her mood had softened under Manson's influence that night at Nicolsons', so it did once more when she faced him in the study. There was that about Manson's very person, his bigness, the gentle strength of him, which made all hasty flare-ups seem like wasted emotion and hypocrisy absurd. You felt that the latter in particular was something to which he never stooped. He did not *need* to. He placed a chair for Jean, saying quietly, "Now, my child, sit down and tell me all about it."

With a vague feeling of guilt, as though she had misjudged him, nonplused, stammering, half crying, Jean did so. She told him everything. She could not help it, for he drew it out of her. This was well, like ridding her heart of poison. Nothing could have been more genuine than Manson's amazement. His brown eyes opened wide, his jaw took a firmer line.

"Jean," he asked when she had finished, "do *you* think that I would discuss any of my parishioners with others like that?"

A CHILD OF DIVORCE

Jean's guilty feeling rose another notch. "No," she murmured, for now, in his presence, such a thing did seem impossible. She was ashamed of her willingness to believe it, yet naturally perplexed. "Then I wonder—what made Mrs. Walton—I wanted to tell you—if—if—I've embarrassed you—I'm sorry. I guess it's because I'm alone—with no one to tell things to except people who go and tell some one else—that I come to you so much. You always help me—but I never thought of people thinking—*that!* I never did—oh, you believe me, don't you?" It seemed just then that if only he believed her, nothing else would matter.

"Of course I do, Jean," he assured her, "and I'm sorry, too, my child, very sorry for your sake, that our friendship should have been so misconstrued. I've wanted, as your pastor, to give you all the help and encouragement I could, more than usual perhaps, because you've been denied so much of it from the quarter where it should have come from. It hurts, I can tell you, to think it has resulted in such embarrassment for you as this."

"But it wasn't anything—*you* did—" Jean faltered, "It was *me*—Mrs. Walton said —or the committee you chose—"

"I chose? That is entirely a misquotation," Manson asserted as kindly as possible.

BABBLING TONGUES

"Jean, I appreciate any exertion my people make on behalf of the good of my work, but if any such strange committee as this has been formed, it is entirely without my knowledge and its effort is misdirected. Jean," he continued bluntly, as always when his feelings were stirred, "since this has happened, I may as well tell you that over-zealous women can sometimes cause more annoyance than help to a man in my position. Their intentions—or attentions—may be of the best, but when they become concentrated upon my personal life, they are superfluous. I don't know why it is that so many people can not seem to recognize the distinction between a pastor's *work* and the man himself. This doesn't happen in other professions. A business man, or lawyer, even a doctor, can be married or single, and, so long as he gives good service, no one is concerned about his connubial or other intimate affairs, but a pastor—somehow people seem to look upon *all* of him as their common property, unwilling to grant him the reservations that even a coal-heaver is allowed to keep. It's really annoying and it hinders his best work, for you know, Jean, it's the cinder in the eye that hurts worse than the load on the back. Perhaps I'm saying too much," he softened it with a little smile, "but, though I'm a preacher, I'm human, and such things as this make me impatient. It would please me a great deal more and do more for the cause if they'd turn that energy into making new Christians. And, Jean, I don't want you to let this worry you. It's not worrying me. Don't you think"—his eyes twinkled with a return of his saving sense of humor—"I'm big enough to take care of myself? I don't need any nursemaids—*I'm not afraid of you!*" Jean smiled, too, and wiped the last of the mist from her eyes. What a dear, honest, wonderful friend he was! Her heart swelled with a speechless longing to *do* something for him, something in atonement for having ever doubted him.

"This about your father," he changed the subject, reversing to soberness: "It's too bad, Jean—another nail in the cross. God help you to bear up under it, my child, as you have under the rest. I heard about it early yesterday and—I meant to tell you to-day—I went over to see him at the Tombs—we had a long talk."

Jean's breath caught. "Is he there now?"

Manson shook his head. "No, Jean, he's gone—up State—this morning." Another of those sick waves swept over the girl. She gripped the chair arms. "And I never knew," she moaned; "I could have gone, too—poor *papa!*"

BABBLING TONGUES

Manson looked at her sadly for a moment, then went on: "They managed to keep it pretty well out of the New Jersey papers till the last minute. The sentence was in New York. He seemed glad to see me, Jean. He opened up his heart to me. I think it meant a lot to him to be able to do it to some one. He seemed to be thinking a great deal about you—begged me to look after you—"

"*You!*" she interrupted bitterly.

"Yes, Jean; having so long thrown that responsibility on others, he at last found himself where he could not do otherwise, and, Jean, I want to tell you this because, though it may hurt, I think you should know it. He was repentant. He said he could see now that his downfall was not alone the result of recent circumstances, but that it began with his separation from your mother—by that he meant the *loosening of his moral sense which always results from a broken oath.* He blames himself as much as your mother. He believes now that if he had refused to consider a divorce and stuck it out through the crisis, your mother would have seen the right sooner or later and the *discipline resulting from that determination* would have saved him from his slow decline ever since which has really led to his present end. I fear his second marriage was never what he expected it would be."

"And my mother is no happier than she was with him!" Jean exclaimed.

"Happier, Jean? There can be no true happiness founded on broken vows. It is impossible. Happiness, Jean, is elusive. Those who deliberately leave obligations to set out after it never catch up with it. There may be a moment when they think they have done so, but it's only a moment of gratified passion that burns itself to death—one bright flame, then ashes. But in the path of duty, in the way of service, where self is secondary, before we know it, we find it waiting for us. It may not be so thrilling and romantic that way, Jean, but it's a lot more durable and satisfying in the end."

"I believe it," Jean agreed humbly, "and that's the way I want to have it.'

"All right, I hope with all my heart you may, Jean." Manson stirred and smiled again. "Now, shall we work?"

They worked, Jean with a heart lightened immeasurably by the reassurance of this interest which meant so much to her, notwithstanding all that had gone before.

When, some time after five, she returned home, Mrs. Webber's door stood wide open, the light streaming out across the hall to touch her own threshold. At the sound of Jean's steps she struggled from the depths of

BABBLING TONGUES

a Morris chair to come and meet her, "The Autobiography of a Disembodied Soul" still open in her hand. Spiritualism was her latest fad.

"Oh, Miss Laval," she panted, winded by her resistance to the force of gravity, "you should of stayed home! There was a nice young man here to see you—brought a bunch of flowers, he did. I told him I'd take care of 'em for you and I put 'em in water in your pitcher. Thought you wouldn't mind if I went in your room for that. He was awful disappointed. He wrote a note. It's in front of your pitcher, and there's a letter for you—"

"Thank you," Jean acknowledged, and, full of wonder, hurried in to be greeted by the sweet, unusual incense of a dozen white and crimson carnations all embellished with ferns and asparagus greens. She paused, entranced, then breathed, "Oh, how lovely! who—was—he?" She seized the two letters, one typewritten, the second addressed in an unknown hand which augmented the mystery. Yet she read the typewritten one first, postponing the surprise, as girls will. It was from a chemical concern in Watsessing, a response to one of her applications for a stenographic position. They were interested because of her approximate residence and would like to have her call for an interview. The other she

A CHILD OF DIVORCE

turned over several times, speculating as to the identity of its writer, ere she finally tore it open. It was just a note, apparently scrawled under difficulties:

"DEAR MISS LAVAL:

"Am sure disappointed that you're not home. I'd like to see you again sometime, if you don't mind. I have heard about some of your troubles and would like to have you know how sorry I am about them. I guess you know I'm your friend whenever you want me for one.

"Since I got mustered out I have my old job back and am getting on fine. More pay and good prospects. I hope you're getting along all right. Won't you please call me up sometime? With best wishes,

"TOM DALY."

Jean sank on the cot with strangely mingled sensations. Her feelings toward Tom had always been neutral. He neither attracted nor especially repelled her. She was both touched by his thoughtfulness and faintly disappointed. Yet why the letter? What had she expected? She arose once more and reapproached the flowers to inhale greedily of their generous perfume.

CHAPTER XVII.

THE SOUL OF A WOMAN

ONE is sometimes led to wonder why the far-seeing Creator, in planning for the twentieth century, did not add to the animal kingdom a peculiar species of being to fit into boarding-houses and the routine underworkings of the modern business world—not a woman with the eternal croppings out of the heritage of Eve to encumber her "efficiency," but some sexless creature of supermentality whose heart would serve only the purpose of a blood-pump. Jean obtained the position with the Watsessing Chemical Corporation. It paid sixty dollars a month and was as good as anything available to her. When she had become accustomed to the factory's pungent odors and familiarized her brain and her typewriter with such simple terms as "cerium nitrate," "zirconium," "beryllium," "lanthanium ammonium," "neodymium," and so on, time dragged along uneventfully, days, weeks and months of confining, monotonous office work, conscientiously discharged, but internally loathed, because chemistry held not the slightest interest for her, and, while diplomacy required that she act as if it did, she could not pretend so to herself; weeks and months of lonely nights and exasperating mornings when she awaited her turn to wash in the "bathroom brigade" on the stairs, hating more each day this vulgar, communistic existence. It mattered not how early she arose, some one with shaving outfit or curling-iron always beat her to that popular resort, due to which, morning after morning, she raced for trains to catch them by a hair's-breadth, chewing as she ran the last hasty bite of a half-eaten breakfast, usually swallowing it as she dropped, breathless, into the red plush seat of a coach. Watsessing was the next station. Weeks and months of washing, on the sly, things she could not afford to send to the laundry; of mending old clothes over and over by gaslight, or raking the stores for the cheapest necessities; of choiceless menus repeating themselves as regularly as the seasons, only much oftener, which the boarders all criticized behind the landlady's back, and kept right on eating; of Mrs. Nicolson's resentment when overtime work made her late to meals, manifested through slopped-over, lukewarm tea and cold portions bumped grudgingly down in front of her; of curious, idle gossip about her own affairs and every-

THE SOUL OF A WOMAN

body else's with no genuine interest behind it, and no one really caring whether she ever returned or not! *Were these the much-lauded glories of economic independence?*

She might have moved, but where to? Who is in the boarding-house business for the altruistic purpose of making real homes within the means of working-girls? Some institutions claim to exist for this, but their waiting-lists are endless and even their boasted privileges are apt to be shadowed by prison-like rules and regulations. Of course all institutions must have rules and regulations—except, apparently, the institution of the family. That, in Jean's case at least, had not had enough of them to hold it together. But having access to the cottage on Greenwood Avenue, which in less than a year would become her own, offered a solution, when she finally thought of it, so far as laundry was concerned. On Saturday afternoons, too, when not otherwise employed, she could sew there, undisturbed, on Mrs. Burnett's old machine. Full of sad associations as the little house was, almost haunted though it seemed to her imagination, as time and activity dulled the edge of her sorrow, it became more bearable in daylight, when she kept busy. Habit at length accustomed her even to the presence of the letter which she never moved or touched, except to dust it reverently.

A CHILD OF DIVORCE

In about the same way as she had turned to the cottage for refuge from the prying eyes of Mrs. Nicolson, she had let herself drift into accepting the friendship of Tom Daly, who made himself a willing means of diversion. One neither wanted to spend all one's spare hours in a furnished room or over a washtub, nor yet to go about unescorted, and Tom was clean and honest. Perhaps it was not quite fair to him. Jean had threshed this out with herself once or twice and concluded that he enjoyed it—as much as she did. Was she not returning in equal measure all that she could ever accept from him—her companionship? Never could he reach the depths of her nature which Truman had so easily stirred. Even the occasional intrusive idea of comparing them thus she would reject at once as something sacrilegious.

Women of some marked genius, or highly specialized ability—women fortunate enough to have had the financial or disciplinary backing which has made them the recipients of, or enabled them to earn for themselves, a full college course along the lines of some profession—find it difficult enough to battle on alone toward the achievement of that rather abstract thing, a career; but what of girls like Jean? Girls with no special talent, unless it be for affection and home-making, and to whom the opportunity for both of these is so obviously denied?

Again the calendar was torn off at April. Came nature's resurrection with its message to all who would read of life for evermore. Life! A continual rotation between a malodorous chemical plant and a human hostelry —was that life? No longer was self-reliance a novelty to Jean. It was a cold, grim, painful necessity, and she discovered that, though one might earn the money to pay for all of one's bread, no such thing exists as absolute independence; for the physical is only one phase of living. There is an inner life which, despite the possession of goods, is contingent for happiness upon its relationships with others congenial to it. In Jean this inner life was like something trying to grow against rocks, crying out for space in which to expand, for understanding and kinship, too strong to die, yet not quite strong enough to overcome conditions, just alive enough indeed to suffer acutely from these cramped quarters. For suffer she did, although a "self-supporting member of society," and she was full of unrest. She could not analyze the reason, though she tried to. Surely there must be more to *life* than just keeping one's vital organs in function—but what? Her problem was to find that *more*. Often she felt that the fault lay in her surroundings. Environment, especially that of one's home, should be the expression of individuality, though material things are needed to crystallize it, and Jean felt that her own nature was being smothered, smothered by the influences—and cast-off furniture—of absolute strangers. She had summoned the courage to approach Mrs. Nicolson about new paper for her room, wanting it so much that she even offered to meet half the expense. The landlady, however, evinced no enthusiasm. She grunted: "Huh? new paper when things are so high you can't hardly see 'em? Why, I was just thinkin' that if things keep goin' up the way they are, I'd have to raise the board anyway. I'm losin' money now. What's the matter with what's up there? You ought to be glad you got a room as good as that at the price *these days*. No, I can't afford that, and, if I could, I'd have to do the whole house, not one room. If you want to pay for it yourself, though, I'll give you permission to do it."

This was, of course, out of the question. For Jean to pay half would have meant sufficient sacrifice. She did buy the cretonne curtains and enough of the same goods to make two pillow covers, but, alas! these only served to betray more flagrantly the blemished wallpaper! This discouraged her. It seemed to

THE SOUL OF A WOMAN

her that even the ants in the earth had more chance for self-expression. . Their abodes were *ants'* abodes. No circumstance forced upon them ancient dressers, kitchen tables and other such outrageous combinations utterly foreign to their taste. Was not a *woman* entitled to the rights of an ant? She thought of the Gypsies—poor nomads! Were they poorer than herself? They lived the life they chose in the way they chose. They would have scoffed at meddlers' efforts to "improve" their lot, and they could afford to! No, it was only the ultra-civilized wage-earner who existed with less freedom of choice than the Gypsy—or even the ant.

Last Saturday night she had gone to a dance with Tom, after three refusals, and found she liked it. She had never taken any lessons, but the steps were easy and Tom knew them well. He was a good leader—and a good "sport." He introduced her to some gay young people who seemed never to have had a trouble in their lives. The colored lights, the "snappy" music, the exotic flowers; the beautiful, if daring, dresses; the punch that tingled down her throat and warmed her heart; the flattering attention in public of Tom and several other young men—all excited her, shot her again with the reckless feeling of that night when she and Dixie paraded

A CHILD OF DIVORCE

Washington Street in Hoboken, joked and giggled conspicuously, flirted with the clerk at the soda fountain. *To be young!* That was what she wanted! She had never been young. To throw all her problems to the winds and leave the sober-minded Jean back in her room, if she pleased to stay there, with the bedstead for company! She knew that through each dance Tom held her a little closer; that with the contact his blood pressure heightened and his breath drew hotter and shorter, and, strangely, none of it was repulsive to her. She knew he had brought her home very late, or rather quite early in the morning, but it was not until the cool, gray dawn awoke her at the habitual hour that the thought of their parting returned to her with shame. He had crushed her in his arms and she had yielded. He had begged her for a kiss and she had given it—she who had told Mary Dugan her kisses were not for sale! Had not that one been sold—for a "good time"? What else? Why had she done it? Not for love. She did not love Tom. Why had she not remembered Truman, whose specter seemed then to stand accusingly beside her bed? and Manson—the ideals he had given her? *Was she degenerating?*

Next time Tom called she was rather distant, and he did not stay as long as usual.

People were beginning to talk, seeing them together so much. Tom was really a nice young man. Nothing brilliant about him, not much vision, nothing at all of the dreamer, just steady and practical, the sort who would never startle the world by either sinking or rising, but always be able to support a family in comfort, under normal conditions. He was pleasant and well-mannered, without a single conviction strong enough to excite himself over or create enemies. Everybody liked him, especially old ladies. He worked as an accountant with a cream-separator company and often boasted to Jean of his "great prospects," though in truth he was likely to remain just a good accountant for the rest of his days. He had a nest-egg, though, which his father had begun for him in infancy, and the existence of which he impressed upon Jean by incidental, but frequent, references to it. Jean supposed she should have been glad to hear him praised, but, oddly enough, it irritated her to hear him discussed at all. It insinuated something that he, and every one, seemed to be taking too much for granted.

Notwithstanding her diffidence of Wednesday night, as if, indeed, he had forgotten it, the following Sunday he came as usual, with the usual box of chocolates, in the usual "flivver" he was buying on payments, and suggested a spin to Pinewood. "There's a new development there, Jean, I'm interested in—some nifty bungalows. Wouldn't you like to see 'em?"

The alchemy of a beautiful day had mollified Jean toward both him and the world. She would as soon have spent the afternoon looking at brand-new bungalows as in any other way. She loved to day-dream of how she would fix them up. It seemed as though that was the nearest she would ever come to doing it. As she was getting ready, some faint intuition tried to warn her against such a trip with Tom, but she ignored it. She was growing sick of the demands of a conscience which could supply nothing in place of the things it was always denying. Why not with Tom as well as with any friend, or alone?

Pinewood was less than an hour away, a fast-growing, typical commuters' town. They parked the car in a garage and started off for a stroll through the newly cut streets, bordered with fresh green sward and baby maple-trees. Bungalows in various stages of erection faced them from many of the lots.

"Aren't they nifty?" Tom enthused.

"Yes," Jean agreed, "I like them because they're not all the same. I'd hate to live—" She caught herself up so quickly that Tom turned toward her with an expression that

THE SOUL OF A WOMAN

struck them both into self-conscious silence. Nervously Jean tried to break it by diverting his attention to a neat corner house, finished all but for the painting, and made matters worse, which she realized the instant the words were out.

"Yes," echoed Tom, "I'll say it's a peach. Wonder how much. Come on, let's look inside. They've left the door open." Jean saw that to retract now would imply some reason for further embarrassment. She must go through with it—impersonally—and never do this again. But—

Springtime, in a little, almost finished house; birds outside happily intent on nesting, balmy air wafting their songs through the open windows, woven with the perfume of new leaves and grasses; within, the fresh, clean scent of sweet, new wood, the sun-kissed purity of walls unmarred; an eager young man, a repressed young woman, with the time-old urge of life pounding at their veins, suggestions of homing all around them. The call of sex; if not for Jean, at least, the call of love.

Tom glanced up suddenly from a minute inspection of one of the radiators. His cheeks showed an unwonted color, even for one who had been stooping. He spoke in a queer, thick tone, "Jean—how do you like it?" All at once Jean's heart beat wildly, not from joy, but fright. It rendered her dumb, and a sense of shame stung her for having encouraged Tom. She might have known! In a flash she knew that she really *had* known and deliberately ignored the true situation. She could not meet Tom's eyes. He mistook her manner for acquiescence. In another moment she was fighting against his arms.

"But—why—" he panted, "aren't we going—to get married?"

"Married!" Jean's voice came back in a gasp, "no—no!" It was Tom's turn to be dumbfounded. In sheer shock his arms relaxed. For an interval they stared at each other, breathing hard. Then Jean began to cry: "Oh, Tom—I'm sorry—I—I've been selfish—I've let you care when—"

Tom continued staring. He was pale now. His lips tightened, his cheeks quivered. "When what?" he demanded gruffly.

"When—I didn't—"

"What? *You!* Is *that* the kind of a girl you are?" Pain, incredulity, passion, rang in the words. They stabbed Jean like a sword. She winced visibly, bowing her face in her hands.

"*You!*" derided Tom in the same heart-cutting voice, "when you were always talking about—the sacredness of love—and all that! God! Haven't you taken everything—as if—

THE SOUL OF A WOMAN

didn't you say your kisses were—only for the right man? and the other night—didn't you lean in my arms and kiss me? What d'you s'pose I thought you meant by that? If it had been any other girl—but *you*—why, I thought that night we were good as engaged!"

Jean had no words with which to excuse or justify her guilt. Deep in her heart she knew that had another girl acted in her place as she had acted, she would have despised her. It was true that Tom had never proposed marriage, but an actual proposal is not always necessary to indicate the trend of a man's feelings. Any woman with her normal share of discernment can soon sense the difference between a friendly interest and that of a suitor. Jean had simply refused to acknowledge it, because, in her loneliness, she wanted the attentions she was not able to pay for.

"Catch me trusting any of you women again—you're all alike—all you want of a fellow is his jack—and a good time!" Tom was accusing stridently.

"No, no!" Jean protested. "Don't, Tom; that's not true!"

"Not true?" he sneered. "*You're* a great one to say that, ain't you? And maybe now you think I'll fall for your sob stuff. Nothing doing! I've been too blamed soft already—but I'm wise now!" His crushed hopes, his wounded pride masked beneath this burst of righteous indignation, he strode to the door. There, however, he remembered to be civil. "Come on, we mi's well get outa here—I'll take you home."

It was a most uncomfortable ride. For sometime no further words were exchanged. Jean was diking back her tears while Tom gave grim-visaged attention to piloting the car. But when they were nearly home, Jean ventured penitently: "Please, Tom—*don't* judge other girls by me. I—I'm only a weak thing, Tom—I'm not good enough to be—your wife—"

Tom slowed down and looked at her queerly. "What d'you mean, *good enough?*" he demanded.

"Why, the way I let you come—and do things for me—when I wasn't in love with you—"

"Oh!" and Jean thought he seemed relieved.

"Tom—you wouldn't want to marry a girl —who wasn't in love with you?"

Tom's eyes were again on the road, but his face appeared less taut. Perhaps the air was cooling him off. "I don't know but I'd take a chance—if *I* loved *her*—I might make her love me," he answered with the supreme egotism of the male.

"You're good, Tom—you're awfully good—and—and I wish I *did* love you! But, Tom, there's nobody else—and I don't seem to know my own mind somehow—I might change it yet—I don't know—" Again he looked at her, and now the genuine distress in her tone, the pathos of her face, awoke his chivalry, completely softened him.

"Say, Jean, I begin to get you. You weren't in love with me, but you were lonesome and I kept sticking around. You liked me, though, didn't you, to go with me? Don't you think if—we kept on going together, you'd learn to—care?"

"I don't know, Tom—I don't know!" Which was true. Jean knew what her feelings had been in the past, but, with fate so treacherous, how could she vouch for the future, even of her own variable emotions? "I'd like to—stop going with you for awhile, Tom—and, maybe then, I can tell—"

"All right. But, Jean dear, if you change your mind, let me know, won't you? Call me up. I'll come right off the bat. I'll break all the speed laws!" Jean smiled wistfully. She had seen his free hand move toward hers impulsively, then draw back. "I guess we're quits," he concluded; "I balled you out like a brute back there, didn't I? Excuse me—and we'll forget about—all the rest. I'll let you

A CHILD OF DIVORCE

alone—if you say so—for awhile—only, if there's any way I can help you, I'd like to know about it." At that minute Jean could have married him out of gratitude.

But, alone once more in her room, she knew that Tom's apparent resignation was no resignation at all; that his very cheerfulness was born of his young, self-confident love which, though it might be denied for a time, had no serious expectation of losing its object.

"For awhile—" His words echoed back to her. What then? *What after the while?* Nicolsons'—the chemical plant! Year in and year out. Or if not Nicolsons' and the chemical plant, some other boarding-house; some other office where the less of a *person* she was, the more perfect machine she made of herself, the better she would be appreciated! A stenographer all her life! A human dictagraph to be used at the "boss's" convenience regardless of any feeling she might have, or plans she may have made; to be *borrowed* at any time by one department from another, even as a typewriter or adding-machine is borrowed! Ah! she had seen them—old stenographers. Weary, washed-out, wistful, if you took the trouble to notice it. Perhaps they had waited for "love" to come. What had they gained? Oh, yes, the boss's confidence. That was an honor no doubt—until the young

ones came. Then, one day, a sleek new boss would call in the old stenographer for a private interview:

"Miss Blank, you know these are busy times, and, in order to keep up with them, we must be constantly changing our methods. Yes—ahem!—efficiency, you know—it's very important. Miss Blank, we appreciate your long and faithful service—but—I'm sorry to say—ahem!—you don't quite seem to grasp the latest methods." And the old stenographer, a little more weary, a little more washed out, too utterly crushed to be wistful, would stumble away from the place where she had won the old boss's confidence—and, if it were an exceptional firm, a little bonus—and hunt another job, only to find that everywhere she was hopelessly inefficient! Was *that* worth a woman's life?

All afternoon, in the back of her mind, had persisted the impression of the bungalow. It was as prominent, if not more so, than Tom. She did not try to separate Tom from the bungalow. A slow, subtle temptation was gnawing its way into her consciousness, so slow, so subtle, she did not realize it till it broke out suddenly in the question, *"Why not?"*

Why not? What *was* love anyhow? Jean spread out her hands as if to ward off some

A CHILD OF DIVORCE

threatening foe and nervously paced the length of the stuffy room. By the window she caught a glimpse of the church, and with that there somehow came back to her, startlingly clear out of what now seemed long ago, her own words to Manson, "If I ever love any one, I want to be true—whatever comes—I want to be a woman!" But—emptiness, memories, dreams—could a woman's nature thrive always on these? Can the body live on thoughts of food consumed a year ago, or the anticipation of some feast to come? Then other words suggested themselves, terrific words which she had later, and with reason, pondered much. She sat down at the wobbly table, picked up a pencil, opened a tablet and, as though to force her soul to face them, wrote unsparingly, *"For better—for worse—for richer—for poorer—till death do us part!"* She read them over and over, till, moved by some strange whim, she drew a perpendicular line and began to write on the other side. It looked like a balance-sheet: *"For better—not worse—for richer—not poorer—till death (of our love) do us part!"*

She held the sheet up with a short, half-hysterical laugh. "The new marriage service—the modern ritual! Why don't they have it? Why didn't my parents have it? It's better than *lying*, anyhow—lying to God! And it's

THE SOUL OF A WOMAN

so easy for that love to die. It's so easy to get free. All they have to say is, 'We are incompatible' and 'A marriage that isn't spiritual isn't really a marriage.' It's enough of a marriage to create somebody else, though—and it's funny how some people never think about it being *spiritual* till they want a divorce! Why don't the spirituality they discover all at once help them to make the best of things the way they promised? But if I marry Tom, my love'll never die—because there isn't any!''

What love is we can not tell; yet we always know *when it is not*. Jean did not love Tom. She knew it; furthermore, she felt that she never would. He lacked those sympathetic qualities, that fineness of nature which alone could call out complete response from her own. But—did any woman ever realize her full expectations in any man? Wasn't marriage with most of them based, after all, on a compromise between a partial affection or none? And if such disillusionment must be every woman's portion, wasn't it just as well to go into it open-eyed as to be awakened afterwards? She did not love him; she knew it—because there had been Truman—but he loved her, as deeply as he was capable of loving any one, and oh! it was so good to be wanted. She had never been really *wanted*. Besides, in a way—she

A CHILD OF DIVORCE

owed it to him. She did not love him, yet thus for awhile she abandoned herself to the contemplation of becoming his wife. If she refused—the swift, relentless years would pass. Time is not kind to the woman alone. She could picture herself at the far end of the trail—an old stenographer, weary, wistful, barren, all that her loveless work had yielded about sufficient for the entrance fee into some home for the aged, till she might change even that begrudged shelter for the narrower one of the grave.

Jean shivered and covered her eyes to try and hide that vision. If she accepted—she would become one of the thousands of mediocre wives whose lives are consumed away in humdrum household tasks—but, ah! the bungalow, her own home, and—children, her own children, growing up around her. Oddly, through all this introspection and effort to foresee the future, she never went far enough to allow for possible misfortunes which she might have to share with Tom. In fact, Tom was a minor figure in the dim background of what he could give her. He simply stood as one who held the key to a refuge from unbearable loneliness, one who could help her from drab existence to something more like complete living, though, once she had married him, she felt even then that her strong sense of loyalty would keep her faithful to the vows—though they became as chains. But why that suggestion of chains? Jean tried to suppress the rising fear, the fear that is woman's best warning.

CHAPTER XVIII.

THE WAGES OF SIN

"For whatsoever a man shall sow, that must he also reap."

THROUGHOUT the following week that haunting fear in Jean's heart threatened to dissolve the image of the bungalow—and children, never quite succeeding. This contest between her impulse to grasp at least the husk of a woman's heritage and her instinct against a loveless marriage, left little energy for her work. She was cross, though she dared not show it, for feelings in business "don't go," nor was there any one at home in whom she could confide. Consequently these pent-up emotions poisoned her thought-stream like stagnant waters, soured and discolored her whole view of life. Everything seemed made and done especially to upset her. No one considered her. Her boss was more inhuman than ever, her work more of a burden and the way she had to live an outrage. How long must it last? *Forever?* How many more nights must she wake up in the blackness with that sudden, fearful, nauseating sense of not belonging anywhere or to any one, of being adrift—*alone?*

Tom kept his promise to stay away. He did not even telephone. Habit and his close association with the things in her mind made her miss him. Others missed him also, though no one commented upon it until Saturday at lunchtime. Jean had to work till almost one o'clock, which made her late. She was just starting to eat when Mrs. Webber came puffing in, abject with apologies: "Oh, Mrs. Nicolson, I'm sorry I'm late. I really don't deserve anything. No, don't take any trouble, give me anything you've got—just a little. I'm sorry—I couldn't help it. Jack had to go to New York on business—awful important— and I had to see him off. Oh, don't bother— never mind—I can wait'll dinner-time. I don't deserve anything—" By this time ensconced in her chair at the same table with Jean, she essayed faintly to rise again, sweet resignation written on her face. This was a common performance of Mrs. Webber's. Every one, including the landlady, knew better than to take it seriously, and she always ended by eating everything in sight. The timely reappearance of Mrs. Nicolson with a thick plate of lukewarm stew caused her, as usual, to succumb to the wiles of appetite, smiling

A CHILD OF DIVORCE

blandly on the world in general and Jean in particular.

"It's such a nice day, I s'pose you'll be going riding again with that nice young man of yours," she observed as the last boarder left the room. Jean was finding it hard to be pleasant these days. It must be confessed that fear of losing her job and her room had as much to do with her self-control as any noble spirit. She frowned as she margarined her bread. "No, I'm not going out—with him."

Mrs. Webber's eyebrows went up. "You're not, really? Say, dearie, what's the matter?" confidentially; "he didn't come Wednesday either, did he? You haven't fallen out with him, have you?" Just then Mrs. Nicolson entered again and, hot from the atmosphere of the kitchen, leaned over the back of a chair, inclined to join in the talk. "He took you to see some bungalows, didn't he?" she asked with her customary officiousness. Jean looked up, surprised.

"Oh, he told me," the landlady explained abruptly. "How'd you like 'em? When's it comin' off?" Mrs. Webber, in her interest, nearly forgot to eat; she leaned forward so that the yellow jabot she was wearing (she changed the color each day for luck) dragged its ends in the stew.

"He told you about it?" repeated Jean, beginning to burn inside. Mrs. Nicolson nodded, contrastingly cool. "You're lucky to have a fellow that can afford a bungalow *these* days."

"Isn't that sweet?" dripped from Mrs. Webber. Gravy was also dripping from her, though she did not know it, being unable to see below her bunchy bosom. "Come on, darling, tell us about it—we aren't so lucky, you know." In Jean's present state of mind there was something accusing about their emphasis on the bungalow. Were all women mercenary —and she along with them? For a moment she was too choked to reply, and, to hide this, went on with a pretense of eating. Mrs. Webber winked at the landlady. "The foxy little thing, she's got somethin' up her sleeve, I bet— come on, dearie, we'll never tell a living soul."

"There's nothing to tell," Jean mumbled at random; "if you think I'm engaged to him, you're mistaken. I'm not."

"What?" popped from Mrs. Nicolson, "you ain't engaged and you go round with him lookin' at bungalows and all like that? Did you turn him down, then?"

"Yes—I did—"

"For land's sake—*why?*"

"That nice young man, Miss Laval!" chided Mrs. Webber.

"Because—I—didn't love him—"

A CHILD OF DIVORCE

"*Love!*" scoffed the landlady. "Rats! There's no such thing. If you got any sense, you better marry a man that can support you, and be glad of the chance. Love don't pay no bills. He's got a bank account and a steady income and he can buy a house. That's more'n a lot of fellows can do *these* days—and better'n tyin' yourself up to a poor-as-Job doctor that ain't out of college yet and don't know whether he'll make good or—"

"*Please!*" broke out Jean. This was too much. She pushed back her chair and arose to leave the room. But Mrs. Webber caught her hand, endeavoring to smooth things. "Oh, come now, darling, we didn't mean to offend you, honest. Don't you know you might love him and not know it—like I did with Jack? Jack was just eating his heart out—he'd of given his two eyes to have me—and I thought I didn't care. But there's a way you can tell, dearie, that's always sure. It's the way I found out with Jack—*just imagine him dead!*"

By the grace of a wise Providence, we human beings are so created that sometimes in our most poignant moments we can be struck by the ridiculous and it saves us from what might otherwise prove fatally crushing. To picture Jack dead required no very strong imagination. Jean laughed nervously and the laugh somewhat relieved her, though it rather chagrined Mrs. Webber. The landlady picked up a trayful of dishes and went disgustedly back to the kitchen.

"I—I—can't imagine Tom dead, that's all," Jean resorted to this explanation of her unexpected mirth, whereupon Mrs. Webber smiled also, and squeezed familiarly the hand she held. "That's right, he's a healthy-lookin' fellow, isn't he, dearie? Very much alive, eh? I guess *you* know. Well, then, whyn't you try asking yourself—*would you die for him?*" Again Jean's restless laugh. "I know I wouldn't, anyway. I'm not marrying to die —but *live!*"

"Oh, yes, of course, darling, I know. Then, you're marrying, though, ain't you?"

"Oh, I don't know—perhaps. He's waiting for me to decide." Jean was prompted in this answer by that universal feminine pride which likes the world to know that *some* man is praying for its possessor's favor.

"Well, dear," counseled Mrs. Webber, "you take my advice and marry him. He's a nice young man—well fixed—you could do a lot worse. I can tell; I'm a good judge of men. Maybe you think you're not in love with him now, but it'll be just like Jack was to me —a blessing in disguise."

Jean had been gradually working her hand free, and finally managed to escape. On her

A CHILD OF DIVORCE

way upstairs she almost bumped into the bride coming down. The bride was going out, and she looked like a wax model in a beauty parlor. The hair-bleach, the rouge, the lipstick and the eyebrow-pencil—all found in her an advertising medium.

"Why wasn't I made like that?" Jean wondered irritably as she shut her door, "then these things would never worry me!"

She had some mending to do, but that could not bridle her thoughts. Unhappy as she was, the worldly philosophy of the two older women had fallen on fertile soil. Vaguely she felt that there must be some way out of her problem. Manson had said that the right way held happiness. She knew that she could not be as happy with Tom as she could have been with Truman, but alone she was even less happy. Yet she was following the path of duty in so far as she could see it. And while in her tortured mind she still threshed about for a solution, some one rapped at the door.

It was Mrs. Nicolson. She pushed in and sat down on a corner of the bed, looking a bit more grim than ordinarily. "Miss Laval," she went abruptly to the point, "I just ran up to tell you—I'm sorry, but by the first of the month I'll have to have this room."

Jean's breath drew heavily. "W-why?" was all she could stammer.

"Well, you know when you come here you told me you didn't have no men friends. But you've had 'em right along, first that doctor and then this Mr. Daly that you say you ain't goin' to marry. I don't see why a girl should run around lookin' at houses with a man if she ain't goin' to marry him. It looks kind of bad—it makes my house look bad. Besides, there's the bother of it. You know I told you when you come, and I think I been pretty patient, but so long as I thought you was engaged and would be movin' to get married soon, I made up my mind not to say nothin' about it. But if you ain't goin' to get married and are figgerin' on staying here, I thought I better tell you. You ain't seemed satisfied lately, anyhow."

All this soaked slowly into Jean, into a spirit already too harassed to resist. And anyway, resistance would have availed her nothing. Her fingers went on sewing and she said simply, "All right, Mrs. Nicolson; I'll be out by the first." The landlady's face showed a slight surprise. She had evidently anticipated some protest. She opened her mouth to speak again, shut it, stood up, hesitated, and went out.

Alone once more, Jean flung her sewing aside. So she must hunt another hostelry—as if things were not bad enough! She had not

A CHILD OF DIVORCE

protested to Mrs. Nicolson, but fiercely now there blew up within her a tempest of rebellion toward life. She swept the room with a look of bitter irony. Her home! The only spot in all the spacious world that she might call so, though it offered few enough of the privileges of home. And she was not wanted even here! What was the matter with her? What was the matter with everything? Now, where would she go? *Tom!* Her hands clenched. Yet why not Tom? He wanted her. He was the only human being on earth who did want her. Then, who was she to reject him for the sake of a whim? What did she expect? What chance had a girl in her position to meet any better men than Tom? Love? What had it ever brought her but grief—and dissatisfaction with the one chance she had? What did it matter anyway—about her feelings? Tom had feelings too—and other things more substantial. He had more to give than she—yet he wanted her. There was her work, then—to make a home for the man who needed her and earn one for herself. Why, it was as plain as thrusting the key into a lock! She would do it—now—to-day ere her pestering conscience began again to weaken her resolve—yes, she would marry Tom!

Like one propelled by some external power rather than inward volition, Jean descended the stairs to the telephone. She had begun to tremble, and her trembling increased as she lifted the receiver: "—don't say! You're sure it was Adele Manson?" "Positive. I was coming out of Honslow's. They live on the same floor, you know, across the hall. I'd been visiting—and he was just letting her in." "Bascomb—the lawyer?—in his bachelor apartment?" "Yes, she looked kind of scared, too, when she saw me, but I went on and I'm sure she went in. She's probably there yet—" "Well, what do you know about that? Don't her uncle know where she is?" "I should *hope* not. He's probably out of town. He'd better look after her, though." "Well, isn't that awful! Some one ought to tell him." "Yes, but who wants to do that? It's—" Suddenly Jean realized the breach of etiquette she was committing by "listening in" on the busy party line. So struck had she been by the unexpected sound of Adele's name that she absorbed mechanically what came after without at once getting the full import of this alarming scrap of gossip. But it came to her swiftly, with a force which chased all former matters, even her late agitation, from her mind. She clicked the receiver into place and hurried back to her room, unable to think of anything now but the jeopardized happiness of Dr. Manson. What could this mean? And what should she do? She had craved, prayed indeed, for an opportunity to serve, in some special way, her benefactor. Was this her answer? Hardly aware of doing it, she slipped on her wraps and left the house. She happened to know Bascomb's address. She had looked it up after Mrs. Burnett's instructions concerning the package. But what mad thing was she bent on? What did she expect to accomplish by going *there?* Yet, though reason tried to assert itself, her steps never lagged. If her plan was not quite clear, her object was.

Just as she reached the Orchard Street Station, the gates of the crossing lowered and the train from New York thundered in. She waited impatiently while it stood, panting, to discharge the usual Saturday load of passengers.

'Why, hello, Jean! Are you getting some fresh air?" Startled, she turned toward the voice and saw Dr. Manson. He had alighted from the forward coach, not twenty feet away. Confusion overwhelmed her, and, because Jean had the kind of a countenance which registers every emotion, he noticed it. Instead of passing on, he stopped to inquire if anything was wrong. And then in some way, she never knew just how, except that there seemed nothing else to do, Jean told him what she had heard and of her purpose. Manson's face blanched and there gleamed in his eyes the sudden dangerous light which had frightened Mrs. Kingston on a previous occasion. His tone, however, was calm as he said: "I'll go with you, Jean. Come, let's take a taxi."

Bascomb maintained living quarters on the second floor of a new apartment house not far from his office. Other tenants, passing in and out, had left the street door unlatched, so that Jean and Manson were able to go directly to the lawyer's rooms. The pastor gave the bell a sharp, peremptory ring. In a moment the door was opened slightly by Bascomb's valet, a Swiss boy in his late teens. He informed them that his master was "varry beesy." Manson, however, entered boldly. He was still calm, but with that calmness which forebodes the brewing storm, and the valet shrank like a blade of grass beneath the wind. Jean followed, and thus they came upon Adele lounging with Bascomb before an open fire, while neglected "briefs" lay near them on the table. Her consternation paralyzed her; even the lawyer's ever-ready tongue was stricken dumb at first. Manson approached his niece with an outreaching hand. "Adele," he said quietly, "come home." She started to obey, when Bascomb intervened. "May I ask, sir, by what right you intrude like this upon my privacy?"

Manson turned on him angrily. "Let's not waste any words," he exclaimed; "the intruding has never been on my side. I may well ask by what right, sir, *you* have intruded into *my* home and enticed my ward into this compromising position!"

"Your ward, I have the pleasure of announcing, is my promised wife!"

"Your wife!"—it was Jean's voice, shrilly impulsive—"how can she be your wife when you already have one?" For the first time Bascomb noticed her. He gave no sign of recognition, only of mild surprise. Adele, however, was visibly shocked. *"I* have one?" the lawyer repeated coolly; "indeed, that's news!"

"News!" All Jean's long-stored bitterness seemed at last to find vent in her defiance of this man she had always detested. "Is that the way you remember your wives? I suppose next thing you'll be asking *which* wife? Well, I don't know which it was, but I know you *said* she was your wife—the girl I took breakfast to that morning in the limousine!" At this, for all his sophistication, Bascomb could not hide an instant's embarrassment. Adele, watching him intently, perceived it, and her heart turned sick.

"So you are that young lady?" Bascomb recovered composure with a slightly crooked smile. "I recall the morning. Well, that *was* my wife—I had the misfortune to lose her." He turned to Adele, throwing into his voice a pathos which thrilled the infatuated girl: "Addie, is being a widower a crime?"

"Why—didn't you tell me?" reproached Adele, on the verge of tears.

"I meant to, but it was hard to speak of when we were so happy. Come, Addie, *you* won't misjudge me? You are all my world. How could I think of any one else while I had you?" He lifted pleading arms. Adele, of course, did not remember his long court practice in the "mechanics of emotion." For a moment she wavered in painful uncertainty, then yielded to the magnetism she had for months been powerless to resist. She clung to Bascomb, sobbing: "Oh, Jerry—I—I—love you! I b—believe in you—whatever any one says!" and from the circle of his embrace, through their tears her eyes flashed on Manson, as she cried: "You were always prejudiced! You'd never give him a chance—but I'm of age—I'm eighteen now—and this is the man—I love!"

Manson went livid to the lips; only a lifetime of self-discipline enabled him to keep in leash the elemental rage provoked to exasperation by the glance of tolerant triumph Bascomb shot him over the gold-bronze head upon his breast. Agony, too, darkened his eyes. He could not speak. Of all four now, Jean had the most presence of mind. "When did your wife die?" she demanded, but Bascomb ignored the question, still gloating toward Manson.

"*When did your wife die?*" Jean forced his attention.

"When? Oh, not long after you saw her."

Jean stepped nearer to him. From the petulant, self-pitying girl of an hour before, this episode had transformed her into a woman, a woman strong and resolute, with the consciousness of power to defend the ones she loved and the almost uncanny insight which that power awakens. "Look here, Jerome Bascomb! You can't look me in the eye and tell me your wife is dead!" The lawyer's disdain showed a tinge of amusement. Nevertheless, he could not meet the challenge. Before her direct gaze his eyes shifted as he declared haughtily, "My wife is dead—to me."

Adele started.

"*To you!*" echoed Jean. "Ah, Mr. Bascomb, quite a few things seem dead to you that are not dead to other people!"

"What do you mean, Jerry?" whimpered Adele. He looked down at her with all apparent tenderness. "I mean, little girl, that I am legally divorced from my wife—free by every law of the land to marry you—that she is no more to me than if I'd never met her. It was a sad experience, Addie, and that's why I never told you. I wanted to forget it—to be happy with you, the first one who ever made me so. I didn't want even the thought of that woman—who was never a real wife to me—to mar our happiness. She was my wife in name only—not my own true wife as *you* will be— she never understood me as *you* do. *You believe me, Addie?*" The last words had more the effect of a hypnotic suggestion than an entreaty. With a little, quivering sigh of relief, Adele once more dropped her head against his shoulder.

"You see?" exulted Bascomb in a low tone to Manson, whose corded temples and convulsive hands betrayed his terrible effort at self-mastery; "I'm willing to marry her if she wishes it."

"*Willing!*" Manson lunged forward then. "You're willing, are you? I'd see her in the grave first—yes, in hell! There are hells on earth and with you she will find one! Let go of her! You're not fit to touch her! She is my ward, and do you think I'll consent to her damnation?"

"Your consent is immaterial, Manson."

"Adele," Manson grasped her arm, in his passion more roughly than he intended, "come away—come home—do you hear?" But the girl,

A CHILD OF DIVORCE

in hurt anger, tried to jerk away. "I *won't,* Uncle Paul! I'm not a child. Stop it!—you pinch me—oh-h-h-h!" She ended in a low scream as her eyes swept the doorway. All turned toward it—and stood galvanized.

No one had heard the bell ring. No one knew how the stranger had entered. It might have been through closed doors, he was so wraith-like. Disheveled, ashen, with a fresh, flaming scar across one cheek, a form on whom the clothes hung as on a skeleton, he strode directly toward Bascomb, in his great staring eyes no longer sunbeams, but the lightning flash of insanity.

Jean uttered one shriek, *"Truman!"* but he neither saw nor heard her. He saw no one but Bascomb. Crushed in his thin right hand was the wad of a white letter. Speechless with fright, Adele shrank away, fleeing instinctively to her uncle for protection.

"Hello, father!" cried the ghost, and laughed. None present had ever heard such a laugh. It curdled the blood. "Hello, father! I've always wanted to meet you—now I have a chance! Take a good look at me, father—before you go—for I'm going to send you where you sent my mother—only you won't meet her *over there!* No, you won't meet her over there—you'll never get to where she is again—thank God! Come on, father—be

brave—be brave if you've got any manhood in you—be brave as my poor little mother was, anyhow—'' Like the fiendish claws of an octopus, the youth's hands, with fingers spread and curled, suddenly gripped the throat of the stunned lawyer, the paper falling from them to the floor. Bascomb roused to a terrific struggle, but the strength in those tentacles was the strength of a madman. He twitched, he cuffed, kicked and gurgled in vain, till Manson, pushing Adele toward Jean, got a jiu-jitsu hold on Truman. The death-dealing fingers relaxed as the youth fell back with a snarl of pain.

"You crazy fool!" gasped Bascomb, trying to adjust his crumpled collar, above which the finger-marks grew redly visible, "who are you anyway? What do you mean by this?"

"You'd better be thankful for your life," exclaimed Manson, trembling all over; "I happen to know this poor young fellow, if you don't, and, before you condemn him, we'll find out—"

"Let go!" raved Truman; "say, let me go —will you! That man ruined my mother's life—I tell you he ruined her life! Wouldn't you kill the man that ruined your mother's life? He's my father—*God damn him!* I hate to think it, but I've got his blood in me. If you don't believe it, read that letter my

A CHILD OF DIVORCE

mother wrote before she died! She's dead—my mother's dead—*my little mother's dead!*" he broke off in a wild fit of crying, fighting ineffectually against the peculiar wrench of Manson's big hands, each movement shocking him with pain.

"Hush, Truman," Manson humored him; "you mustn't do this thing—you *must not!* What would your mother think of you? Her spirit is watching you, Truman—hush, my boy—be quiet—justice will be done."

"*Justice!* It's no justice when that man is left to live and my mother's dead! She's dead, I tell you—*she's dead*—and it's his fault. She was as young as he—but she was like an old woman—because he ruined her life—he ruined her life, I tell you—he never married her at all—I know it now—it's in the letter—and I—I'm—nothing but a bastard! God kill me—but let me kill him first!"

"You'd best get out of sight," said the pastor to Bascomb, and perhaps nothing could have better portrayed the lawyer's true caliber than the facility with which he acted upon this suggestion by edging into the next room.

"Now, Truman," Manson warned firmly, "if you don't keep quiet, I'm going to tie your hands."

"*No!* Don't you dare! Who are you, anyhow? What're you stopping me for? If you

THE WAGES OF SIN

don't let go—I'll kill you too—*I'll kill all of you! Let me alone, I say!—let me go!*"

"Adele," directed Manson, "give me your belt." The cringing girl obeyed meekly. It was one of those very narrow, but tough, leather belts worn loosely with one-piece dresses. Not without a tussle did Manson manage to bind it several times around Truman's wrists and fasten the buckle. Thus handicapped, the frantic youth raged harmlessly till his frail physique became so exhausted that he dropped on the lounge weeping and sobbing. It was then Jean saw her chance to go to him, her heart nearly bursting with its rush of mingled feelings—joy, anguish, tenderness, pity. Nothing she could say or do, however, brought to his face one gleam of recognition, though a woman's ministrations obviously soothed him. She piled up some pillows and persuaded him to lie down while she knelt beside him, smoothing his rumpled hair, caressing his hot forehead with her gentle hand. Manson, who had picked up the paper, followed Bascomb. She could hear the buzz of their voices, but what they said was nothing to her. Everything now was nothing to her, save that Truman, her own Truman, had come back from the dead. Yet was this Truman, or only the poor shell of the man she had loved? Each minute he grew weaker, more childlike. He closed his eyes and the tears gushed from under their quivering, black-fringed lids, down the wan cheeks to the parted, twitching lips. With her handkerchief she wiped them away. His breath came hard, in frequent sighs. The flaming scar, so repulsive to Adele, she bent over and softly kissed. He stirred at the touch. "Is that you, Mom? It's all right, Mom—Jean'll take care of you—I asked her to—" Her heart sprang up in hope, but though he babbled on, sometimes of "Jean," he knew not that Jean was near.

"—it's a frameup—I don't believe it—the fellow has no proof!" With startling unpleasantness Bascomb's raised voice cut into her consciousness. No proof? Jean arose slowly then and turned toward the next room.

"Oh, Jean! don't leave me alone—*with him!*" cried Adele, springing from a huge armchair in which she had been huddling. Jean looked at her sadly. "He won't hurt you, Adele. He's too ill to hurt any one." Adele gave a timid glance toward the prostrate form with hands pathetically bound by her belt and felt a sting of self-reproach. Her eyes were streaming. Suddenly she flung her arms around the older girl. "Oh, Jean! I've been so wicked—so mean to uncle! How can he—or God—ever forgive me? Oh, Jean—if only I'd never met him—" meaning Bascomb.

THE WAGES OF SIN

Jean stroked her hair and patted her shoulder. "Never mind, 'Dele; it could have been worse—a lot worse."

"Yes, yes—I know it," Adele sobbed on. "Oh, Jean—if you hadn't come—I—I—was going away with him—to-night!" she shuddered. "Oh, Jean, it's terrible! I thought he was a good man, Jean—I thought he was all right and uncle was wrong—he could make me do anything—but *this*—oh! I feel as if I was falling—and everything was falling—and there wasn't—any bottom!" Jean's lips set grimly. "We've got to be brave, Adele. We're women. You know you said you were of age." Adele's words had brought to her mind the sudden memory of what she, too, had planned to do to-night. It seemed very far away, like something long ago, something foreign to her own true nature. Her manner strengthened Adele. "Yes, I know, Jean, and I—I'll try and be a woman. If only uncle'll forgive me—I'll never—cross him again. Jean, if you want to go—in there—I—I'll stay with Truman."

Bascomb had slunk down into one of the dining-room chairs. Manson stood opposite him, the rumpled letter on the table between them an object of scorn to the lawyer. "That's no evidence," he was defying; "any one could have written that. Where are his witnesses? Where is his *proof?*"

"His proof is with me!" The two men started and turned toward Jean. "His mother left a package in my care when she died. She told me to bring it to you, Mr. Bascomb, in a year if Truman did not return. I don't know what's in it, but I'm sure it contains proof that will back up anything written in that letter. And I know Truman's mother wrote that letter. She gave it to me to leave in the house, for him, because she thought he might come back. I've seen it—almost every day—since she died."

"You seem to have been appointed my recording angel," Bascomb sneered at her.

"There's a record for all of us, Bascomb," Manson said, "and sooner or later our sins find us out."

"That's right, brother; remember your profession"—the lawyer took a mocking tone—"if a preacher ever earned his living, *you* do!"

"And you've earned yours, Bascomb, in the way you chose. I've wanted God for my partner—but you seem to have preferred the devil. I've tried to keep homes together—it seems to please you to destroy them."

"Yes, I know all about your efforts there—and the consolation you've offered to a victim of one of the wrecks"—he looked insinuatingly at Jean—"you may not know it, Manson, but your own record isn't lily-white—if there's anything in rumor, and you know the good old adage, 'Where there's so much smoke, there must be fire'—oh, well," he shrugged, "I suppose even a saint may have his weak spot."

Manson did not strike him, though he had a pristine urge to do so. Perhaps it was that reference to fire which oddly brought to his mind the text, "A bruised reed will he not break and smoking flax will he not quench." This wretch, this dupe of self-deceit and misspender of talent, with a mind too poisoned to believe in purity, would sooner or later break and quench himself. What need for a stronger man to do it? His fists knotted, but he kept on the main track, insisting: "Didn't you know this Laura Burnett?"

Bascomb toyed nervously with a napkin ring. He finally admitted: "Oh, yes, I *knew* her."

"Rather well?"

The other glanced up again, his lips curling: "As well as she knew me."

"I doubt that," Manson answered; "as well, perhaps, as she *thought* she knew you. You seem to hold moral obligations rather lightly."

"How should I know there was any child? I never heard of it."

"You might have taken the trouble to find out—under the circumstances. Nature is nature, you know."

A CHILD OF DIVORCE

"I don't see it. She came halfway—and more than half. She was the kind of woman you couldn't get away from, always sticking around—I got sick of it. I tried to end it; that's why I left her and went up-State for several years. I don't know whether she followed me up there, but she was the kind who could do it if she wanted to. This letter shows she found out my address here, so she could have found me—when it happened. Why didn't she let me know before this?"

"The letter explains that, Bascomb, and you know it. She was faithful to you as the man to whom she had given herself, yet she did not want to hurt your career. She kept hoping—even praying—poor woman!—that you would come back to her of your own volition. That's why she tried to keep near you and yet didn't bother you; that's why she struggled on alone through all these years to support your child—that, and for the boy's sake—she had him to think of, too, and she even tried to make him respect his unknown father! Such love, such faith as that, is rare, Bascomb, *mighty* rare, and I don't wonder that you can't understand it. Still, you could hardly expect the son to share the same feeling."

"That's right, Dr. Manson," Jean came to his support; "that's just the way she talked

THE WAGES OF SIN

before she died, and Dr. Manson, look—can't you see the resemblance—his eyes?" She had been studying Bascomb as he slouched there in assumed indifference while the slanting rays of the afternoon sun threw his features into sharp relief, betraying, too, the network of age lines not usually so noticeable. In beauty of setting and color his eyes were indeed like Truman's. The only difference lay in their expression. On women Bascomb looked with either unconscious tolerance or a kind of confident intimacy; on members of his own sex, with cynicism. The eyes are well called the windows of the soul, and it was borne to Jean with swift clarity why, on that morning in the shadowy corner of her stepfather's inn, she had experienced the transient sensation of having long before looked into Bascomb's eyes. Truman had inherited his father's "windows," but through them, thank God, shone his mother's intrepid, faithful, reverent soul. Women are much more apt than men to observe such details, but, with his attention called to it, Manson nodded: "You're right, Jean. Bascomb, there's a point you can't gainsay. The boy bears a striking resemblance to you."

Bascomb spread out his hands and sneered again. "Have it the way it pleases you, but the law, my dear people, requires more than

A CHILD OF DIVORCE

insinuations. A man may even look like another without being his father. Let the fellow gather up his evidence and proceed through the regular channels. I shall prepare to meet his suit." He climbed to his feet, his whole manner indicating that he wished the discussion ended.

Manson and Jean returned to the library, where Adele sat near the couch, anxiously watching Truman. The strain of her ordeal sounded in her voice. "I'm afraid he's very sick. He keeps muttering things, and look how his face is beginning to flush."

Tenderly now Manson unwound the belt from the youth's limp wrists and Jean tried to chafe away the marks of it. His hands were hot and dry. Manson felt his forehead and his pulse. "He's running a fever," he reported quietly. "I'll 'phone for an ambulance. He'd best be taken to a hospital."

"No—no!" pleaded Jean; "take him home to his own house—and let me nurse him!" Now that she could see him, touch him, she could never let him go again. In the great surge of her yearning she felt that, though he should die, her love and prayer must quicken with consciousness that dear, fragile body. Manson, however, shook his head. "That wouldn't do, Jean, never in the world. But I tell you what. There's plenty of room in the manse—there's a big spare room upstairs with a little one opening off from it where we can put you both, and Mrs. Kingston is as good as any trained nurse who ever graduated. She'll help you and so will Adele. We'll have him taken there, then; shall we? I'll 'phone Mrs. Kingston to get things ready.''

So it was arranged. Jean thought there was never anything finer, bigger or more effectively disarming than Manson's calm indifference to gossip which had no foundation. Perhaps there is no profession that makes a man more of a target for criticism than the ministry. If he openly pays some particular attention to those who discretion and sympathy tell him need it, he is accused of partiality. If he withholds it, he is unchristian. But Manson had long since discovered that the pastor who always worries about pleasing every one in little things, consumes time and energy needed for the really big tasks of his calling and is hardly more popular at that. He simply raised his head above it, and, undisturbed, kept in sight the vision, pursuing his duty according to his light, incidentally commanding, even in those of opposite opinions, the respect he never angled for. Thus what evil rumors may have been started by jealous tongues to besmirch his interest in Jean, soon died a natural death for lack of truth to feed on, especially in the presence of this new development.

Before sundown Truman was tossing restively in the big white bed in the spare room of the manse, with a doctor attending him, Jean and Mrs. Kingston carefully noting or acting out the latter's orders. To Jean it was as if three years had passed rather than three hours since the time she had left Nicolsons'.

Adele retired early to her own room, too completely miserable and shaken to longer face the world. By and by her uncle came up to her, and, after one plaintive look, she flew to his open arms in a paroxysm of contrition. Till darkness fell, he sat by her, listening to her confession and pleas for his forgiveness, a quiet, loving, understanding presence. He did not scold her. He had had his own days of hero-worship and known the fearful shock of youthful disillusionment. He knew that her lesson had been severe enough; furthermore, that, away from the influence of Bascomb with his unique and hectic fascination for very young women, she would grow into the realization of that serener happiness which wisdom alone can teach. He did say once, though not in a tone of rebuke: "I was surprised, 'Dele; I thought you had forgotten him."

"I thought so myself, Uncle, during the war—with all the excitement and everything

—but afterwards—there was nothing left to do—special, I mean—and when he called up again—''

"Mr. Paul!" interrupted Mrs. Kingston's voice from without; "Mr. Paul—the telephone!"

"All right—coming." Manson kissed his niece gently, told her not to worry, but eat the supper Mrs. Kingston would bring her and go to bed.

"Mr. Paul," the housekeeper imparted mysteriously in the hallway, "it's the police station."

"All right, Mrs. Kingston." He went on down to the landing and took up the instrument. "Yes—hello—*this* is Manson—" Then, after a pause, "*What—you don't tell me!*—very well, I'll be there directly."

It was nearly ten o'clock before he returned home, pale from the nervous exhaustion peculiar to large-framed, sensitive men, and asked Mrs. Kingston to call Jean to the living-room.

When the girl came in, he walked toward her, heavy-footed, sad-eyed. "Jean, you've been so brave—you've been more level-headed than I have. It was really you this afternoon who kept me from losing my temper with—that man. Jean, can you bear one more shock—and I hope the last?"

A CHILD OF DIVORCE

Jean steeled herself and nodded.

"It's Bascomb—he's dead."

"*Dead!*" The girl put her hand to her forehead, her brain reeling. Was there no end to tragedy?

"Yes, Jean, he's dead. He shot himself to-night, and it's all true, Jean. Truman is his son. He left a confession which shows that he knew of the boy's existence, though he denied it. He must have planned it right after we left there. He went out this very afternoon and added a codicil to his will, bequeathing all he had to Truman, came back and wrote his confession to the police. His valet heard the shot and found him dead. Poor wretch! Think of it, Jean—going to face one's God like that! If I'd only known, I'd have tried harder to reach his soul—but we never know, Jean, we never know! There were three letters near him, the one to the authorities, one to myself and —this one to Truman—" He drew a sealed envelope from his inside pocket and held it toward her. "Give it to him, Jean, when he gets well enough to stand it." Jean took it numbly, disliking even then to touch it, and Manson advised: "You'd better go to bed now, child, and get some rest. Remember, to be a good nurse you must keep up your strength." This brought her back to the loving task at hand. "Dr. Manson," she asked shakily, "you were talking to the doctor. What did he say —about Truman?"

"He said, Jean, that it was a bad case of nervous shock in addition to his war experience; that he is seriously, but not dangerously, ill."

"Then he will get well!" she cried, with an impulse to fall on her knees and thank God.

"Yes, Jean—with the kind of nursing he'll get here—home surroundings—people wanting him—he'll get well. I'm glad now we didn't send him to the hospital, poor lad! I fancy he's had his fill of hospitals in the last few months! To be where folks love him— where he's made to *want* to live—will make a lot of difference in his case."

CHAPTER XIX.

WHAT IS LOVE?

"Love seeketh not her own."

THIS time Jean did not merely ask for a few days off from her work. She resigned her position at the chemical plant with the option of returning if it had not been filled when she was ready to do so. In the latter case she understood she must await her turn, or look elsewhere. She did this both at her own inclination and the advice of Dr. Manson. "You know," the pastor told her, smiling, "you should invest your time and strength into what will count most for the future. Just now your future lies in the spare room upstairs."

Jean, however, thought little now of her own future and less of her new task in the light of an investment. Always it was Truman and Truman's need that filled her life. All that he might later provide for her in the way of those material things which constitute love's outer shell was secondary to her possession of *him*. Subconsciously she felt that mundane problems would solve themselves. There were no questionings in her heart as there had been with Tom Daly; there was no doubt, no fear, and she accepted her obvious destiny as though it had been so from the beginning, and she had never known aught else but union with Truman Burnett.

Truman's delirium had at last surrendered, released him again to the realm of the sane. He had ceased to rave and moan, to jumble together in disconnected mutterings the trenches, shells and "Heinies" with bastards, the world's injustice, "that rotten Bascomb" and "Mom." He had fallen asleep and awakened with his face turned toward a young woman sewing near him and he had murmured wonderingly, *"Jean!"* and Jean had laid down her sewing to kneel by the bed in grateful ecstasy.

"Jean, are you dead too?" he asked so weakly it was scarcely audible.

"Dead? No, dear, I'm very much alive."

"But where are we, Jean?—isn't this—heaven?" His forehead puckered as his eyes roved slowly about the shaded, restful room.

"No, Truman, it is the world, dear, but I feel as if it was heaven because you're getting well."

"Well? Was I sick, then, Jean? Where's Mom?"

A CHILD OF DIVORCE

"She's resting, Truman—I'm taking her place."

The young man sighed. "Oh, Jean! I had such an awful dream—I thought Mom—was dead!"

"Hush, darling, you mustn't talk. You aren't strong enough yet."

"But Mom's alive—she's all right?" he persisted anxiously.

"Yes, dear, she's all right—everything's all right." Again he sighed and closed his eyes. "I'm tired," he whispered.

After that he asked no further questions, seeming content to sleep or lie watching Jean as she moved about the room in her felt-soled slippers, noiseless as an angel, or sat by his side to sew or read; yet it was inevitable that with passing time he should be puzzled by the non-appearance of "Mom." This was the thing Jean dreaded most. But as he regained interest in life, so in proportion did his strength return, and with it memory. He began to evince that hopeful sign so welcome in every convalescent, an appetite. Mrs. Kingston could prepare dainties which Manson said "any one would turn back from the grave to eat," and she lavished affectionate skill on the dishes she fixed for Truman, Indeed, that was about the only thing Jean would let any one else do for him, except on the occasions

WHAT IS LOVE?

when she was persuaded to take a walk or a nap by the argument that it would render her more fit for service. Then she reluctantly left him to the housekeeper or to Adele.

Adele was eager to help, and her "home nursing" lessons during the war stood her in good stead. Her uncle liked to have her mind and heart thus nobly occupied in hours when she might have brooded over her own disappointment; for she put her heart into it. She was the sort of girl who is ready to love those dear to her cherished friends. The technical demands of nursing she managed to execute well, but the poor child proved unequal to other demands made by her bewildered patient. Of course she thought all along that he knew of Mrs. Burnett's death, and when, one day during Jean's short absence, his awakening suspicions made him insist upon extracting the truth from her, her countenance betrayed her amazement. By what followed she was greatly distressed and upon Jean's return hurried to meet her in tears. Jean, too, felt badly about it, but she comforted Adele by saying: "Well, dear, he'd have to know soon anyway. We couldn't keep it from him much longer."

She found Truman with his face buried in the pillows; nor did the touch of her hand arouse him.

"Truman," she said earnestly, "I'm sorry, dear, so very sorry, but she was tired, Truman—she's gone to rest—"

"Why didn't you tell me before?" came in muffled tones from the pillow; "why is every one—trying to—trick me?"

"Darling, no one is trying to trick you. We love you—we want you to get well. You weren't strong enough to bear it—" He turned toward her then, his cheeks wet, his lips quivering. "Oh, yes, I am," he asserted despondently; "I'm too strong—I'm too tough—I live through everything—if only I could die!"

"Don't, dear; you mustn't talk so."

"I've been nearly dead twice—once they put the tags on my wrist and ankle—but here I am—while other men with everything to live for—"

"Have you nothing to live for, Truman? Don't you love me any more?" A rush of tears filled his eyes. "Love you, Jean!" he husked; "oh, if you knew how much! You've been with me everywhere—the thought of you. But what have I got to give you now—for all you've done for me—and Mom?"

"Do you really want to know, Truman? I'll tell you, then! Give me yourself—strong and well—oh, Truman, I love you—I want you so—just you—*you!* If you leave me again I can't bear it. Make your arms strong—and take me in them—that's all I want—your arms around me again—your strength to help me live—with you—and there's life, Truman. Your mother's work was finished, but yours and mine have just begun—you're going to be a doctor—to save lives and make people happy—you're going to make up for all the wrong that's been done! Isn't that something to live for, Truman?" The throbbing intensity of her voice, her vivid face, stirred Truman even in his weakness; the words struck a challenge in him, the challenge of youth and life warring against despair and decay. He reached up a hand to clutch the one on his shoulder, and into his pale cheeks crept the first faintest touch of normal color.

"Just the fact that you *were* almost dead and have been brought back to life," Jean went on ardently, "doesn't that prove that God has a work for you—and me?"

"I guess—maybe you're right, Jean," he admitted slowly; "I—I've been selfish, I guess—lying here—and Jean—when she—Adele—told me about Mom—it all came back to me—like a flash—everything—even the letter she left there—poor Mom! She asked me to forgive her—*me* to forgive *her!*" he choked.

"I know, darling, I know all about it—and you know why she did it, don't you, dear?

A CHILD OF DIVORCE

And, Truman, it's not the least bit worse than the lie *my* mother told—than any one tells who says 'till death do us part' and then goes and gets divorced—only *she* did it for a more unselfish reason!''

"Then, Jean—you don't think—well, since I knew the truth I got to thinking—it seemed to me—I didn't have any right to be living."

"*Right!*" Jean's hazel eyes suddenly snapped. "Truman, dear, you've as much right to be here as I have, or any one on earth. *You* couldn't help being born, could you? And it's *God* who creates folks—*laws* don't do it! I'll tell you what I think determines people's rights to live—it's whether they make their lives *worth while,* and you still have your chance to do that. Idle, good-for-nothing parasites who take all they can grab and do nothing for any one—*they're* the only kind who have no right to live, I don't care if their parents had twenty weddings! You ask Dr. Manson, darling, and see if he don't think so too. And now, dearest, if you don't live and prove your right to live, if you insist on dying, do you know what I'm going to do? I'm going to make them bury me alive with you—like they did to the women in India—for it's a funny thing, Truman," she turned serious again, "I can't seem to live myself—really *live*—without you."

WHAT IS LOVE?

"And I should like to see the man who could stay *dead* with you—even in his grave!" exclaimed Truman. He was smiling, his voice was stronger, his color more pronounced.

"Isn't it funny, though?" Jean marveled, "that with you to love and work with I feel so strong and capable—and alone I feel so weak—oh, so weak and miserable—I'll tell you sometime, dear—it's not important now, and we're going to have so much time together, aren't we? But it just seems funny. I wonder why it is. I wonder if all women are that way."

"I don't know, beloved, about all women—it's enough for me that one is so and that she is mine! Jean, kiss me." She leaned over and their lips met long and fondly. When she drew away she felt a little frightened, he was so flushed, and there was something else, something nameless, felt far more than understood between them both.

"Now," she said repentantly, "I'm afraid all this talk has excited you too much. You must take your medicine and sleep till suppertime." He complied, but it was the last time he succumbed to orders without some rebellion. In fact, from that afternoon on he began to grow quite unruly.

Instead of watching beside him as he slept, this time Jean dragged the rocker to the dormer window and sat there, looking dreamily out at the sky. She could neither sew nor read, she could only think. It was really the first chance she had had to think—about the future. Whence came that strange feeling which had gripped her as she kissed him? Was it from the "man-feel" of his black, uncropped beard? Partly that, but why should she be frightened? Yet it was not a fright she wanted to escape from; the rather she would have liked to repeat the sensation, drifted farther into it. He was getting well, his virility was returning, and she felt her own vibration to it in other chords than the maternal. She felt again the exalted thrill of that day at Eagle Rock, though more intensely, for suffering and trial had strengthened her nature since then, deepened her capacity for true, well-balanced love. She did not understand it altogether, but at last she was blissfully, flawlessly happy.

That evening Truman ate an unusually good supper, and the next day he wanted to get out of bed. The doctor forbade this for another day or two, but said he might sit up. He felt of his beard, made a wry face and asked Jean for a mirror. When she brought it to him, he flushed, exclaiming: "My goodness, Jean, I look like a bolshevist! Would Dr. Manson be kind enough to loan me his razor?"

WHAT IS LOVE?

"I shouldn't wonder," laughed Jean; "when he comes up here you might ask him."

"Honest, Jean, I guess I've shaved about three times since I saw you last. I've spent most of the time in hospitals—one after another—on account of my game leg. It got shot and infected, but it's all right now, I guess—anyhow it feels so—and I got discharged at last—but they didn't have time to shave all the fellows, and to see us you'd think you were in a synagogue or something."

"You were shot in the leg, Truman?" asked Jean, with mixed feelings of horror and gratitude that it was no worse.

"Yes, and it bled so much before they got to me that I fainted and they thought I was dead. Anyhow, I guess they reported I was—and when I came to life they shipped me to a hospital for awhile—and then to another one—oh, all around. I don't know where I was most of the time, Jean, and neither do lots of the fellows—and now I don't care, it's so good to be back with you—here in this big, clean room with folks so kind and everything. Jean, I'm afraid it's a dream and I'll wake up dead after all. Oh, it was fierce, Jean—worse than I ever thought war could be, and—let's not talk about it—I want to forget about it. Isn't it funny, though, that you should turn out to be my nurse after all—like we said when we were kids?"

"I suppose it is, darling," answered Jean, "but it don't seem so to me any more—it seems where I belong."

"Does it, Jean?" Truman reached out his hand for hers, his fine eyes eloquent with tenderness. "Come nearer, Jean; you're the best medicine a fellow ever had, and all day that little verse Mom taught me has been running in my head. Jean—do you like poetry?" He asked this a bit timidly, as if he feared she might laugh at it. She sat down on the edge of the bed, just as she used to with his mother. "Indeed I do," she assured him softly; "what little verse was it, Truman?"

"Straight through my heart this thought to-day
    By Truth's own hand is driven—
God never takes one thing away
    But something else is given."

"Oh, Truman!" Jean sobbed, too touched for further words. His own eyes were misty. For a long time they sat there in full-hearted silence, hand in hand. At last he murmured, "Jean, you're just like Mom." Jean's heart swelled. "Am I, Truman?" she asked eagerly. "Oh, darling, I'd rather have you think that than call me beautiful—I'd rather hear you say 'I need you' than 'I love you'!"

WHAT IS LOVE?

"But I do both, Jean. I need you because I love you and I love you because I need you, and now when I start life again I'll need you more than ever. Jean, I don't think that I could stand being alone—with no one to love or care—any more than you can. I should lose heart and vision—even the vision that Mom gave me for my work. You know, she wanted me to be a doctor—and I wanted to be myself—because I could do some good just as you told me. I don't want to get material in my work. I don't want to lose sight of people's souls, Jean. Some doctors do, you know, just because they see so much of the body—and the fool things people do to spoil their bodies. But Mom used to say, 'Truman, if you want to be a doctor, remember that folks have souls as well as bodies that need to be healed sometimes, and that often by healing the soul you can save the body, and sometimes by healing the body you can reach a person's soul. If you're not able to do this, Truman,' she used to say, 'you'd better not try and be a doctor, for you won't make a really good all-round one.' But, Jean, I like it, I've always liked it—all sides of it and I've been thinking a lot lately—after I graduate I'd like to start practicing in a small town somewhere—somewhere where there aren't enough doctors and I could get to be friends with my patients—

some mining or lumber town maybe, where they really need me. Would you like that sort of life, Jean?"

"Truman, dear, my first choice is to be with you wherever you feel you ought to go, and wherever that is I want to make it cozy for you, and I'll make up my mind to love your patients—even if they're ugly as sin."

"Sin is the only thing that makes people ugly, I think; don't you, Jean? Aren't we serious for young people like us? But it's our lives, I guess—yours and mine—the way things have been—we couldn't help *thinking*. And, Jean—there's another thing"—she saw the gray-blue eyes turn suddenly dark with feeling—"in her letter Mom said—I remember now—something about my living and working to redeem her sin. *Her* sin, Jean! I don't believe my mother was sinful—I don't care what the world says! She was weak—poor little Mom—she'd just do anything for those she loved—and he took advantage of it —that blackguard—Bascomb!"

"Hush, Truman, dear, you mustn't get excited like that," warned Jean, for she could feel his increased pulse by the surge of blood through his hand, "and can't we try, Truman, to forgive the past? We have each other, that's all that matters now."

WHAT IS LOVE?

"*Forgive! You* wouldn't ask me to forgive my mother's betrayer? Why, Jean—I mean to avenge her yet—whatever happens! I will—I will! I couldn't hold my head up if I didn't!" In an instant he was resentful. He pulled his hand from Jean's to clench it, his cheeks reddened and paled again, his eyes glittered, all of which, with his stiff, dark stubble, lent him an aspect of fierceness incongruous with the soft background. Jean only looked at him earnestly, and said: "Truman dear, I may as well tell you the truth now. You can't do anything to your father. He is dead."

"*Dead!*" Truman winced as if struck, and fell back speechless.

Simply Jean related all there was to tell. Then she withdrew the sealed envelope Manson had given her from its hiding-place in the dresser drawer and brought it to him, but he shrank away from it.

"Truman dear, I think we *ought* to read it —even the worst person deserves the right to a last word."

"I don't want to hear from him!" cried Truman, stubbornly.

"Very well, darling—some other time." But as Jean turned to replace it, he childishly changed his mind, conceding: "All right, then; I suppose it may as well be now as ever—if

A CHILD OF DIVORCE

you think it's so important. Read it, will you, Jean?"

Jean resumed her seat, tore open the missive and read aloud:

"To My Son Truman Burnett:

"When you read this, it may be of some satisfaction to you to know that I have gone to that oblivion into which you wished to send me this afternoon, without the necessity of your hands being stained by my blood and your name by murder. I have for some time been sick of life, and, after careful consideration, came to the conclusion that this is an opportune time for me to drop out of it, as my decease is probably what you will seek and eventually accomplish anyway. In a way, I do not know that I blame you. Your position is not an easy one in the eyes of a hypocritical civilization which, despite its boasts of 'freedom,' still clings slavishly to stupid scruples and superstitious conventions which it tries to force on all its members, ostracizing those who dare to ignore them. I do not know but that you have a right to resent being put there by those who are responsible for your existence. At any rate, you are the least to blame in the matter.

"As far as I know, your mother, Laura Burnett, was what the world calls a good woman, until she met me, and, I believe, afterwards. You have no reason to be ashamed of her, even in the eyes of society. She was more 'moral' than a good many married women, though it might be hard to convince the average person of this.

"In the past few years I have managed to accumulate some property, real estate, investments and capital, all aggregating about one hundred thousand dollars, perhaps a little over. I am bequeathing this to you.

WHAT IS LOVE?

See McKenzie, with whom my will is filed. You will hear from him anyway. No, this is not done in atonement. I despise that sloppy word. I have simply no one else to leave it to—no descendants other than yourself, to my knowledge. Use it according to your judgment.

"Do not waste any sentiment over this. When you reach my age you will realize the futility of sentiment —if you have any left. I simply return to oblivion, and, if it does not worry me, it should not worry you.

"Your natural father,
"JEROME BASCOMB."

Jean dropped the page with a shudder. "Oh, Truman—how fearful! what a miserable man —so hard and cold and loveless! Could any punishment be worse than that?"

But Truman's thoughts were running in a different channel. He flared up again. "And does he think I want his money—his dirty money? I won't touch a cent of it! No, I won't! Hasn't he insulted me enough without that?"

Jean laid her hand on his, the awful barrenness of that human life they had been discussing still the uppermost thing in her mind. Somehow it made her want to be more tender to Truman—and to every one.

"Dear, I wish you wouldn't work yourself up so," she pleaded; "when you're well, things will look so different. Then I know you'll see that because *he* shirked his responsibility is no

A CHILD OF DIVORCE

reason why you should shirk yours. Money and things have no personality. They can't carry a taint from one person to another, but I think they are an obligation, Truman, if they come to us. I don't think you'll be a bit nobler in throwing this money away than you will in using it for some good purpose. Some one might even get it who would do more harm than good with it. You won't have to answer for the way it was earned, only for the way you use it when it's yours, Truman dear; and remember—*your hospital.*"

For another long while Truman was silent, reclining wearily among the pillows, his eyes downcast. Finally he laced his fingers into hers once more, drawing her toward him.

"Jean," he yielded, "perhaps you're right—I didn't think of it that way—but I don't want to think at all—till later—I'm so tired of it all, Jean—I'd like to forget it. I just want you, beloved. I'll do whatever you say. Come here—kiss me and hold my hand—and let's not talk any more."

The circumstances of Jean's life, the repression forced upon her by lovelessness and necessity, had saddened what had begun existence as a hopeful, if not a buoyant, temperament. Now, with a normal means of outlet for her individual gifts, an object for her innate powers of affection, she seemed to rebound to

WHAT IS LOVE?

her own true nature, and her optimistic influence had a great deal to do with Truman's rapid recovery. Truman was sensitive as a chameleon to his environment, more moody than herself, and this was apt to be augmented lately by the gloomy reactions too often resulting from nervous disorders. Through those many hours when Jean kept her vigil over him, thinking of him sometimes proudly as her mate, and again tenderly as her little boy, she frankly determined to feel for that key which every wife must discover to her husband's inner self if she would be happy. Some successful wives call the possession of it "managing," but Jean detested that term; it implied a monopoly in the marriage relation wholly disagreeable. Better she liked that mutual-sounding word "understanding." She had observed enough also to realize the folly and futility of trying to "remodel" any man, even with the hands of love, and she made up her mind to accept Truman's faults with his virtues as part of himself, though to find, if possible, an antidote for his fitful and cranky turns.

All convalescents come to a time when they rise from bed to find themselves not nearly so strong as they felt themselves to be while lying in it. This is discouraging, and it is likewise demonstrative of how physical reactions

A CHILD OF DIVORCE

can affect one's mental outlook. Truman grew more and more impatient for the doctor's permission to get up and (behind that whiskered gentleman's back) resented his fashion of deferring it "for a day or so." "That's what he said last time, Jean!" he would cry irritably. "If he's going to keep me an invalid forever, why don't he come out like a man and say so?" and then he would punch the pillows, kick at the covers, toss himself into a hopeless-looking tangle, till Jean, while trying to extricate him, would say firmly: "Truman, you know it's rest you need—for your heart and nerves. If you work yourself all up like this, you'll just have to keep on lying here!" Whereupon he would begin to pout, accuse her of being in league with "the old pill-roller," snatch at her hand when she came close, beg her to pet him, fret, fume, use baby-talk, do all the utterly silly things that only a young fellow under those restive conditions ever does. He frequently gave her the sensation of trying to hold in an unbroken stallion, and, as dearly as she loved him, sorely tried her tact and patience.

What do young couples really know of each other whose acquaintance is limited to short-timed visits or outings in Sunday clothes and Sunday manners? Could every engaged girl have this test of nursing her prospective mate through an illness, or every man that of seeing his "divine one" in a similiar state of depletion from her superficial charms, there would probably be fewer divorces, for there would be fewer marriages to result in disillusionment. "In sickness and health"—the lovers repeat it glibly after the preacher, too seldom, alas! conjuring up any image of what sickness really means. Old-fashioned novels were wont to represent the repining maiden, or declining hero, as sort of angelic creatures hovering on the threshold of the next world; mediums for celestial messages, who only thought about God, cherubim and heavenly bells. Even yet some hypochondriacs try to affect this pose. They only deceive themselves, for in reality we are all just at our ugliest, both in looks and manners, when we are sick.

But when the great day came for Truman to rise up triumphantly from bed, he was overwhelmed by weakness. He had not tottered five steps ere everything began to swim around him, and, leaning heavily on Jean's shoulder, he barely gained the big rocker which she had made comfortable with blankets, in time to sink, half fainting, into it.

"Hang it all!" he whimpered, "I thought I was getting well, and I feel like a consumptive jelly-fish! Oh! what's the matter with me anyhow? How long's it going to last?"

A CHILD OF DIVORCE

"Not very much longer, darling," Jean consoled; "now that you are up, you'll get well fast. The exercise will help. Dr. Morris said so. It's only the first day, dear, from being in bed so long."

Her prediction came to pass, though not as fast as Truman wished. Daily he crawled about the room, perceptibly gaining strength and getting chagrined with himself whenever he needed aid. For hours at a time she read aloud to him from the books he chose. His taste here was inclined to be studious, for a sick person heavy, and Jean was disappointed to note that this form of recreation did not appear to refresh him very much. He even tried to start arguments over questions raised in the books. One day, when he was crosser than usual, a favorite epigram of Dr. Manson's occurred to her, with seeming irrelevancy at first, but a slowly dawning significance— "Faith, repentance, *humor* and baptism." "These are the things we are saved by," the pastor was sometimes wont to observe with a twinkle, and she remembered how her foolish threat to have herself buried with Truman had lifted him, smiling, out of his dejection. Humor. Was that the antidote? She went to the public library and came back with one book of light, witty stories and another of after-dinner jokes. More readily than she had dared

414

WHAT IS LOVE?

to hope, Truman took to this literary diet. The result was a marked improvement both in his health and temper. Nor did he, during the remainder of his convalescence, ask again for the serious reading. They varied this with cheerful discussions of their future. They planned to be married the following month, and spend the summer in some quiet section of the New York hills where Truman might fully recuperate. The bed was strewn with catalogs of such resorts, and time-tables. The little house on Greenwood Avenue, with its sad associations, they decided to offer for sale. Both felt the need of starting their new life in fresh surroundings. In the fall Truman would enroll for his last year at the College of Physicians and Surgeons, and they would keep house in a little apartment till he graduated and finished his interne course. Then—the small town of their dreams and his own "shingle"!

Jean had been back occasionally to her room at Nicolsons', which would remain hers until the first of May, arousing great interest and curiosity among the other boarders, the more so because she kept her own counsel. She had already transferred many of her small belongings to the manse, from which she and Truman were to go forth as man and wife. Once she found a letter from Tom Daly. It ran in part:

A CHILD OF DIVORCE

"I've heard of your good luck, how your friend has come back, so I know it's all off with me, but I'd like you to know I'm glad you are happy."

Jean refolded it thoughtfully. "Poor old Tom!" she reflected; "he was fairer to me than I was to him. What a great injustice I nearly did him—and myself. How could I ever have thought seriously of *marrying* a man I didn't love!" For in these latter days she had been given a very graphic glimpse into some of the realities of living with a mate.

When Truman could get dressed again his glee resembled that of a youngster upon his premier appearance in trousers. His first outdoor exercise was on the veranda or about the grounds with Jean, Adele and sometimes Dr. Manson. Despite the difference in their ages, his studious trend of mind, his fine, clean ideals afforded a basis of comradeship between him and his host. The shadow over his birth, even while unknown to him, had resulted in a life of considerable isolation, but those who learned to know him felt his irresistible claim upon their affections—he was such a unique mixture of sage and little boy. Friends of both Jean and the Mansons had been solicitous throughout his illness, sending flowers and more tidbits than a well person could eat, let alone a sick one—

WHAT IS LOVE?

though Truman wanted to eat them! Even Mrs. Webber waddled in one day with a lump of fig-pudding by which to excuse her presence. The Dennisons, and one or two others who owned cars, sometimes came to take the young pair riding. The sensational suicide of the "prominent lawyer" was swiftly succeeded in the local news columns by some other sensation, and the relation between Bascomb and the ex-soldier guest at the manse, repressed, at the pastor's urging, by the authorities, remained a secret in three loyal hearts and the city's archives.

One of the first places Truman wanted to visit was, perhaps naturally, his mother's grave. On the Sunday beginning the week in which their wedding was to occur, he begged Jean to guide him to that tiny spot in Sylvan Lawn Cemetery. Jean wished he would postpone it, but she saw that her refusal would upset him as much as anything else she might fear, and so they went.

All the way on the trolley he was very quiet, and the minute they passed through the wide gates of Newark's great necropolis, she saw in him the depression she dreaded. There was as yet no stone to mark Mrs. Burnett's mound, only a temporary wooden cross, but it was green now, and at her own expense Jean had had the gardener plant it with pansies

A CHILD OF DIVORCE

and crocuses. She stopped before it mutely. He gave her one questioning look, and, as she bowed her head, a kind of spasm passed over his features. His bosom heaved, then from his lips the low cry that pierced Jean like a dagger, "*Mother!*—oh-h—Mother—*Mother!*—" In another moment he had dropped down against the grave, his thin body shaking with sobs like to wrench out his heart. It seemed to Jean that never in all her own sufferings had she felt such agony as then—and her sympathy was so impotent! Dear God! if only she were big enough to take him in her arms and comfort him! If only she had the power to comfort him! She turned away, unable to bear the sight, and walked blindly down the gravel path, leaving him alone for a time with his grief—a pathetic, quivering, orphan figure mourning above the bones of her whose folly had brought him into being. How strange life was! Those bones—that moldy dust below—had been a woman once —a woman like herself, who had breathed and moved and loved—and loved, ah, yes! too well! And Bascomb, the suicide, had breathed and moved—and loved in his own lustful way—and they had given her Truman. They had been when Truman was not; now they were no more, but Truman was. Oh! how life hurt her when she thought of it like this—the bigness of it—the pressure of it on her heart! Who could understand it? Then came another thought, more personal, full of embittered wonder, "His mother is more to him dead than mine is to me alive!"

When at length she returned to the grave, she found Truman standing upright, his hat still in his hand, his face, for all its marks of sorrow, strangely resolute, almost harsh. He did not notice her until she could have touched him, then he started and drew back as if he were afraid of her.

"Truman—what—?" she asked, shocked by the fear that the strain had been too much for his mind. But the tone in which he spoke was normal, except for being harsh like his face: "Jean, I don't know what's been the matter with me all along—not to have faced the truth about things. I can't —of course I can't—accept your love!"

Jean was stunned, her breath caught, but she marshaled all her resources, forcing herself to demand quietly, "Why not, Truman?"

"Oh, Jean!" he looked away as if he could not stand the light in her eyes, "you've always understood. Help me—help me—by understanding now! What kind of a man would I be to let myself marry you? Don't you know I'm nothing—nothing but a bastard?"

A CHILD OF DIVORCE

"No, Truman, I don't know anything like that"—she tried to keep her emotions in check, for his were running away with him—"I only know that you're the man I love and I'm going to marry you this very week. I thought *that* was settled long ago!"

"But, Jean, I can't let you do it—I can't! Jean, I've been thinking here—about Mom—and things came back to me that I didn't realize the meaning of once—but I do now—the price she had to pay—because of me—the way people snubbed her—cut her—oh, Jean! I couldn't help it then, but what a cad I've almost been to take your love and expose you to things like that!"

Jean moved slowly toward him, took gentle hold of his two lapels, looked straight up into his tortured face. He tried to draw away, far more afraid of himself than of her, but she moved with him. Only the tremor in her voice and a certain smoldering fire in her eager hazel eyes betrayed her real agitation. "Truman, if I didn't know that you love me as much as I love you, I might even let you have your way. But, Truman, be sensible. Two people are crumbling back into dust. No one will ever hear their voices or see their faces again—but because, when they were on earth, they did something wrong, is that a good reason why two innocent people should be lonely all their lives? Truman, I feel somehow as if I'd as much right to refuse to marry you because my parents are *legalized bigamists,* as you have to reject my love because your mother was an unlegalized wife—because she failed to have said over her those same few words which *my* mother has made profane! Oh, Truman—my dear love! You've been face to face with death—you've been where the flimsy lines men draw are nothing in the eyes of God—where nothing counts but what is sincere! Tell me—tell me—what *is* the difference between you and me? Your mother was faithful to an 'unlawful' love—and paid the price; mine was faithless to a 'lawful' one—and doesn't want to pay the price! Which is worse, Truman? Does God mean *'thou shalt not' more than He means 'thou shalt'?"* Her breast was throbbing now like his own. Suddenly he crushed her to him and they clung together there, two bewildered victims of wrongs which they had taken no part in, yet of which civilization made them the brunts, each heart crying out for life in its fullness, nothing but the stoic dead around them.

Truman's arms were the first to loosen. "But, Jean," he gasped, "I can't—I can't! Oh, I feel that way too—but the *world,* Jean —it don't see things so! Oh, I know, I know,

Jean—I saw what it did to Mom! It can make you suffer, Jean—the world can make you suffer! Why, Jean—I haven't even a legal name to give you!''

"I love your name, the name you have— it's the only one I want, and you can make it legal, Truman, as legal as any one's; you know it, dear. Names are not of much importance, so far as I can see. My mother changed hers twice, my father gave his to another woman and dragged it into prison! Oh! I shall be glad to drop it for yours. And the world— my parents kept all its conventions. Yet it's made me suffer as much as if they hadn't— oh! but it's driven it home to me, Truman— everywhere I've gone—that I'm homeless— an odd number—*the result of a mistake!*"

"Has it, Jean? Have they treated you that way?" His arms tightened again with an impulse of protection, his eyes struck a spark of defiance.

"Yes, Truman, it has—it has! Yet—if you leave me now—you'll be crueler even than the world!"

"You mean it, then? You're *sure*—you're not afraid?" His voice was tense.

"Far less afraid than I would be alone!"

The tense voice broke in a sob. "Then, come to me, beloved, and God forbid I should refuse so great a blessing!"

CHAPTER XX.

HOME

"Be it ever so humble."

EVENTIDE. Another Spring, just that time in Spring when nature shows us how many different shades of green are in her paint-box; when the lilacs, like purple-cassocked acolytes, waft their incense before the altar of the sunset, and the golden flames of the dandelions are smoldering into smoke. An upward road, mysteriously winding, low, mossy banks on either side, staunch old trees clinging with roots like the talons of huge eagles through whose sun-tinted wings the breezes softly stir. The end of the road, a house—no, not just a house, a home—glimpsed between giant ash-trunks all crimson down their western sides. A brown house, quaintly restful, with spots of cheerful color in the window-boxes, with branches shading it, leaves softening it as stray curls soften a careworn face. A porch, comfortably spacious; a cataract of wisteria tumbling over the edge of its roof to meet the ramblers climbing up. A step, with

A CHILD OF DIVORCE

an old-fashioned "scraper" on it; a cat with paws curled in toward its furry breast, blinking.

The front door opens. A young woman comes out, crosses the porch and leans against a post. It is Jean, and her face is sweetly restful. The cat uncurls its paws, rises, yawns, glides toward her, rubs against her ankles, back arched, purring. But Jean does not notice. She had an apron on, but that, too, is forgotten. She is watching the sunset—the beautiful sunset far over the sloping land before her. Behind her, much nearer, is all that she loves, in her heart the whispering hope of a greater joy to come.

She has left the door open and soon some one follows her. It is Truman—yet can it be Truman, this tall, bronzed, virile man? Yes, for he slips his arm around her and they stand together, watching the sunset. Their words fall on the silent air:

"Gee! I'm glad we've got those books all up—that's a good job done! And the office looks like a regular clinic, don't it, Jean? And I've got three appointments already for to-morrow. Isn't it great?"

"Yes, dear, and you'll soon have more. That nice old woman who brought us the chicken said the whole town was tickled that a doctor was going to settle here at last."

HOME

"Did she, Jean? Bless her soul! She ought to know—I guess she's the kind that keeps her finger on the whole town's pulse."

"Naughty boy—to make fun of her!"

Smiles exchanged and a stillness; then, "Isn't it beautiful, Jean?"

"Yes, dear."

"Jean—maybe I'm childish, but I like to think—Mom's over there."

"So do I, darling."

Above the sunset a mackerel sky has been forming. A fan of filmy, creamy cloud sprays out from the west, spans the zenith, its tip where the sun will rise to-morrow. Jean lifts her eyes to it. "Look, Truman—it's like a great wing over us!"

"So it is; you can almost see the feathers." A fine light beams across his face, his voice sinks lower: 'He shall cover thee with His feathers'—what's the rest, beloved? Do you remember?"

Jean remembers: "—'and under His wings shalt thou trust.'"

THE END.